MAKING
FURNITURE

Attractive easy-to-make furniture designs for every room in the house

MAKING FURNITURE

Attractive easy-to-make furniture designs for every room in the house

Edited by David Thomas

ORBIS PUBLISHING·London

Acknowledgments

The items of furniture in this book were designed by:
Harry Butler: Window Box (Photo: Mike Leale, Artwork: Venner Artists) pp 125–6; *Roy Day:* Kitchen unit (Photo: Orbis/John Rawlings, Artwork: Venner Artists) pp 16–20; *Formica Limited:* Bathroom storage unit (Photos: Orbis/John Rawlings, Artwork: Venner Artists) pp 106–10; *David Goodwin* and *Peter Wheeler:* 'Bed-sitter' (Photos: Orbis/John Rawlings, Artwork: Batesons Graphics) pp 78–82; Decorative Screens (Photo: Orbis/John Rawlings, Artwork: Venner Artists) pp 52–5; Picnic Table (Photos: Terry Trott, Artwork: Studio Briggs) pp 112–5; Playpen (Photos: Orbis/Dudley Reed, Artwork: Ed Stuart) pp 84–7; Room Divider (Photo: Orbis/John Rawlings, Artwork: Venner Artists) pp 34–9; Unit seating (Photos: Orbis/John Rawlings, Artwork: Venner Artists) pp 56–61; Wardrobe (Photo: Orbis/Terry Trott, Artwork: Hayward Art Group) pp 66–72; *Handiboard:* Chest of drawers (Photo: Orbis/John Rawlings, Artwork: Venner Artists) pp 73–7; *David Knight:* Pine table and benches (Photo: Orbis/Terry Trott, Artwork: Studio Briggs) pp 24–9; Playboard (Photos: Orbis/Terry Trott, Artwork: Venner Artists) pp 91–5; Tile top table (Photo: Orbis/Terry Trott, Artwork: Ed Stuart) pp 112–15; *James Kyriacou:* TV cabinet (Photo: Orbis/Terry Trott, Artwork: Venner Artists) pp 62–4; *Roger Limbrick:* Dressing table (Photo: Orbis/John Rawlings, Artwork: Venner Artists) pp 100–4; *Chris Oakley:* Corner cabinet (Photos: Orbis/Dudley Reed, Artwork: Hayward Art Group) pp 45–51, Fireplace surround (Photo: Orbis/Dudley Reed, Artwork: Advertising Arts) pp 40–3; *Orbis:* Canopy deck-chair (Photo: Orbis Verlag, Artwork: Venner Artists) pp 121–4; Mini shelf unit (Photo: Orbis/Terry Trott, Artwork: Venner Artists) pp 22–3; Mirror frame (Photo: Orbis/Terry Trott, Artwork: Peter Weller) p 44; Pet hutch (Photo: Orbis Verlag, Artwork: Venner Artists) pp 96–9; Pine wall unit (Photo: Orbis Verlag, Artwork: Venner Artists) pp 30–2; 'Recliner' (Photos: Orbis Verlag, Artwork: Venner Artists) pp 116–20; Rocker cot (Photo: Orbis Verlag, Artwork: Venner Artists) pp 88–90; Towel Holder (Photo: Orbis/Terry Trott, Artwork: Advertising Arts) p 21; Kitchen (Photo: Elizabeth Whiting Agency) p 10.

First published in Great Britain by Orbis Publishing
Limited: London 1980
© Orbis Publishing Limited 1980

Printed in Czechoslovakia
ISBN: 0 85613 255 1
50118

Contents

Introduction

Making your own furniture is not only cheaper and more satisfying than buying ready-made items, it also gives you complete control over the quality of materials used. Another advantage is the scope the handyman has to tailor new furniture and fittings to suit the space and storage problems of his own home.

With economy and high quality as its theme, this totally practical book gives clear step-by-step guidance on the assembly and fitting of a wide selection of household furniture. We have chosen these designs to meet the requirements of modern living. Some provide storage, some save space, some are dual-purpose and some are just fun to make and fun to use. They are all designed to be made as inexpensively as possible and with the minimum effort but, at the same time, retaining strength and character that are missing in a lot of modern furniture and toy designs. Although they are made as simply as possible, they are built to last and will give you years of service.

For the kitchen there are tables, wall and shelf units, a large kitchen unit with a built-in electric hobplate, and, for a quick and easy task, a set of matching wooden holders for roller towels and paper kitchen rolls. We show you how you can divide your sitting room with a useful shelving unit or with attractive screens; we give very practical designs for zip-together seating, or you can make your room more attractive with a fireplace surround and corner cabinet in warm pine. In the bedroom section we show you how to make a wardrobe, a chest of drawers and, for those in small bed-sitters, an ingenious space-saving bed. We provide both practical and 'fun' designs for the children, ranging from an ideal teenage dressing table to a playpen and playboard for the younger members of the family. For the bathroom there is just about everything you need in one free-standing unit. Moving outside, there are attractive designs for garden furniture; a deckchair with its own canopy, a 'recliner' and a fold-up table.

With a little experience anyone can tackle the projects in this book. All you need is a very basic tool kit and plenty of spare time. You will not only save a lot of money but you will gain a great deal of satisfaction from putting your skills into practice. Start with some of the easier projects and, as you gain confidence in your own ability, try some of the larger, more difficult designs. At the back of the book you will find clear instructions and illustrations covering all the joinery techniques used in these projects. All dimensions are in metric only, so we have included conversion charts which you can check at a glance, as many timber merchants still deal in imperial units. Never mix metric and imperial measurements once you have started work.

Stage-by-stage instructions for every project, accompanied by detailed diagrams, enable you to see clearly how each piece fits together. We even tell you where to drill the clearance holes for the screws, giving precise measurements. Providing you cut the timber accurately and do not hurry any one stage, you will achieve professional results every time. It is not difficult—just take your time and check your work constantly against the instructions and diagrams to make sure you are doing the right thing.

The measurements in the cutting lists are worked out from standard timber sizes although these may vary slightly from timber yard to timber yard. We have therefore used average sizes so, if the timber you buy differs in width and thickness from the timber we used, you must make the necessary adjustments to compensate. When a project requires a great deal of timber or boards, there are cutting plans showing the easiest and most economical way to cut them up. You want to make it and we tell you how—it's as easy as that.

The
kitchen

The tile top table, shown opposite, would make an ideal addition to this strong, simple kitchen design. The lines of the table are clean and sturdy and the colour of the tiles used in the design can be easily matched to any existing tilework.

The kitchen furniture designs given in this section of the book have been specially selected to fit in happily either with the modern fitted kitchen or with the increasingly popular kitchen design shown here, in which second-hand pieces of furniture are cleverly blended with the new. The owners of this workmanlike kitchen, for example, have borrowed several ideas and products from industry. The floor-standing unit was once a shop counter; now covered with a run of sleek wood, it makes an ideal storage and work area.

Restaurants learned long ago that there is no reason why the hob must be over the oven — or why you have to choose between gas and electricity; if space and budget allow, why not have both and set them where you find most convenient? Also inspired by professional catering, strips of metal are fastened to the wall, so often-used implements will always be within easy reach. Strong illumination (preferably overhead to avoid shadows) is an absolute necessity in the kitchen. These plain, spun aluminium shades are white inside to reflect the maximum light.

Tile top table

This is the ideal table for your kitchen. It has a
heatproof ceramic tile top, giving a durable wipe-clean
surface, and includes a lot of valuable open storage space.
Use white or coloured tiles to match your kitchen colour scheme.

Cutting list for softwood & plywood

Description	Key	Quantity	Dimensions
Long border rails	A	2	940 × 98 × 22mm
Short border rails	B	2	786 × 98 × 22mm
Side rails	C	2	809 × 124 × 22mm
End rails	D	2	654 × 44 × 22mm
Legs	E	4	740 × 54 × 54mm
Stiffener	F	1	730 × 98 × 12mm
Support battens	G	4	765 × 16 × 16mm
Tile bed (plywood)·	H	1	770 × 610 × 6mm
Shelf (plywood)	J	1	825 × 642 × 6mm

Tools & materials

timber (see cutting list)
measuring tape, pencil and try square, sliding bevel
marking and mortise gauge, marking knife (as needed)
fine-tooth panel saw, tenon saw, coping saw
sharp trimming knife, metal straight-edge, 9mm chisel
medium fine, fine and flour glasspaper, sanding block
rebate plane (as needed), block plane
frame or web-clamp, two sash-cramps
hammer and nail punch
screwdriver, bradawl, countersink bit
hand or electric drill, 6 and 10mm bits
water-resistant woodworking adhesive and clean cloth

For assembly
panel pins 12mm long, oval nails 25mm long
No 10 brass countersunk screws 32mm long
twenty 150mm square ceramic tiles
epoxy tile grout

For finish
matching plastic wood or stopping
clear matt polyurethane lacquer, 25mm paint brush

It is advisable to purchase all the timber at least two weeks before starting this project so it can be stored indoors to season. If you do not do this, there is a risk the timber will shrink, causing joints to come apart after a short time and form a gap.

Purchase all the tiles at once; if you intend to make a chequerboard pattern, the different colour tiles must all come from the same manufacturer. This is because the tiles tend to vary in thickness between one manufacturer and another and therefore cannot usually be mixed successfully.

stage 1

Measure and cut all the softwood pieces with a tenon saw according to the dimensions shown (**see cutting list**). Measure and mark out the cutting lines onto both sides of the sheet of plywood according to the dimensions shown (**see cutting list**). Score along these lines through the surface veneer with a sharp trimming knife held against a metal straight-edge. Cut the plywood to size with a fine-tooth panel saw, keeping slightly to the waste side of the line to avoid damaging the surface veneer. Rub smooth all cut edges of all the pieces of timber with medium fine, then fine, glasspaper.

Using a marking gauge, mark

Assembly diagram

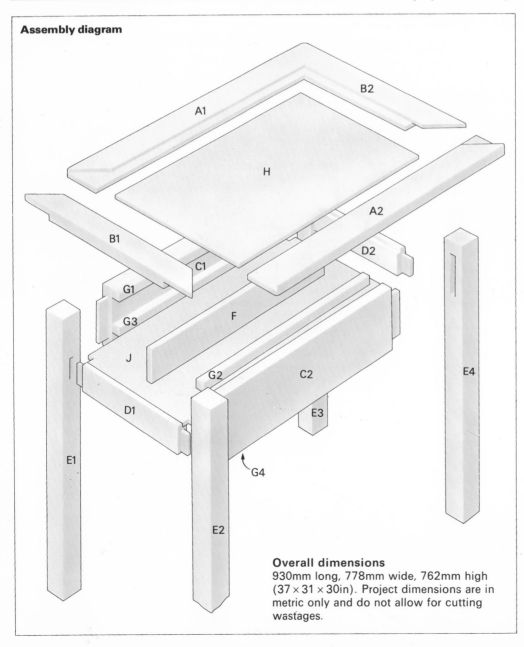

Overall dimensions
930mm long, 778mm wide, 762mm high (37 × 31 × 30in). Project dimensions are in metric only and do not allow for cutting wastages.

out the rebate onto both of the long border rails A according to the dimensions shown (**see 1**); the depth of the rebate is the tile thickness plus 6mm. Remove the waste from the rebates with a rebate plane; if you do not have one, clamp a long straight piece of scrap wood against the marked line of the rebate and use this as a saw guide, marking the required depth of the rebate with a pencil onto the blade of the tenon saw (**see 2a**). Turn the rail on its side, nail the scrap wood to the waste in the rebate and use it as a saw guide as before (**see 2b**).

Smooth the cut edges of the rebates with medium fine, then fine, glasspaper wrapped round a square sanding block.

Mark out the rebates in the short border rails B according to the dimensions shown (**see 3**) and remove the waste as before (**see 2**). Lay out all the tiles on a flat surface with five along one edge and four along the other, leaving a 2mm gap between each tile. Measure the length and width of the area covered by the tiles and add 4mm to each dimension. Mark the measured length of the rectangle of tiles (adding on 4mm) centrally onto the long border rails A and the width (again adding on 4mm) onto the short border rails B. Mark out the mitred halving joint at each end of all four rails, using a sliding bevel set to exactly 45 degrees and a trimming or marking knife to

mark out the joint lines. Mark out the depth of the halving joint onto all four rails; the depth of the joint must be exactly the same as the rebate already cut. Cut out the waste wood with a tenon saw, but don't cut the rails to length at this stage. Bring each joint together (without adhesive) and rub them over with medium glasspaper; trim them with a sharp chisel, if necessary, to obtain a perfect fit.

Apply water-resistant woodworking adhesive to the joint faces of the long and short border rails and tighten a frame or web-clamp round them, making certain the joints remain square. Tighten a G-clamp over each of the mitred halving joints and wipe

stage 2

Using a mortise gauge, mark out the tenons on the side rails C and end rails D according to the dimensions shown (**see 5 and 6**). Mark out the rebate on both end rails D according to the dimensions shown (**see 6**). Cut them out with a tenon saw, using a long straight piece of wood as a saw guide. Cut all the tenons with a tenon saw, keeping slightly to the waste side of the line in each case. Mark out the required positions of the mortises with a mortise gauge in the legs E according to the dimensions shown (**see 7**), remembering two of the legs will be on the left-hand side and the other two will be on

Elevations
(dimensions in millimetres)

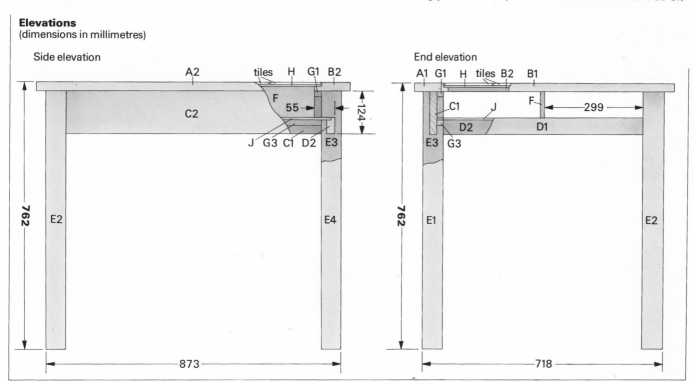

Side elevation

End elevation

1 Long border rail detail

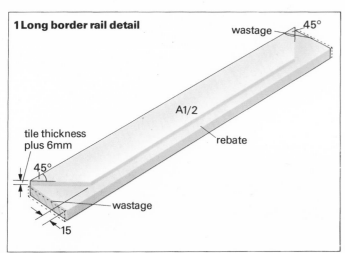

off all excess adhesive with a clean dampened cloth. Check again all joints are square. When all the adhesive has set hard, cut off the waste wood at each joint (**see 4**), marking out and cutting the small curve with a coping saw at each corner. Clean up any protruding edges at the joints with a sharp block plane and rub all surfaces smooth with medium fine, then fine, glasspaper. Apply three coats of clear matt polyurethane lacquer, allowing plenty of time for each coat to dry before applying the next.

the right. Chop out the mortises to a depth of 22mm with a 9mm chisel.
Put the joints together (without adhesive) to check for fit; trim the tenons of any joints which are too tight with a sharp chisel. Apply adhesive to the tenons of one of the side rails C, push the tenons firmly and squarely into the mortises in two of the legs E and tighten a sash-cramp round them until the adhesive has set. When you have tightened the clamp, make certain the legs are square with the side rail and

13

2 Cutting the rebates

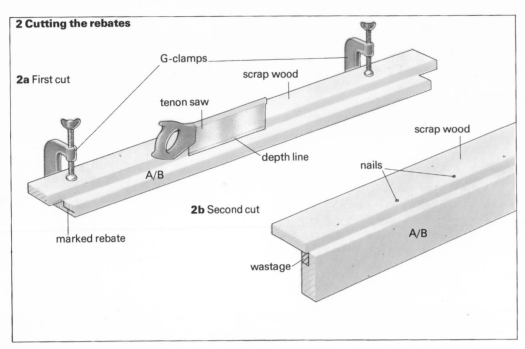

2a First cut

G-clamps

scrap wood

tenon saw

depth line

scrap wood

nails

A/B

2b Second cut

marked rebate

wastage

A/B

rebates in D1 and D2. Apply adhesive to the insides of the rebates in the end rails and to the top edge of the support battens G3 and G4 and fix the shelf firmly in position with the 12mm long panel pins, spacing these at about 100mm intervals and punching all pin heads below the surface of the plywood. Wipe off excess adhesive.

Drill six 10mm diameter holes through the shelf J and through the support battens G3 and G4 together at the dimensions shown (**see 9**). These holes are to take the blade of your screwdriver when fixing the long and short border rails in position so the screwdriver can be made to line up with the screw heads.

Drill three 6mm diameter clearance holes in the two remaining support battens G1 and G2 50mm in from each end and one in the centre; countersink them to take No 10 screws.

Glue and fix G1 and G2 with 25mm long oval nails, countersink downwards, to the inside face of the two side rails C so the top edges are flush (**see assembly diagram**). Punch all nail heads below the surface of the timber and wipe off

3 Short border rail detail

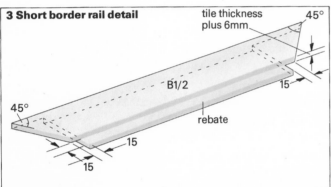

tile thickness plus 6mm

45°

B1/2

15

45°

rebate

15

15

assembly diagram), so the top edge of each batten is on the marked line on each side rail. Punch all nail heads below the surface of the timber with a nail punch and wipe off all excess adhesive. Mark out the rebate in all four corners of the shelf J according to the dimensions shown (**see 8**) and cut them out with a tenon saw. Plane down the ends of the shelf until they fit neatly inside the

4 Shaping corners

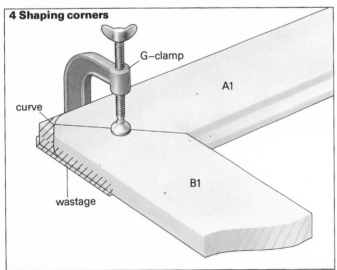

G-clamp

A1

curve

wastage

B1

wipe off all excess adhesive. Glue and cramp the other side rail to the two other legs in the same way. When all the adhesive has set hard, fix the two end rails D following the same method. When clamping the end rails, check both frame diagonals are the same length.

stage 3

Using a marking gauge, draw a line along the inside face of both side rails C exactly level with the bottom of the rebates in the end rails D. Glue and nail the support battens G3 and G4 in position using 25mm long oval nails (**see**

5 Side rail detail

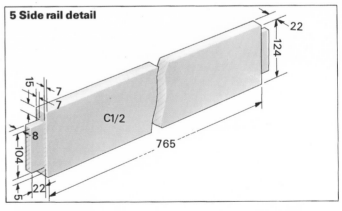

22

124

15

7

7

C1/2

765

8

104

22

5

6 End rail detail

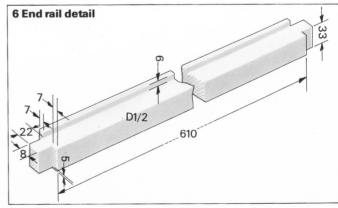

33

6

7

7

D1/2

22

610

8

5

excess adhesive.
Rub smooth the top surface of the shelf J with medium fine, then fine, glasspaper and rest the table top (long and short border rails) in position on top of the frame. Slide the stiffener F into position (**see elevations**) and mark onto each end of F the position of the bottom of the rebates in the short border rails B. Join these marks together with a pencil and straight-edge and plane down to this line (**see 10**) so the bottom face of the tile bed H will rest on the stiffener when the table is assembled.
Glue and nail F in position on top of the shelf J at the dimensions shown, using the 25mm long oval nails (**see plan and elevation**). Punch all nail heads below the surface of the plywood and wipe off all excess adhesive. Fill all holes, cracks and abrasions in the frame with matching plastic wood or stopping, paying particular attention to the joints and the holes left by the nail heads. Give all surfaces of the frame (except the shelf J) a final rub over with flour glasspaper and apply three coats of clear matt polyurethane lacquer.

stage 4

Place the table top (long and short border rails) upside down on a clean flat surface and position the frame upside down on top of it.
Make sure the frame is central on the top and fix it firmly in position with the 32mm long No 10 screws, placing the screws in the 6mm clearance holes drilled in the support battens G1 and G2; tighten the screws by passing the blade of the screwdriver through the 10mm diameter holes drilled in the shelf J and the support battens G3 and G4. You will notice the clearance holes in the support battens G1 and G2 are oversize; this is to allow for the inevitable expansion and contraction of the table top due to the constantly varying temperature and humidity in a kitchen. Don't use any adhesive when fixing the table top, for the same reason. Turn the table the right way up and plane the edges of the tile bed H until it fits perfectly inside the rebates in the border rails. Fix the tile bed in position with the 12mm long panel pins, spacing these at about 100mm intervals.

stage 5

Position all the tiles on the tile bed H, making certain there is an even gap between each tile. Stick the tiles in position one by one, pressing them down with a twisting movement to ensure the base of every tile contacts the plywood tile bed; this gives a flat top surface. Use woodworking adhesive – not tile adhesive – to fix the tiles, otherwise you would have to allow extra depth. When the adhesive has dried, mix up and work some epoxy grout into the gaps between the tiles according to the manufacturer's instructions. Wipe off any excess grout from the tiles with a clean dampened cloth.

See **Mortise & tenon joints**
See **Halving joints**

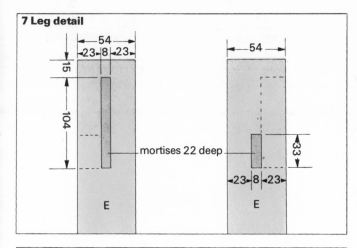

7 Leg detail

mortises 22 deep

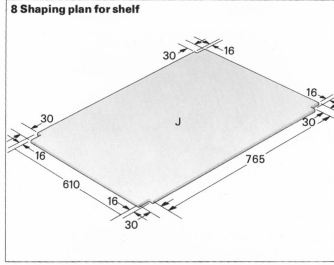

8 Shaping plan for shelf

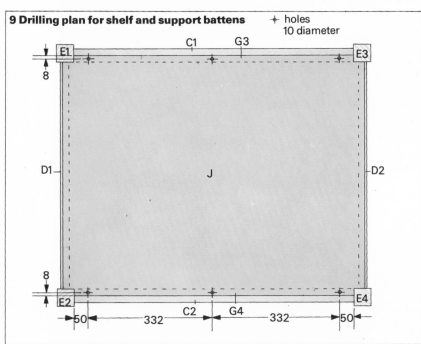

9 Drilling plan for shelf and support battens + holes 10 diameter

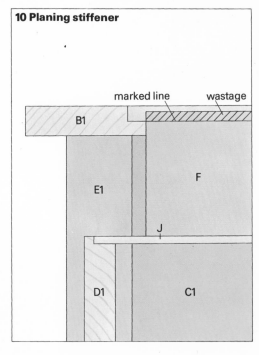

10 Planing stiffener

marked line   wastage

15

Kitchen unit

A narrow space-saving cooking unit designed for any kitchen or bed-sitter. Make it up in wipe-clean, heat-resistant decorative laminate and white – or coloured – melamine panels to suit your room scheme. It's complete with cupboard, drawer and open shelves for all your pots and pans.

Cutting list for Timesaver panels

Description	Key	Quantity	Dimensions
Base	A	1	1470 × 533 × 15mm
Ends	B	2	880 × 533 × 15mm
Divider	C	1	790 × 533 × 15mm
Plinths	D	2	1470 × 75 × 15mm
Lower open shelf	E	1	995 × 457 × 15mm
Top open shelf	F	1	994 × 381 × 15mm
Lower cupboard shelf	G	1	459 × 457 × 15mm
Top cupboard shelf	H	1	459 × 381 × 15mm
Cross rail	J	1	460 × 50 × 15mm

Cutting list for chipboard & hardboard

Description	Key	Quantity	Dimensions
Top	K	1	1506 × 532 × 18mm
Fascia	L	1	995 × 110 × 18mm
Drawer front	M	1	455 × 107 × 18mm
Door	N	1	650 × 455 × 18mm
Back (hardboard)	P	1	1500 × 825 × 3mm
Drawer base (hardboard)	Q	1	476 × 431 × 3mm

Cutting list for decorative laminate

Description	Key	Quantity	Dimensions
Top	KK	1	1512 × 538mm
Fascia facing	LL	1	1512 × 135mm
Drawer facing (front)	MM	1	461 × 98mm
Drawer facing (back)	MMB	1	458 × 110mm
Door facing (front)	NN	1	656 × 461mm
Door facing (back)	NNB	1	656 × 461mm

Overall dimensions
1505mm long, 532mm wide, 898mm high (59 × 21 × 35in).
Project dimensions are in metric only and do not allow for cutting wastages.

Tools and materials

Timesaver panels, decorative laminate, timber
  (see cutting lists)
electric hobplate
measuring tape, pencil and try square
panel saw, fine tooth veneer saw
jig or pad saw (for cutting hobplate aperture)
screwdriver, cutting knife and metal straight-edge
chisel, block plane, fine flat file
hand or electric drill, 2 and 5mm bits, countersink bit
1520mm length of batten, medium fine and fine glasspaper
one litre impact adhesive

For assembly
14 joint blocks
four white panel joints, 12 white shelf supports
No 8 Pozidriv countersunk chipboard screws, 38mm long
eight white plastic Pozi tops
No 6 countersunk chipboard screws, 12mm long
No 6 round head chipboard screws, 12mm long
round wire nails, 25mm long
two unsprung lay-on hinges, mini automatic latch
5.5m of 18mm edging strip (see laminate cutting plan)
primer, undercoat, matt paint (if hardboard back painted)

For drawer
1.5m × 100mm profile of 15mm Formica Timesaver drawer system
two 100mm corner posts and two 100mm front plates
1m length of matching plastic drawer runner profile
500 × 430 × 3mm lacquered or plain hardboard or
  birch plywood (for base)
350mm of 12 × 9mm plain fillet (for base support)

For our unit we chose Formica laminate in Fresh Olive with white Timesaver panels of melamine-surfaced chipboard, and a Neff double electric hobplate.

stage 1

Mark lightly with a pencil all the cutting lines on the Timesaver panels according to the dimensions shown **(see cutting list and cutting plan for Timesaver panels)**. To avoid confusion label each panel with the appropriate code letter. Scribe along the cutting lines with a sharp knife and metal straight-edge to avoid damaging the melamine surface when sawing the panels to size. Cut all these Timesaver panels with a panel saw. Cut all the chipboard and hardboard squarely to size with a panel saw according to the dimensions shown **(see cutting list and cutting plan for chipboard and hardboard)**. Smooth all cut edges with a block plane.

stage 2

The two plinths D are attached to the base A and ends B with five joint blocks each. These are fixed to the inside faces of the plinths so they cannot be seen on the finished unit **(see front elevation/side section)**. On each plinth screw one joint block flush with each end and equally space the other three between these flush with the top edge. Now screw plinths to base A through the joint blocks at 25mm in from the front and back edges of A so the base overhangs the plinths. Before fixing the end panels, drill four 5mm holes at the bottom of the two end panels according to the dimensions shown **(see 1a and 1b)**. Countersink the holes to take No 8 screws. Drill all the holes needed for the shelf supports (according to maker's instructions' to dimensions shown **(see 1a and 1b)**. There are only two holes for shelf supports in the open shelf end B2 as the lower shelf E here is fixed with panel joints. There are 12 holes in the door and drawer end B1 so the height of the two shelves can be adjusted as required.

Cut the 1m length of plastic drawer runner in half using a fine tooth veneer saw. Fix one half to the inside of end B1 using five 12mm long No 6 round head screws. Screw through the runner into the chipboard to the dimensions shown (**see 1a**). Cut a 50mm length of drawer runner to use as an end stop and screw this across the back end of the drawer runner to the dimensions shown (**see 1a**). Now fix both ends B to the base and plinths assembly.

Place one of the end panels squarely and accurately against the base and, using the previously drilled 5mm holes in the bottom of the end panel as a guide, mark with a bradawl where to drill the pilot holes into the edge of the base. Then drill 2mm pilot holes 25mm deep. These prevent the chipboard splitting when the screws are driven into place.

Follow the same procedure for the other end panel. Screw the two ends B into position using No 8 countersunk screws.

Warning Don't overtighten

Assembly diagram

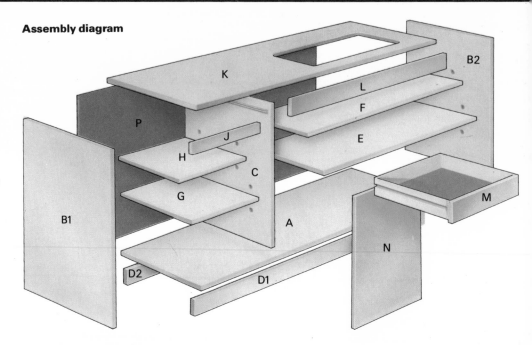

Plan, elevation and sections
(dimensions in millimetres)

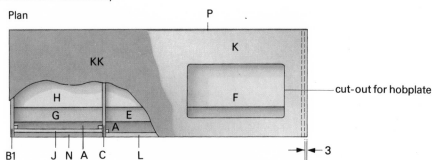

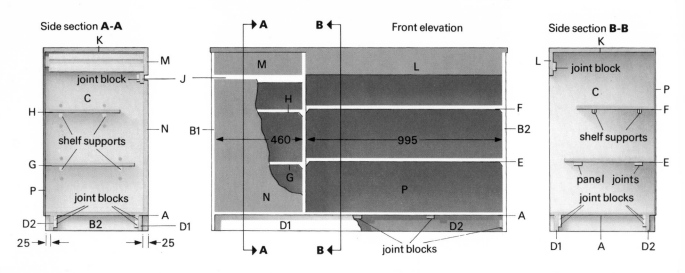

the screws as this would cause them to work loose inside the board and give you a weak joint.

Carefully turn the structure upside down and screw through the joint blocks at the ends of the plinths into the two end panels B.

Drill holes in each side of the divider C of the correct diameter and depth for your chosen supports (**see 2a and 2b**). There are only two holes to be drilled in the open shelf side as the bottom shelf E is fixed with panel joints. There are 12 holes on the drawer side so the height of the shelves G and H can be adjusted. Screw on the other half of the plastic drawer runner to the drawer side of the divider with a stop as before (**see 2a**).

Mark with a pencil on the base the position of the divider according to the dimensions shown (**see front elevation**). Drill four 5mm holes through the base (having removed the divider) and countersink them to take No 8 screws. Place the divider accurately and squarely in position and, using these holes as a guide, drill 2mm diameter pilot holes following the method given for fixing end panels. Screw the divider into position using No 8 countersunk screws.

stage 3

Turn the structure the right way up and keep the end panels and divider braced

until the top is fixed by nailing a batten to the top edges along the centre line of these three components.
To fix on the cross rail J, screw a joint block at each end of the back of the cross rail at dimensions shown **(see 3 and door and drawer side section).**
Screw in position so top edge of rail is 105mm down from the top edge of panels and the front face of the cross rail 21mm in from the front edges of the panels.
Drill 5mm fixing holes all round top K at dimensions shown **(see 4)**. Countersink these to take No 8 screws.
Place the fascia L accurately in position so the front face is flush with the front edge of the top K and 18mm in from the outer end of the top **(see 4)**, supporting the underside of the top at the back with a suitable prop or some books.
With a bradawl, mark through the 5mm holes into the top edge of the fascia and drill 2mm pilot holes at these points.
Glue and screw the top and fascia squarely together using No 8 countersunk screws.
Apply a layer of woodworking adhesive to the fixing edge of

Cutting plans

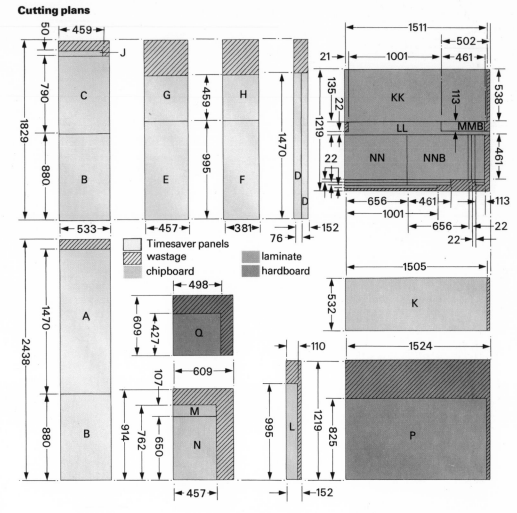

Timesaver panels
wastage
chipboard
laminate
hardboard

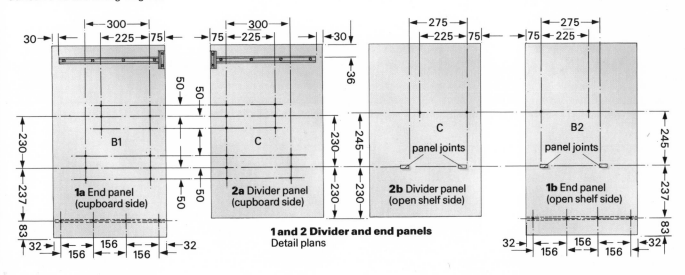

1a End panel (cupboard side)

2a Divider panel (cupboard side)

2b Divider panel (open shelf side)

1b End panel (open shelf side)

1 and 2 Divider and end panels
Detail plans

the fascia and screw together while still wet. Wipe off any excess adhesive with a clean dampened cloth.
Screw two joint blocks, one to each end of the inside face of the fascia, 12mm up from the bottom edge.
Cut and glue the laminate edging strip to the ends of the chipboard top and the bottom edge of the fascia

with impact adhesive and trim back flush on all four edges with a block plane and file.
Cut all pieces of laminate to size **(see cutting plan for laminate)**. We have given 22mm widths for the edging strips as this allows for cutting waste and trimming back when covering the edges of 18mm boards.

Glue the laminate fascia facing into position and carefully cut off the surplus with a fine tooth veneer saw – this waste is used for the drawer facing MMB. Saw off the surplus at the other end and trim all edges as before.
Now place the top section (K and L) accurately and squarely in position. Drill 2mm pilot holes through the

5mm holes in the top and into the two ends B and the divider C before screwing the top down with No 8 countersunk screws, making sure to sink them below the surface.
Turn the structure upside down and screw through the two joint blocks, already on the fascia, into the end panel B2 and the divider.

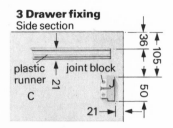

3 Drawer fixing
Side section

plastic runner
joint block
36
105
21
50
C
21

4 Top panel
Detail plan

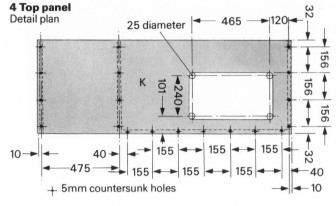

25 diameter
465
120
32
156
156
156
32
K
240
101
10
40
155
155
155
40
475
155
155
155
155
10
+ 5mm countersunk holes

stage 4

Decide whether you want to paint the front face of the hardboard back P before fixing it in position. If so, apply a coat of primer to the smooth side, then an undercoat and a matt top coat (preferably white to match the Timesaver panels) and allow to dry.
To fix the hardboard back, turn the structure on its front and use your try square to ensure all joints are square. Hammer the long wire nails through the hardboard, into the back of the two ends B, base A, divider C and top K at about 100mm intervals. Make sure the top edge of the hardboard is flush with the chipboard top.
Trim all edges with a block plane. Glue the laminate top KK into position with impact adhesive. Make sure there is sufficient overlap at the back to cover the top edge of the hardboard back panel P.
Trim all laminate edges with a block plane; file as before.
Fix the lower open shelf E into position using the four panel joints **(see 1a and 1b)**. Mark the position of the top and bottom of the shelf on the outside of the hardboard

back from the dimensions given **(see open shelf end side section)**. Turn the whole structure on its front and hammer long wire nails through P into the back edge of this shelf.

stage 5

Construct a three-sided Timesaver drawer **(see Techniques)**. Our kitchen drawer has a concealed finger pull for a handle, giving a flush front surface. For this you need to cut a rebate and fillet (which also acts as a base support), the gap in the fillet strip allowing for the finger-pull area **(see 5 and inset)**.
Place the drawer front M against the three-sided assembly and mark off exactly where the hardboard base will enter the rebate. Draw a line along the length of the drawer front at this point. Cut very carefully along this line with a panel saw to half the thickness of the chipboard and then

remove the waste by sawing from the bottom edge.
Cut the 350mm length of fillet in half using a fine tooth veneer saw and smooth all edges with fine glasspaper. Glue and screw each half, one at each end of the bottom inside face of the drawer front M, using No 8 countersunk screws. Countersink the screws and wipe off any excess adhesive immediately with a clean dampened cloth. There will be a 105mm gap between the two lengths of fillet for the finger pull area.
Cut and glue the laminate edging strip to the edges of the drawer front M and trim back flush on all four edges with a block plane and file. The laminate for the back drawer facing MMB has already been cut out as waste from the fascia facing LL. Glue this to the inside face of the drawer front, with the bottom edge of the laminate flush with the top of the rebate, and trim off as before. Glue the drawer front facing

MM onto the outside face. Fix the chipboard drawer front to the front plates of the three-sided drawer assembly, slide the hardboard base into position and then fix the front plates into the ends of the side profiles.

stage 6

Cut and glue the laminate edging strip to all four edges of the door N and trim flush. Glue the door front facing NN and back facing NNB into position and trim as before. Mark the position of the two lay-on hinges with a pencil on the inside of the door. One should be 60mm down from the top edge and the other 60mm up from the bottom. There is no need to cut a recess as they are fixed directly onto the laminate **(see 6)**. Mark through the hinges with a bradawl to show the position of the screw holes before fixing firmly down with No 6 round head screws.

stage 7

We built a rectangular electric hobplate into the laminated top. To make the aperture, drill 12mm diameter holes in each corner **(see top plan)** and cut out with a pad or jig saw.
Lower the hobplate into position and screw down according to manufacturer's instructions. Depending on the type of hobplate used, you may have to build up the surface mounting with pieces of scrap wood. You could make use of scrap pieces of the Timesaver panels for this. To finish, insert the Pozi tops into the screws where the two ends B are attached to the base A. Wash off any pencil marks with soapy water and fix the unit in position in the kitchen. Fix the touch-latch by screwing the body to the divider C 20mm down from the lower edge of the cross rail J and screwing the latch roller plate to the door with the screws provided **(see 7)**. Push the shelf supports into position at the desired height and insert remaining shelves.

5 Drawer front fixing

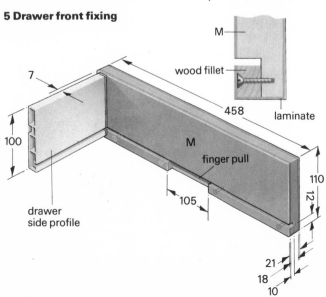

7
M
wood fillet
458
laminate
100
M
finger pull
105
110
12
drawer side profile
21
18
10

6 Hinge fixing

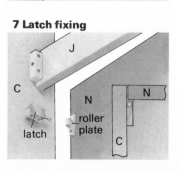

M
J
50
B1
B1
N
lay-on hinge

7 Latch fixing

J
C
N
N
C
latch
roller plate

Towel holder

Designed to take standard roller towels or kitchen rolls, these attractive holders are an ideal way of using up any pieces of scrap wood.

stage 1

Cut a piece of softwood or hardwood measuring 506 × 73 × 22mm for the back using a tenon saw; the length of this should be reduced to 242mm to make the paper towel holder.
Cut two pieces measuring 132 × 73 × 22mm for the sides. Mark out the curve on the front of both sides by drawing a semi-circle with a pair of compasses set to a 36.5mm radius. Cut off the waste from each one with a coping saw and smooth over with a spokeshave or block plane. Drill a 12mm hole and three 5mm diameter clearance holes in each side piece at the dimensions shown (**see side detail**), placing a piece of scrap wood under the drilling area to prevent pieces of wood breaking away from the bottom surface as the drill bit bursts through. Countersink the 5mm holes to take No 8 screws.

Make two cuts with a tenon saw from the top edge of each side piece to the outside of the 12mm holes (**see side detail**) to form the slots. Hold the two side pieces in the required position against the back and mark with a bradawl through the clearance holes in the sides onto the back. Make pilot holes with a bradawl at these points.
Apply woodworking adhesive to both ends of the back and fix the sides in position with three 38mm long No 8 countersunk brass screws. Wipe off all excess adhesive with a clean dampened cloth.

stage 2

To accommodate a roller towel cut a 504mm length of the 25mm dowel to make the roller; this length must be reduced to 240mm if you are making the paper towel holder. Drill a 12mm diameter hole, 10mm deep, centrally in

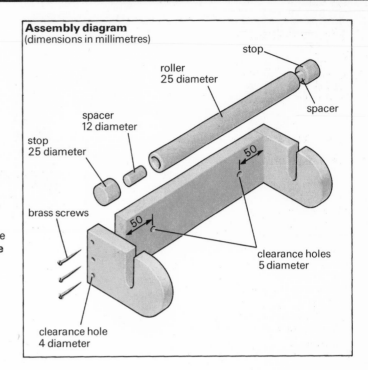

Assembly diagram
(dimensions in millimetres)

stop
roller 25 diameter
spacer
spacer 12 diameter
stop 25 diameter
brass screws
clearance holes 5 diameter
clearance hole 4 diameter

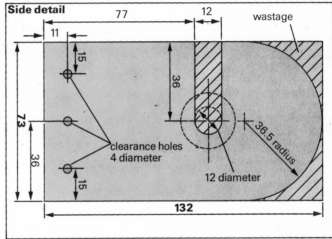

Side detail

77
12
11
wastage
15
36
73
36
clearance holes 4 diameter
12 diameter
36.5 radius
15
132

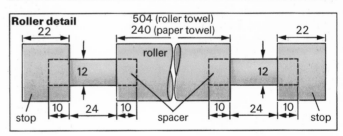

Roller detail

504 (roller towel)
240 (paper towel)
22
22
roller
12
12
10
24
10
10
24
10
stop
spacer
stop

each end of the roller.
Cut two 22mm lengths of the 25mm dowel for the stops and two 44mm lengths of the 12mm dowel for the spacers. Drill a 12mm diameter hole, 10mm deep, centrally in one end of both of the stops. Pour some adhesive in all the 10mm deep holes and fix the spacers and stops in position (**see roller detail**), making absolutely sure the gap between the roller and the stops is 24mm in both cases. Wipe off all excess adhesive.

Fill all holes, cracks and abrasions with matching plastic wood or stopping. Rub all surfaces smooth with medium fine, then fine, glasspaper and apply two coats of clear matt polyurethane lacquer, allowing plenty of time for the first coat to dry. When the lacquer has dried, drill a 5mm diameter hole 50mm in from each end of the back (for the wall fixing screws) and countersink them to take No 8 screws.

Mini shelf unit

This unusual shelf unit is especially useful in the kitchen. It can be fixed to the back of a door to save space; and the dowels stop things sliding off the shelves as the door is opened. It is easy and inexpensive to make; two of these units can be made from a standard 1219 × 1219mm sheet of plywood as you can see from our cutting plan. If you wish to make only one unit, you should be able to obtain an offcut from your local timber merchant.

stage 1

Measure and mark out the cutting lines on both sides of the plywood sheet to the dimensions shown (**see cutting plan**).

Score along these lines through the surface veneer with a sharp trimming knife held against a metal straight-edge, then cut the various parts to size with a panel saw, keeping to the waste side of the line. Cut thirteen 424mm lengths of the 9mm diameter dowel with a tenon saw. Smooth all cut edges with medium fine, then fine, glasspaper.

To make the curves on the uprights, mark a point 45mm in from the front edge and 45mm down from the top edge for one curve and the same up from the bottom for the other (**see drilling plan inset**). Set your compass to a 45mm radius, draw the curve then cut off the waste with a coping saw.

Cutting plan for 9mm plywood
(dimensions in millimetres)

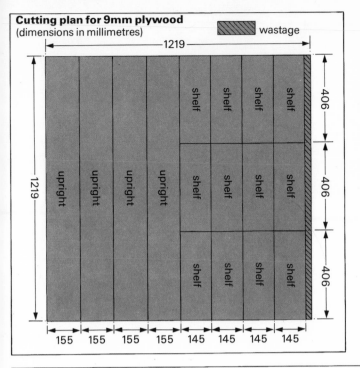

▨ wastage

Mark out the 3mm diameter clearance holes and the 9mm diameter dowel holes on one face of one of the uprights according to the dimensions shown (**see drilling plan**). Check the uprights are exactly the same size then clamp them together with two G-clamps so all edges are flush, making sure the clamps do not cover any of the hole centres you have marked out.

Drill all the clearance holes with a 3mm diameter bit and the dowel holes with a 9mm diameter bit, drilling through both uprights at the same time – this ensures perfect alignment of the shelves and dowels.

Always place a piece of scrap wood under the drilling area to prevent pieces of the surface veneer breaking away as the drill bit bursts through. Remove the clamps and countersink the clearance holes on the outside faces to take No 4 screws.

stage 2

Smear some woodworking adhesive inside all the dowel holes in one of the uprights, insert the dowels and wipe off excess adhesive with a clean dampened cloth. Smear adhesive inside the holes in the other upright and push the other end of the previously fixed dowels in position, making sure the ends of the dowels are flush with the outside faces of the uprights.

Hold one of the shelves in the required position between the two uprights, flush with the back edges, and mark with a bradawl through the clearance holes in the uprights onto the shelf. Drill 2mm pilot holes at these points, apply adhesive to both ends of the shelf and screw it firmly in position with the No 4 screws 32mm long. Wipe off excess adhesive with a dampened cloth and fix the other five shelves in the same way.

stage 3

Fill all holes, cracks and abrasions with cellulose filler or plastic wood and rub all surfaces smooth with medium fine, then fine, glasspaper.

For the finish apply a coat of primer, an undercoat and two gloss top coats. A natural finish would look untidy since the ends of the dowels, glued in position inside the uprights, could not be hidden.

Screw mirror plates close to the top and bottom edges of both uprights, then screw the shelf unit to the back of a door or to a wall.

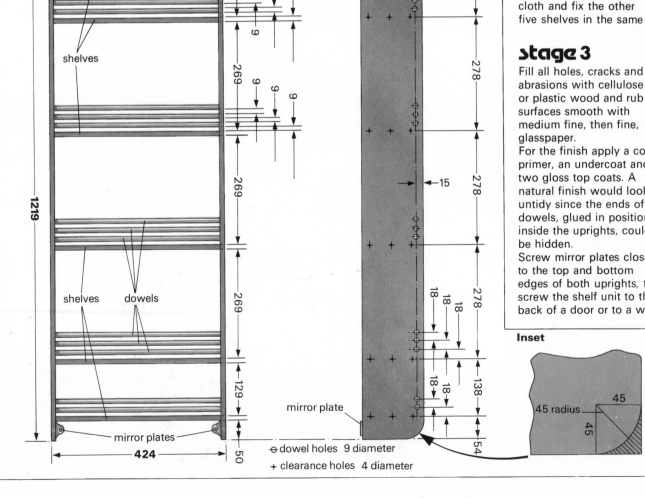

23

Pine table and benches

Make this table and benches for your kitchen. We used tongued and grooved timber for the table and bench tops, making them easier to construct and amazingly inexpensive.

Tools and materials

timber (see cutting list)
measuring tape, pencil and try square, pair of compasses
fine-tooth panel saw, tenon saw, coping saw
smoothing plane, spokeshave, marking gauge, mortise gauge
three sash cramps, four G-clamps
coarse, medium fine, fine and flour glasspaper
hand or electric drill, 2, 5 and 10mm bits
12, 16 and 22mm chisels, mallet
screwdriver, bradawl, countersink bit
No 10 countersunk screws 50, 57 and 64mm long
brass screw cups for No 10 screws
matching plastic wood or stopping, clear matt polyurethane lacquer and 50mm paint brush (for finish)

For this project to be a success it is vital you buy the timber with the utmost care. The table top planks A, the table leg planks B and the bench top planks H are made from tongued and grooved floorboard timber. These must be straight-grained and free from twists.

Any knots must not be dead (black) and the edges of the planks must be absolutely knot-free. The tongued and grooved edges must be completely undamaged.

Arrange half the planks with the grain flow running in one direction and the other half with the grain flow running in the other direction (**see 1**).

All the floorboard timber for A, B and H should be purchased at least 50mm longer than the finished lengths quoted in the cutting list; be sure to check there are no splits in the ends. Allow all the floorboard timber to season indoors for at least two weeks; there must be a complete airflow round all surfaces. This process is very important; if you do not season the timber, the table may warp after it has been made. After seasoning the timber you will probably find the planks have warped a little, but it is better it happens at this stage than after the table is assembled.

Assembly diagram for table

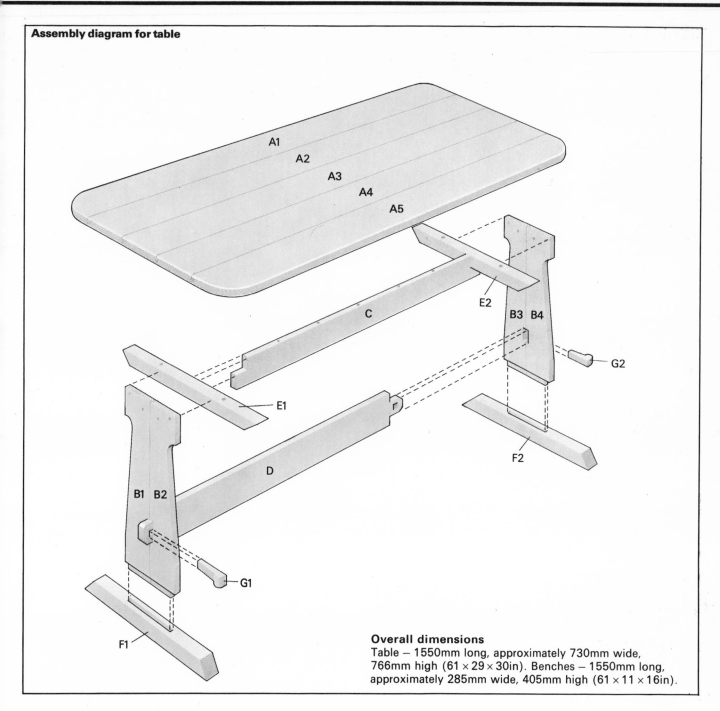

Overall dimensions
Table — 1550mm long, approximately 730mm wide, 766mm high (61 × 29 × 30in). Benches — 1550mm long, approximately 285mm wide, 405mm high (61 × 11 × 16in).

Cutting list for softwood

Description	Key	Quantity	Dimensions
For table Top planks*	A	5	1550 × 149 × 22mm
Leg planks*	B	4	725 × 149 × 22mm
Spine	C	1	1050 × 102 × 22mm
Brace rail	D	1	1200 × 149 × 22mm
Cross rails	E	2	600 × 44 × 44mm
Feet	F	2	600 × 44 × 44mm
Wedges	G	2	100 × 35 × 16mm

Description	Key	Quantity	Dimensions
For benches Top planks*	H	4	1550 × 149 × 22mm
Leg planks	J	4	395 × 149 × 22mm
Spines	K	2	1200 × 73 × 22mm
Brace rails	L	2	1350 × 98 × 22mm
Cross rails	M	4	235 × 35 × 35mm
Feet	N	4	235 × 35 × 35mm
Wedges	P	4	70 × 30 × 12mm

*tongued and grooved floorboard timber

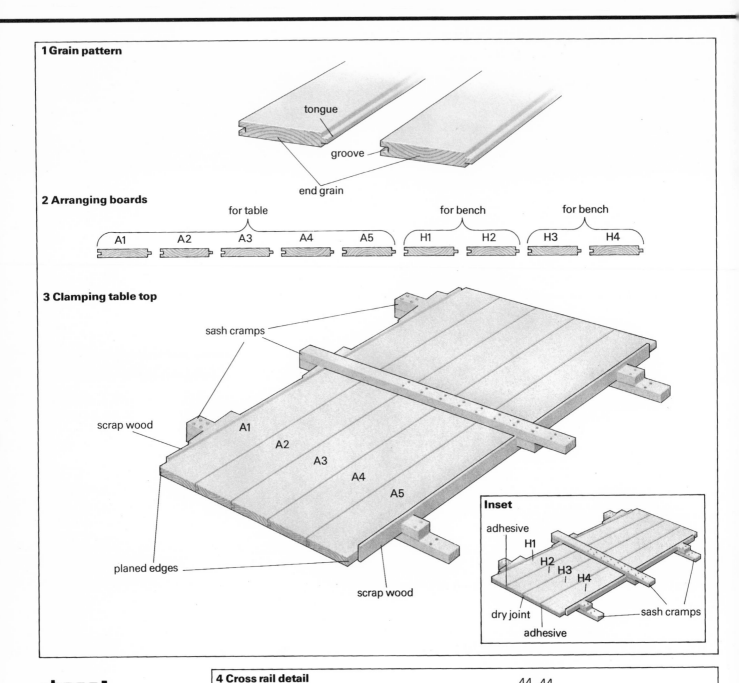

1 Grain pattern

tongue

groove

end grain

2 Arranging boards

for table

A1 A2 A3 A4 A5

for bench

H1 H2

for bench

H3 H4

3 Clamping table top

sash cramps

scrap wood

A1
A2
A3
A4
A5

planed edges

scrap wood

Inset

adhesive

H1
H2
H3
H4

dry joint

adhesive

sash cramps

stage 1

Measure and cut with a fine-tooth panel saw all the pieces of timber to the dimensions shown (**see cutting list**), remembering the floorboard planks for parts A, B and H must be cut 50mm too long at this stage. Arrange the larger lengths of floorboard timber side by side with the end grain running in opposite directions (**see 2**). Juggle the boards about so five of them present a good grain figure on either the top or bottom face; label these boards A 1–5 and place the remaining four aside for the bench tops.

Plane off the tongue and groove on the two outer boards with a smoothing

4 Cross rail detail
(dimensions in millimetres)

Table

44 44

E1/2

44

600

44

Bench

35 35

35

M1/2/3/4

235

35

plane, leaving the outside edges square and straight in both cases. Apply woodworking adhesive along the joint faces of all five boards and position them in two sash cramps, placing a long piece of scrap wood down each side to protect the

boards and to distribute the pressure evenly.
Make absolutely certain the boards stay flat down on the base of the cramps, using weights if necessary to hold them down. Position a third sash cramp over the boards as shown (**see 3**), then

tighten all three cramps firmly to ensure the joints are closed. Some adhesive will be squeezed from the joints due to the pressure; wipe this off immediately with a clean dampened cloth.
While the adhesive is drying (leave it to dry for at least 12

26

hours), mark out and cut off the ends of the two cross rails E to the dimensions shown (**see 4**) and smooth the cut edges with medium fine, then fine, glasspaper.

stage 2

When all the adhesive in the table top planks A has set hard, remove the cramps and check if the table top has a twist or a bend in it; if it has, this can be corrected gradually by placing it on a flat surface, clamping it at the edges with G-clamps and placing weights on it until the twist has gone. You will have to leave the table top in this position for several hours. Carefully inspect both faces of the table top, select the best looking face and label this 'top'. Place it, top downwards, on a clean flat surface and hold it firmly down with G-clamps; protect the boards with pieces of scrap wood. Using a very sharp smoothing plane flatten the surface, first of all working across the grain, then at 45 degrees, then with the grain. You will probably find the joints have swollen since they will have absorbed some adhesive; this is the area to concentrate on. Rub the surface smooth with coarse, medium fine, then fine, glasspaper.
Warning Make sure your plane is very sharp since a blunt plane will tear up the surface of the timber. It should be finely set to avoid removing too much wood.

stage 3

Place the two cross rails E in position on the underside of the table top at the dimensions shown (**see 5**). Check for gaps between the table top and the cross rails and mark onto the cross rails where to drill clearance holes so the fixing screws will be over the gaps as shown (**see 6**). Drill 5mm clearance holes at these points and countersink them to take No 10 screws. Replace the cross rails and mark with a bradawl through the clearance holes in them onto the table top. Remove E and drill 2mm pilot holes, 13mm deep at these points.

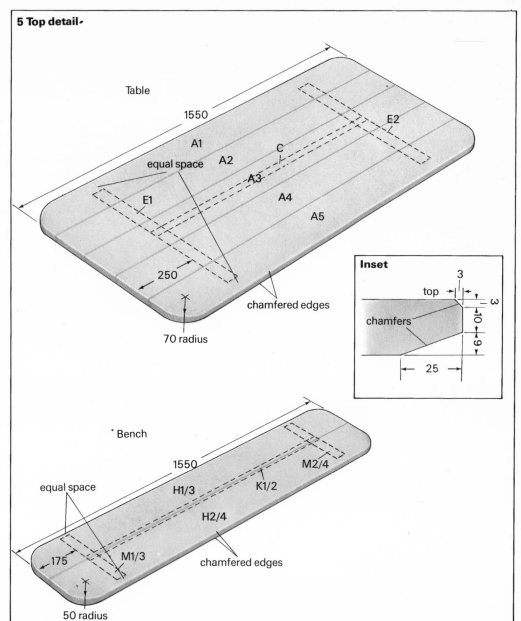

5 Top detail

Table
1550
A1
A2
equal space
E1
C
A3
E2
A4
A5
250
chamfered edges
70 radius

Inset
3
top
3
chamfers
10
9
25

Bench
1550
equal space
H1/3
K1/2
M2/4
H2/4
M1/3
175
chamfered edges
50 radius

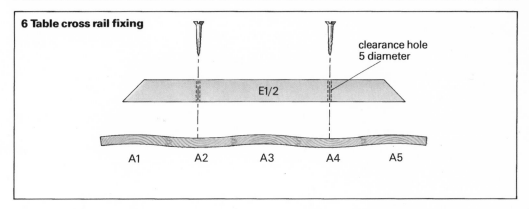

6 Table cross rail fixing

clearance hole 5 diameter
E1/2
A1   A2   A3   A4   A5

Apply woodworking adhesive to the fixing face of both cross rails E and fix them firmly in position to the table top with the 57mm long No 10 screws. Wipe off excess adhesive. If necessary, place weights on this assembly to close any gaps

between the table top and the cross rails.
When the adhesive has set hard mark out the required overall size of the table top, using a pair of compasses to mark the 70mm radius curves at the corners (**see 5**).
Using a tenon saw at a

shallow angle remove the waste from both ends of the table top and cut the curves with a coping saw.
Using a sharp pencil mark the large chamfer on the underside of the table top according to the dimensions shown (**see 5 inset**). Form

this chamfer with a sharp smoothing plane, using a spokeshave for the curves. Plane the long sides first, then smooth the planed edges with coarse, medium fine, then fine, glasspaper. Turn the table top over and clamp it to your work surface and level the top face as before using a very sharp,

finely set smoothing plane. Rub smooth the top face with coarse, medium fine, then fine, glasspaper. Mark out the chamfer round the top edge of the table top to the dimensions shown (**see 5 inset**) and form this chamfer with a sharp smoothing plane, using a spokeshave for the curves.

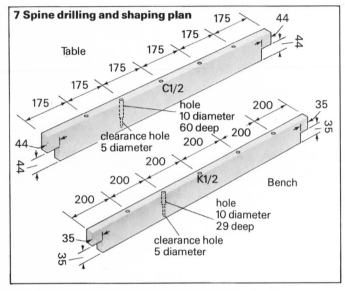

7 Spine drilling and shaping plan

Smooth the planed edges with medium fine, then fine, glasspaper.

Mark out and cut the rebate at both ends of the spine C according to the dimensions shown (**see 7**). It is important the overall length of C is exactly the same as the distance between the outside edges of the cross rails E; also check the ends of C are square to ensure the rigidity of the table. Drill five 10mm diameter counterbore holes, exactly 60mm deep, in the spine C at the dimensions shown, then drill a 5mm diameter clearance hole centrally through each of these. Hold C in the required position on the underside of the table top (**see 5**) and mark with a 150mm nail through the clearance holes onto the table top. Remove C and drill 2mm pilot holes, 15mm deep, at these points. Apply adhesive to the fixing edge and to both rebates of C and fix it firmly in position with the 57mm long No 10 screws. Wipe off excess adhesive and leave it to set. Give the underside of the table top three coats of clear matt polyurethane lacquer allowing plenty of time for each coat to dry; leave the top face until after assembly.

stage 4

Sort the four table leg planks B into two pairs, making sure the planks in each pair fit together with the end grain

going in opposite directions in the same way as for the table top planks (**see Stage 1**). Plane off the tongue from the outer edge of one pair and the groove from the outer edge of the other. Apply adhesive to the fixing edges of each pair and cramp the two pairs together with three sash cramps as before (**see 3 inset**). Wipe off excess adhesive.

When the adhesive has set hard, remove the cramps, separate the two legs and check for flatness; if the planks are slightly bowed, this will be corrected when they are fixed to the feet F with mortise and tenon joints (**see assembly diagram**). Plane the remaining tongued and grooved edges and level off both faces of both legs with a smoothing plane. Mark onto both legs the correct length (725mm) and cut off the waste with a fine-tooth panel saw. Using a mortise gauge, mark out the tenon on the bottom edge of both legs according to the dimensions shown (**see 8**). If the legs are bowed, you must straighten them before cutting the tenons. This is easily done by sandwiching the legs, one at a time, between two thick, strong pieces of scrap wood (**see 9**) while cutting the tenons with a tenon saw. Mark out the central mortise on both faces of each leg to the dimensions shown (**see 8**). Chop out the waste from each one with a 22mm chisel making sure not to make the mortises too big; the tenons on the brace rail D must be a tight fit inside them, if the table is to be rigid. When chopping out the mortises, work from both sides of the legs. Drill the 5mm diameter clearance holes in both legs at the dimensions shown (**see 8**), but don't countersink them since the fixing screws will be used with screw cups. Mark out the shaping lines on both legs according to the dimensions shown (**see 8**), drawing the 50mm radius curves with a pair of compasses. Remove the bulk of the waste with a fine-tooth panel saw, but use a coping saw for the curves. Smooth all cut edges with medium fine, then fine, glasspaper.

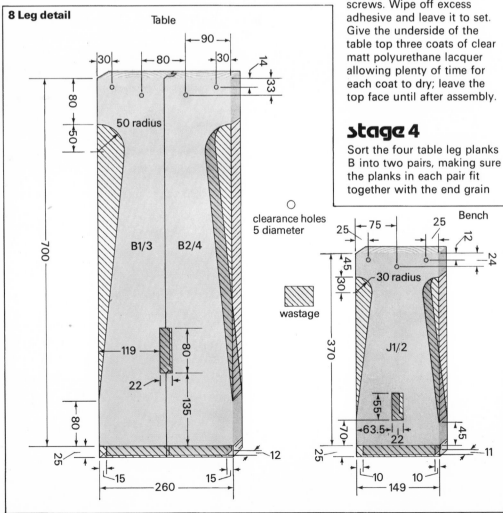

8 Leg detail

9 Straightening table leg and cutting tenon

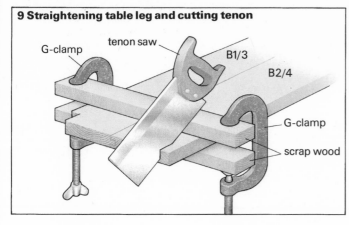

G-clamp · tenon saw · B1/3 · B2/4 · G-clamp · scrap wood

10 Foot detail

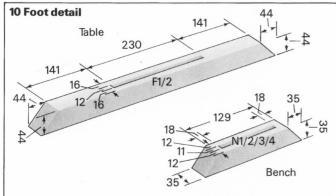

Table

230 · 141 · 44 · 44 · 141 · 16 · 12 · 16 · F1/2 · 44 · 44

18 · 35 · 129 · 35 · 18 · 12 · 11 · 12 · N1/2/3/4 · 35 · Bench

11 Brace rail detail

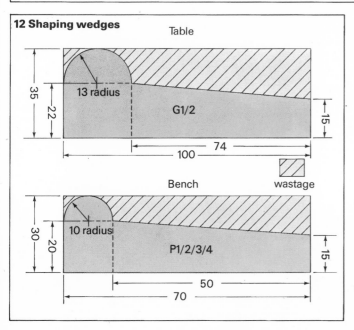

Table

19 · 55 · 35 · 8 · 66 · 16 · 149 · D · 80 · 36 · 19 · 1050 · 75 · 1200 · 19 · 19 · wastage

Bench

75 · 43 · 22 · 22 · 12 · L1/2 · 19 · 55 · 8 · 19 · 1200 · 37 · 1350

12 Shaping wedges

Table

35 · 22 · 13 radius · G1/2 · 15 · 74 · 100 · wastage

Bench

30 · 20 · 10 radius · P1/2/3/4 · 15 · 50 · 70

stage 5

Mark out and cut the mitre at both ends of both feet F to the dimensions shown (**see 10**). Mark out the mortise in both feet with a mortise gauge and chop out the waste, to a depth of 25mm, with a 12mm chisel.
Push the tenons on the legs into the mortises in the feet to check for fit; if they are too tight, remove a little wood from the tenons with a chisel. Apply woodworking adhesive to both tenons and fix these firmly and squarely to the feet, cramping them with two sash cramps until the adhesive has set.
When the adhesive has set hard, remove the cramps; fill all holes, cracks and abrasions with matching plastic wood or stopping and rub smooth all surfaces of the legs and feet with medium fine, fine and then flour glasspaper. Apply three coats of clear matt lacquer as before.
Mark out the tenon at both ends of the brace rail D according to the dimensions shown (**see 11**); the distance between the two tenons must be exactly the same as the overall length of the spine C. Push these tenons into the central mortises in the legs to check for fit; if they are too tight, remove a little wood from the mortises. It is essential this joint is a good snug fit or the table will not be rigid.
Mark out the mortises on both faces of the brace rail tenons to the dimensions shown (**see 11**) and chop out the waste with a 16mm chisel, working from both sides towards the middle of the timber. Cut off both corners of both tenons with a tenon saw to the dimensions shown (**see 11**) then rub smooth all surfaces of the brace rail D with medium fine, then fine, glasspaper. Mark out the two wedges G to the shape shown, using a pair of compasses set to a 13mm radius to draw the curve (**see 12**). Cut the curve on both wedges with a coping saw then saw along the rest of the cutting lines with a tenon saw. Smooth all surfaces of both wedges with medium fine, fine and then flour glasspaper. Apply three coats of matt lacquer.

stage 6

To assemble the table, place the table top upside down on a clean flat surface and fit the brace rail D into the two legs then secure with the wedges. Place this assembly in the required position on the table top, making sure there is an equal gap to either side of the legs. Mark with a bradawl through the clearance holes in the legs onto the cross rails E and fix the leg section firmly in position with the 64mm long No 10 screws, placing screw cups between the screw heads and the timber. Don't use adhesive to fix the legs; this is so they can be removed to enable the table (and benches) to be packed away and reassembled if you are moving house. Tap the wedges firmly home with a mallet. Fill all holes, cracks and abrasions in any unlacquered surfaces and rub smooth with flour glasspaper. Apply three coats of clear matt polyurethane lacquer, allowing each coat to dry.

stage 7

Both benches are made in almost exactly the same way as the table, the main difference being that each leg is made of a single piece of timber. The dimensions for the benches are different (**see cutting list**). When fixing the legs and the cross rails, use 50mm long No 10 screws.

See **Mortise and tenon joints**

Pine wall unit

Make this attractive, all-purpose shelf unit for yourself or for a present.
It is simple – and inexpensive – to make and is especially useful in the kitchen.

This hanging shelf unit can be used to hold bottles and glasses in the living room, herbs and spices in the kitchen, or your favourite paperback books anywhere. It consists of four shelves with three optional guard rails, two sides and a back bearer, glued and dowelled together (or screwed, using decorative dome head screws). If you fix the unit using mirror plates you do not need to make the back bearer. The specially shaped cross-braces are inset into the sides at top and bottom (**see diagrams**).

For a natural finish and to show the wood to its best effect, we applied two coats of teak oil with a lint-free rag. Or you could wipe on a thin coating of matt, clear polyurethane lacquer.

Tools and materials

timber (see cutting list)
measuring tape, pencil
try square, vice
medium and medium fine glasspaper
panel saw, veneer tenon saw
18mm bevel edge chisel
block plane, spokeshave
hand or electric drill
wood and masonry bits
countersink bit
screwdriver and bradawl
woodworking adhesive
teak oil or clear polyurethane lacquer and lint-free rag (for finish)

For fixing shelves and rails
No 8 countersunk screws 40mm long and No 8 decorative dome head screws 20mm long
600mm of 9mm dowel for 26 dowels 20mm long (if used)
320mm of 9mm dowel for four dowels 77mm long

For wall fixing
two mirror plate packs and wall plugs

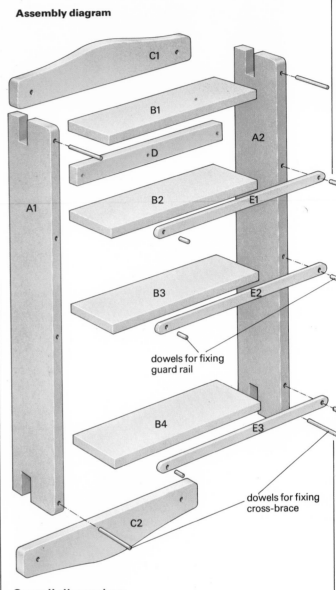

Assembly diagram

C1
B1
A2
D
A1
B2
E1
B3
E2
dowels for fixing guard rail
B4
E3
dowels for fixing cross-brace
C2

Overall dimensions
440mm long, 110mm wide, 850mm high (17 × 4 × 33in)
Project dimensions are in metric only and do not allow for cutting wastages.

Cutting list for softwood

Description	Key	Quantity	Dimensions
Sides	A	2	790 × 100 × 20mm
Shelves	B	4	360 × 100 × 20mm
Cross-braces (cut to shape)	C	2	440 × 75 × 20mm
Back bearer (optional)	D	1	360 × 40 × 20mm
Guard rails (optional)	E	3	420 × 20 × 10mm

Plan, elevation and section
(dimensions in millimetres)

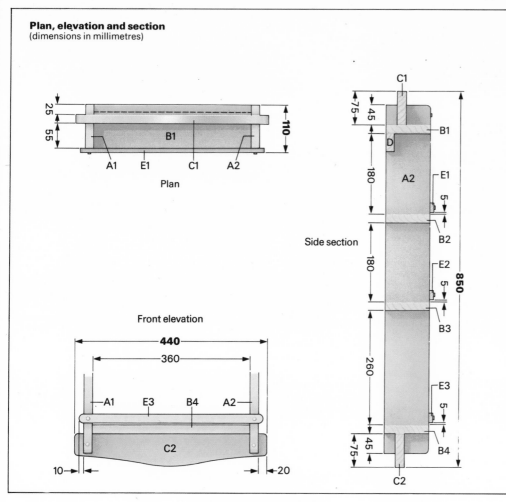

Plan

Front elevation

Side section

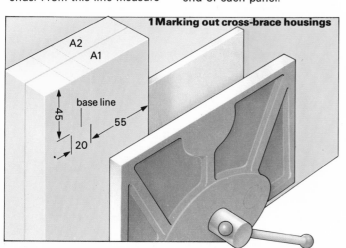

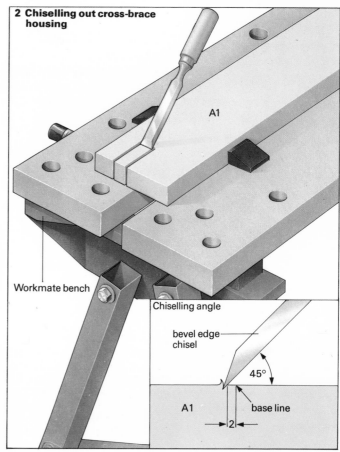

stage 2

To cut out the housings, clamp the two panels together again in a vice and tenon saw down to the base line with the saw horizontal and the waste on the outside of your working hand. Don't go below the base line or your housings will be inaccurate. Turn the panels round to cut down second line. Repeat for other ends. Separate the side panels and lay one flat on your workbench, securing it (to avoid movement while chiselling out) by nailing a piece of scrap wood onto the bench to give the panel something to push against. If using a Workmate, clamp the panel so the housing is over one of the vice jaws, thus providing a firm surface on which to chisel.
Use a sharp 18mm bevel edge chisel to remove the waste or you will be unable to do the job correctly. Place the chisel bevel uppermost and away from you – never towards you – about 2mm above the base line to allow for the cut itself (**see 2 and inset**).

stage 1

Measure and cut timber with a panel saw to dimensions shown (**see cutting lists**), making sure all ends are square. For cross-brace housings, take the side panels A1 and A2 and place them flush together in a vice. On the end grain measure back 55mm from both front edges, mark with a pencil and, using your try square, square across both panel ends. From this line measure

back a further 20mm and square across again. This is the correct thickness and position for the recess to take the cross-braces. Release the side panels from the vice and, taking one panel at a time, mark 45mm down from both lines and square across the timber to join up with these two lines. This makes a 45 × 20mm rectangle ready for cutting out and receiving the brace (**see 1**). Repeat for the other end of each panel.

1 Marking out cross-brace housings

2 Chiselling out cross-brace housing

Warning If you work directly against any of the outer edges of the waste to begin with, the housing will be too big and a neat snug fit will be impossible.

Hold the chisel firmly with both hands, guiding the blade with one hand and pushing with the other. Work at an angle, taking away a little of the waste at a time, until you are halfway through the housing. Turn the panel over and work from the other side until you reach the base line. Then hold the chisel at 90 degrees and shave the bottom of the housing until it is smooth, using a steel rule or try square to check it is flat. Repeat for the other housings.

3 Cross-brace
Cutting and shaping plan

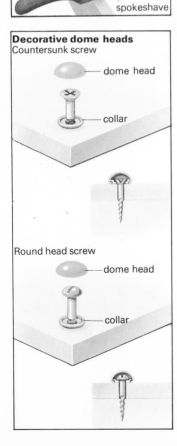

spokeshave

Decorative dome heads
Countersunk screw

dome head

collar

Round head screw

dome head

collar

stage 3

To shape cross-braces (**see 3**), mark the centre of the top edge of the top brace C1 and the bottom edge of C2. Then mark 25mm down from the top edge of C1 and bottom edge of C2 at each end. Join the three points with a pencil line and tenon saw away the waste. First saw from one end to the centre, keeping the waste on the outside of your working hand. Then turn over the cross-brace and repeat from the other end to the centre, having marked the cutting line on the reverse. This keeps the waste always on the outside. Plane smooth and level, checking with your try square. Slightly round all corners and central rise with glasspaper. Use a spokeshave (**see inset**) for further shaping.

stage 4

To assemble the unit, if using back bearer D, drill holes in bearer to take wall fixing screws. Either fix bearer and four shelves B1, B2, B3 and B4 to side panels A1 and A2 with decorative dome head screws or glue and dowel them at distances shown (**see plan, elevation and section diagrams**). For dowelling you need four 9mm dowels for the back bearer and four for each shelf (two for each end). Half of their 20mm length goes into the side panels and half into the bearer or shelves. Next position the cross-braces C1 and C2 in the housings, allowing a 20mm overhang at each end (**see 4**). Drill four 9mm holes for long securing dowels (one for each end of the two braces) right through the front edge of each side panel and into the cross-braces. Remove cross-braces and apply glue to the housings, replace braces and insert dowels. For decorative effect these should be left slightly proud of front edges.

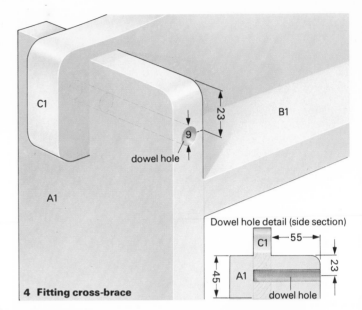

4 Fitting cross-brace

Dowel hole detail (side section)

stage 5

To round front guard rails, mark a 20mm diameter circle (or draw round a one penny piece) at each end of rails E1, E2 and E3. Then use a sharp chisel to pare off the waste round half of the circle. Smooth with medium fine glasspaper. Use the same dowelling technique as before to fix the guard rails to the side panels, drilling 9mm holes 20mm in from each rail end and 8mm into the side panels (**see 5b**).

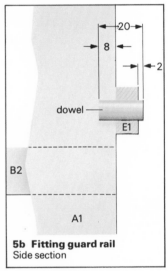

5b Fitting guard rail
Side section

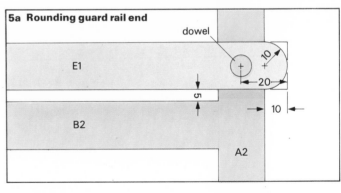

5a Rounding guard rail end

stage 6

To fix to the wall, you can screw into wall plugs either through ready-drilled holes in the back bearer D or through mirror plates fixed to back of side panels (**see 6**).

See **Dowel joints**

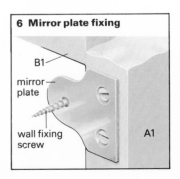

6 Mirror plate fixing

mirror plate

wall fixing screw

The sitting room

Room divider

Whether you want to separate a large room into two areas or just want a free-standing shelving system, our room divider is ideal. It is made in slot-together units so you can make as many as you need and they are easy to take apart if you are moving home. The height of every shelf is adjustable and there are storage cupboards too; make as many cupboards as you want and place them at the required height. There are no knobs or handles on the cupboard doors — they are fitted with auto latches to give a neat finish.

stage 1

Measure and cut all the softwood pieces with a tenon saw to the dimensions shown (**see cutting list**). Smooth all cut edges with medium fine, then fine, glasspaper. Measure and mark the cutting lines on both sides of the sheets of plywood and blockboard to the dimensions shown (**see cutting list and cutting plans**). Score along these lines with a sharp knife held against a metal straight-edge and cut all the pieces to size with a fine-tooth panel saw, keeping slightly to the waste side of the line to avoid damaging the surface veneer. Smooth all cut edges as before. To avoid confusion later, label each part with the appropriate code letter.

Using a marking gauge, mark out the halving joint at both ends of all eight panel uprights A and all eight panel horizontals B to the dimensions shown (**see 1 inset**) and cut them out with a tenon saw. Drill a 4mm diameter clearance hole at both ends of all the uprights A (**see 1**) and countersink them to take No 6 screws. Apply woodworking adhesive to the fixing edges of all the halving joints and assemble the four panels, securing each joint with an 18mm long No 6 screw. Make sure all the joints are square and wipe off excess adhesive with a clean dampened cloth.

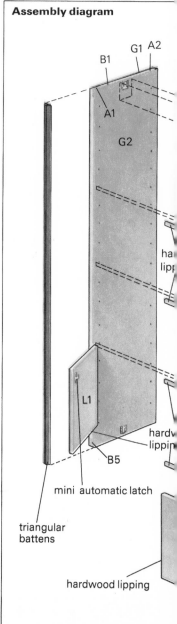

Assembly diagram

G1 A2
B1
A1
G2
ha
lipp
L1
hardw
lippi
B5
mini automatic latch
triangular battens
hardwood lipping

When all the adhesive has set, glue and pin the plywood panel cladding G to each side of all four panel frames using the 12mm long panel pins and spacing these at 50mm intervals. Punch all pin heads below the surface with a nail punch. Wipe off excess adhesive and trim flush any protruding edges of the cladding with a block plane.

stage 2

Apply adhesive to one end of all the brace frame verticals C and fix the brace frame long horizontals D to them in the position shown (**see 2**) with the 38mm long oval nails. Wipe off excess adhesive. Fix the brace frame short

horizontals E between the verticals C in the same way (**see 2**), driving the nails through the verticals into the short horizontals. Make sure you position the nails so they will not interfere with the fixing screws for the flush mounting plates. Sink all nail heads below the surface with a nail punch.

Make sure all the joints are square and, when all the adhesive has set, glue and pin the brace frame cladding H to both sides of each brace frame using the 12mm long panel pins spaced at 50mm intervals. The plywood cladding must overhang the frame by exactly 4mm at both ends but be flush with the top and bottom (**see 2**).

Cutting list for softwood

Description	Key	Quantity	Dimensions
Panel uprights	A	8	1800 × 44 × 22mm
Panel horizontals	B	8	460 × 44 × 22mm
Brace frame verticals	C	12	78 × 44 × 22mm
Brace frame long horizontals	D	6	452 × 44 × 22mm
Brace frame short horizontals	E	6	408 × 44 × 22mm
Fixing battens	F	6	385 × 22 × 12mm

Cutting list for plywood & blockboard

Description	Key	Quantity	Dimensions
Panel cladding	G	8	1800 × 460 × 4mm
Brace frame cladding	H	12	460 × 100 × 4mm
Shelves (blockboard)	J	12	460 × 448 × 15mm
Cupboard backs (blockboard)	K	3	460 × 385 × 15mm
Cupboard doors (blockboard)	L	3	445 × 372 × 15mm

Tools and materials

timber (see cutting lists)
measuring tape, pencil and try square, marking gauge
fine-tooth panel saw, tenon saw, mitre box (or guide)
medium fine, fine and flour glasspaper
sharp trimming knife and metal straight-edge
block plane
hand or electric drill, 4mm bit
screwdriver, bradawl, countersink bit
hammer and nail punch
woodworking adhesive, clean cloth

For assembly

No 6 countersunk screws 15, 18 and 32mm long
panel pins 12 and 25mm long, oval nails 38mm long
32m of 12mm triangular batten
18m of 15 × 6mm hardwood lipping
six joint blocks and 19mm long screws to fit
12 pairs of flush mounting plates
six 38mm brass flush hinges and 18mm brass countersunk
    screws to fit
three mini automatic latches
204 shelf support sockets and 36 supports

For finish

matching plastic wood or stopping
wood dye or stain and lint-free rag
clear matt polyurethane lacquer
12 and 50mm paint brushes

Overall dimensions

1800mm high, 1500mm wide, 460mm front to back
(71 × 59 × 18in).
Project dimensions are in metric only and do not allow
for cutting wastages.

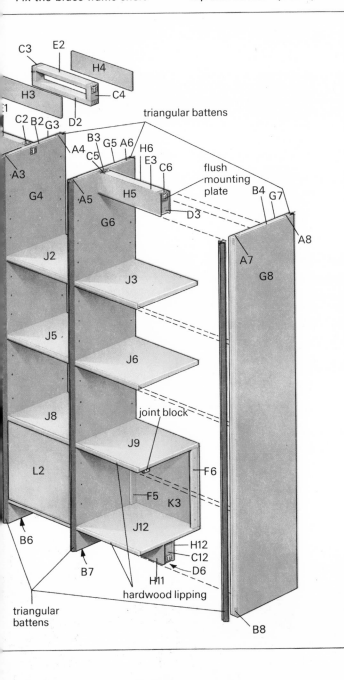

C3 E2 H4 H3 C4 C2 B2 G3 D2 triangular battens B3 G5 A6 H6 A4 C5 E3 C6 flush mounting plate A3 G4 A5 H5 G6 D3 B4 G7 A8 A7 G8 J2 J3 J5 J6 J8 J9 joint block F6 L2 F5 K3 J12 B6 H12 C12 D6 B7 H11 triangular battens hardwood lipping B8

Front elevation
(dimensions in millimetres)

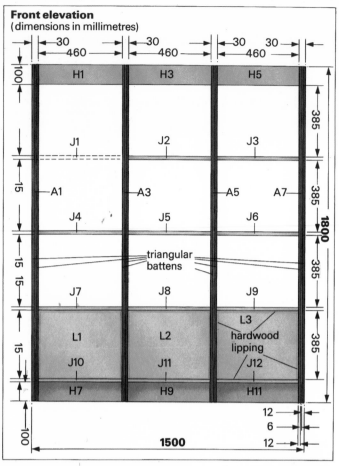

This is to hide the flush mounting plates and to increase rigidity.

On the ends of each brace fix a flush mounting plate in position with the 15mm long No 6 screws. The three braces which will go at the top of the divider have the mounting plates fixed adjacent to the top edge (**see 3**); the three which will go at the bottom have the plates adjacent to the bottom edge (**see 3**). The tongues on the mounting plates on the braces must face downwards in all cases.

Fix two flush mounting plates to both sides of two panels and to one side only of the other two since these will be end panels (**see 4**). The tongues on the mounting plates on the panels must face upwards in all cases. Drill holes of the correct diameter and depth for the shelf supports you are using in both sides of the two centre panels and in the side of the end panels to which the mounting panels are fixed according to the dimensions shown (**see 4**).

stage 3

Cut twenty-four 460mm lengths of the 15 × 6mm hardwood lipping with a tenon saw and smooth the cut edges with fine glasspaper. Apply adhesive to the front and back edges (460mm wide) of one shelf J and fix two of the lippings in position, so all edges are flush, with the 12mm long panel pins at 100mm intervals. Wipe off excess adhesive. Fix the rest of the cut lippings to the other shelves in the same way.

stage 4

Fix the braces in position at the top and bottom of the panels (**see assembly diagram**) so the divider is partly assembled ready to take the cupboards.

To make up a cupboard, use two shelves to form the top and base. Leave three clear shelf support holes between the top and base shelves, push the shelf supports in position and place the top and base on them (**see 5**).

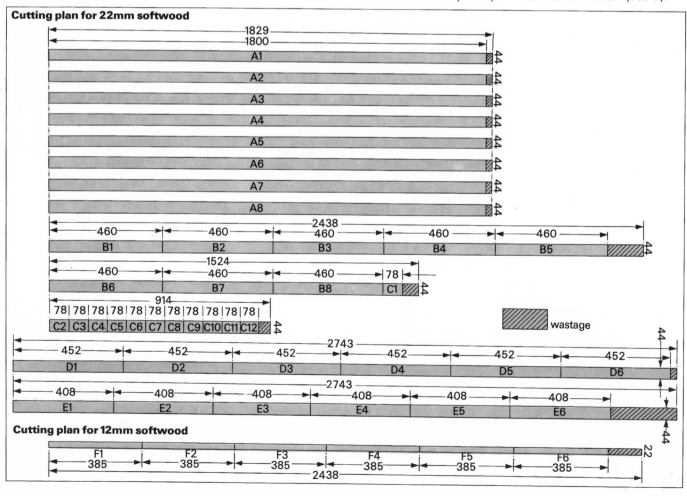

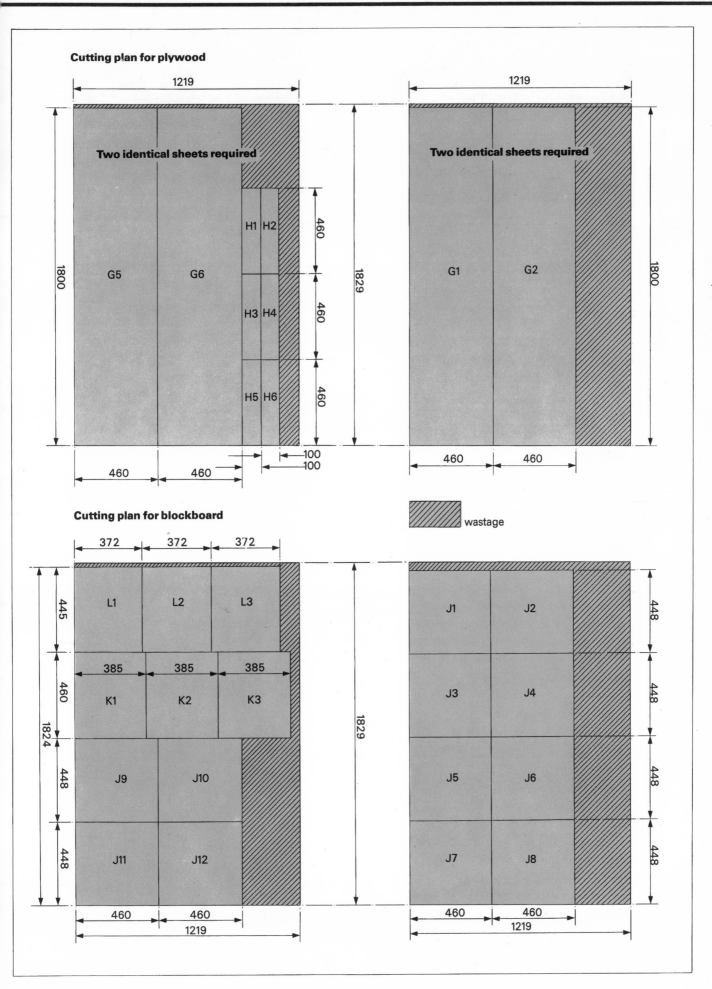

Cutting plan for plywood

Two identical sheets required

Two identical sheets required

G5 G6

H1 H2
H3 H4
H5 H6

1219
1800
1829
460
460
460
460
460
100
100

1219
1800
G1 G2
460 460

Cutting plan for blockboard

wastage

372 372 372

L1 L2 L3
385 385 385
K1 K2 K3
J9 J10
J11 J12

445
460
1824
448
448

J1 J2
J3 J4
J5 J6
J7 J8

448
448
448
448

1829

460 460
1219

460 460
1219

Cut six 457mm lengths of the 15 × 6mm hardwood lipping with a tenon saw and mitre both ends of each cut length (**see 5a**). Cut six 384mm lengths and mitre both ends of each piece as before. Apply adhesive to the edges of the doors L and fix the lippings in position with the 12mm long panel pins at 100mm intervals. Wipe off all excess adhesive.

Drill the 4mm diameter clearance holes in all six fixing battens F at the dimensions shown (**see 6**) and countersink them to take No 6 screws. Hold two of the fixing battens in the required position against one of the cupboard backs K (**see 6**) so the top, bottom and outside

edges are flush and mark with a bradawl through the clearance holes onto K. Make pilot holes with a bradawl at these points, apply adhesive to the back edge of each fixing batten and fix them firmly in position with the 32mm long No 6 screws. Wipe off all excess adhesive. Remove the cupboard top J, and the shelf supports, hold each cupboard back K in the required position between the main upright panels (**see 5**) and mark with a bradawl through the fixing battens F onto the panels. Make pilot holes with a bradawl at these points and fix the cupboard backs firmly in position with the 32mm long No 6 screws. Don't use

adhesive since you may want to remove the backs if you are moving house or rearranging the positions of the cupboards to suit your needs.

With 15mm long No 6 screws fix two joint blocks to the underside of each cupboard top J, flush with the side edges and 25mm in from the front edge. Lay each cupboard top on the cupboard back K and fixing battens F and check there is 385mm clearance between the cupboard top and bottom. Screw through the joint blocks into the upright panels to fix the cupboard tops firmly in place; these can be removed easily if necessary. Screw two hinges to each door at the

dimensions shown (**see 5b**), making sure to fix the larger leaf of each hinge to the door; fix the door onto the upright panels by screwing through the smaller unattached leaf of each hinge. Fix the mini automatic latch in position 50mm down from the underneath of the cupboard top following the manufacturer's instructions.

stage 5

Cut the decorative triangular batten into sixteen 1800mm lengths and smooth all the cut lengths with fine glasspaper. Give them a final rub over with flour glasspaper and apply some wood dye or stain with a lint-free rag.

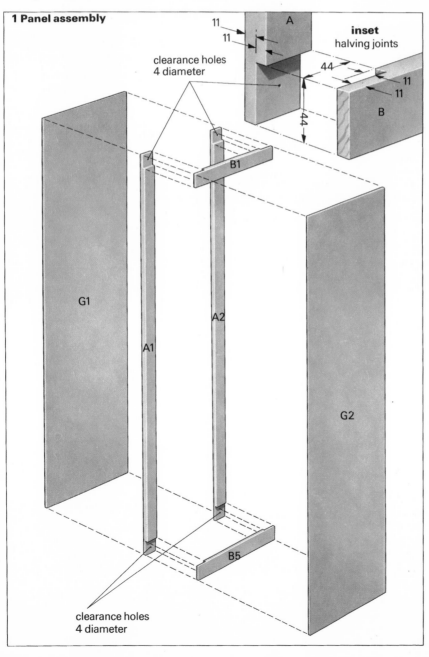

1 Panel assembly

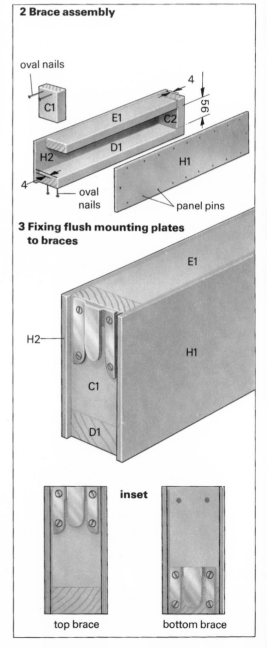

2 Brace assembly

3 Fixing flush mounting plates to braces

When it has dried, apply one coat of clear matt polyurethane lacquer. When the lacquer has dried, glue and pin the decorative battens (using the 25mm long panel pins) to the edges of the upright panels in the positions shown so there is a gap between each one in every pair (**see 7**). Punch all heads below the surface and wipe off excess adhesive. Fill all holes, cracks and abrasions with matching plastic wood or stopping. Rub all surfaces smooth (except the decorative triangular battens) with medium fine, then fine, glasspaper.

Apply two coats of lacquer to all surfaces, allowing the first coat to dry thoroughly before applying the second. Push all the shelf supports in position at the desired height and place the shelves on top of them.

See **Halving joints**

4 Fixing flush mounting plates and shelf supports to panels

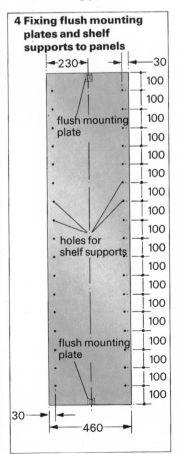

5 Cupboard assembly

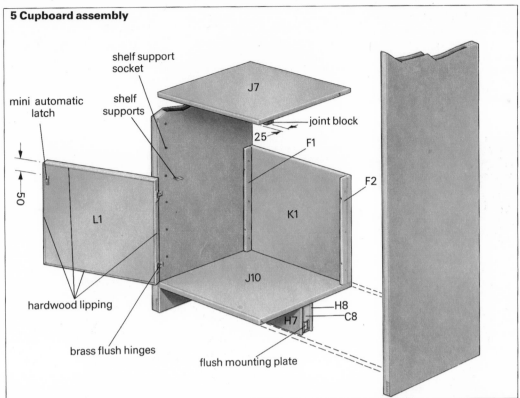

5a Mitre detail for door lipping

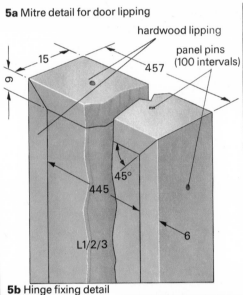

5b Hinge fixing detail

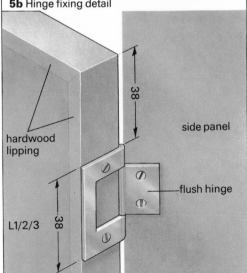

6 Cupboard back assembly

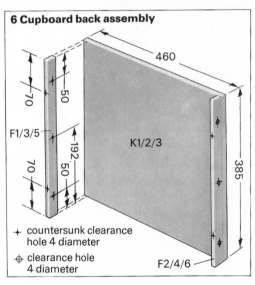

+ countersunk clearance hole 4 diameter
⊕ clearance hole 4 diameter

7 Fixing triangular battens

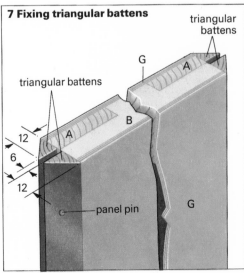

Fireplace surround

This beautiful pine surround including a mantelpiece will fit any
fireplace with a few minor adjustments to the dimensions

Tools and materials

timber (see cutting list)
measuring tape, pencil and try square, pair of compasses
fine-tooth panel saw, tenon saw, coping saw
mitre box (or guide)
smoothing plane and spokeshave
medium, medium fine, fine and flour glasspaper
hammer and nail punch
bradawl, screwdriver, countersink bit
hand or electric drill, 2, 5 and 6mm bits
woodworking adhesive, clean cloth, web-clamp
oval nails 38 and 50mm long
panel pins 25mm long
No 8 countersunk screws 64mm long
No 12 countersunk screws 100mm long and eight wall plugs
  of the required type
10m of 35mm wide softwood half-round moulding

For finish

matching plastic wood or stopping
wood dye or stain (as required)
clear gloss polyurethane lacquer and 50mm paint brush

Cutting list for softwood

Description	Key	Quantity	Dimensions
Outside uprights	A	2	1100 × 44 × 44mm
Inside uprights	B	2	1100 × 44 × 44mm
Front planks	C	2	1100 × 149 × 22mm
Brace rail	D	1	1287 × 149 × 22mm
Cross rail	E	1	1077 × 22 × 22mm
Plinth fronts (to shape)	F	2	187 × 73 × 44mm
Plinth sides (to shape)	G	4	98 × 73 × 44mm
Mantelpiece	H	1	1475 × 162 × 29mm

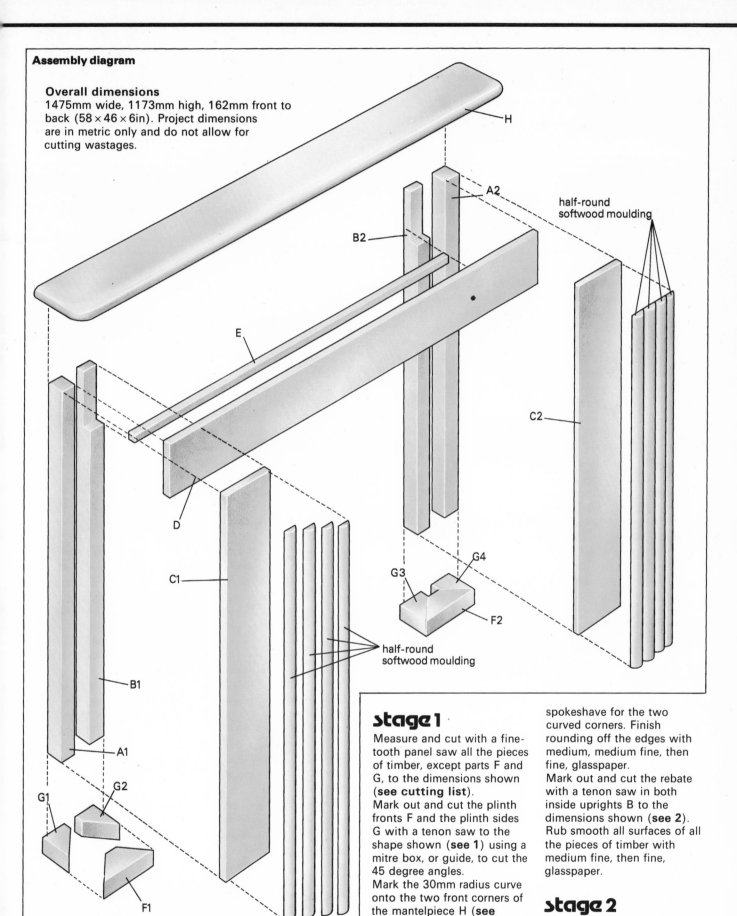

Assembly diagram

Overall dimensions

1475mm wide, 1173mm high, 162mm front to back (58 × 46 × 6in). Project dimensions are in metric only and do not allow for cutting wastages.

H

A2

half-round softwood moulding

B2

E

C2

D

C1

G4

G3

F2

half-round softwood moulding

B1

A1

G2

G1

F1

stage 1

Measure and cut with a fine-tooth panel saw all the pieces of timber, except parts F and G, to the dimensions shown (**see cutting list**).

Mark out and cut the plinth fronts F and the plinth sides G with a tenon saw to the shape shown (**see 1**) using a mitre box, or guide, to cut the 45 degree angles.

Mark the 30mm radius curve onto the two front corners of the mantelpiece H (**see plan**) and cut off the waste from each curve with a coping saw. Round off the front and both side edges of the mantelpiece H with a smoothing plane, then use a

spokeshave for the two curved corners. Finish rounding off the edges with medium, medium fine, then fine, glasspaper.

Mark out and cut the rebate with a tenon saw in both inside uprights B to the dimensions shown (**see 2**). Rub smooth all surfaces of all the pieces of timber with medium fine, then fine, glasspaper.

stage 2

Apply woodworking adhesive to the fixing edge of the rebate in both inside uprights B and fix the inside uprights squarely to the brace rail D at the dimensions shown (**see**

Plan and elevation
(dimensions in millimetres)

Front elevation

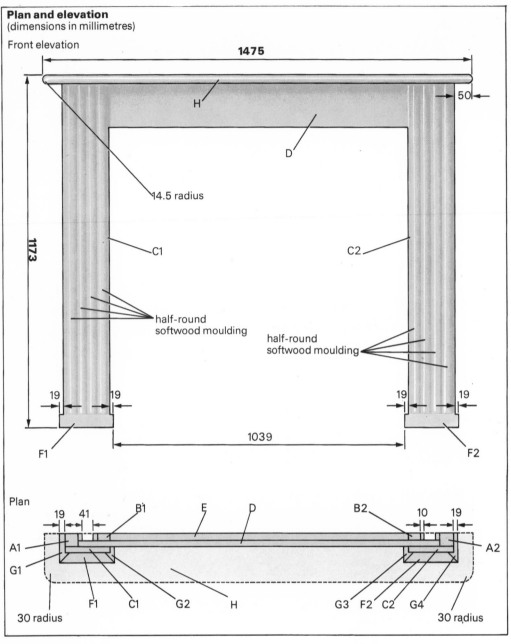

half-round softwood moulding

half-round softwood moulding

Plan

30 radius

30 radius

---

3), securing the joints with the 38mm oval nails. Make certain the joints are square and sink the nail heads below the surface with a nail punch. Wipe off all excess adhesive with a clean dampened cloth.

Apply adhesive to the front face of both inside uprights B and to the part of D to be joined to the two front planks C (**see 3**). Fix C1 and C2 onto this assembly with the 50mm oval nails so the top and bottom and inside edges are flush (**see assembly diagram**). Sink the nail heads below the surface with a nail punch and wipe off excess adhesive.

Apply adhesive to the front face of both outside uprights A and fix these in the required position on the rest of the assembly (**see 3 and assembly diagram**) by nailing through the front planks C with the 50mm long oval nails.

Apply adhesive to both ends and to the fixing face of the cross rail E and fix it onto the brace rail D in the required position (**see assembly diagram**) with the 38mm oval nails so the bottom edges are flush. Punch all nail heads below the surface and wipe off excess adhesive.

stage 3

To fix the mantelpiece H in position, apply adhesive to the top edges of the four uprights A and B, the front planks C, and the brace rail

---

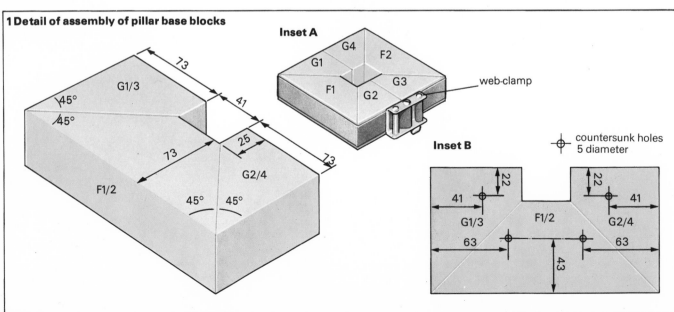

1 Detail of assembly of pillar base blocks

Inset A

web-clamp

countersunk holes 5 diameter

Inset B

2 Cutting rebates on inside uprights

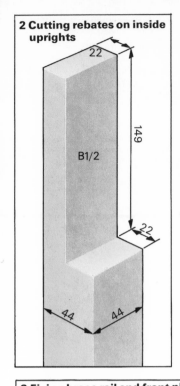

22

149

B1/2

22

44 44

D. Nail through H into these parts with the 38mm oval nails, making certain the back edge of H is flush with the back edges of the rest of the assembly and that there is a 50mm overhang at both sides (**see front elevation**). Punch the nail heads below the surface; the holes that remain can be filled later and will be almost invisible. Wipe off excess adhesive.

Apply adhesive to the fixing faces (mitred) of both plinth fronts F and glue them to the plinth sides G in the positions shown (**see 1**). Wipe off all excess adhesive and place the two plinth assemblies together; tighten a web-clamp round them so they are both clamped squarely while the adhesive sets (**see 1 inset A**). When the adhesive has set hard, remove the clamp, separate

the two plinths and drill four 5mm diameter clearance holes in them at the dimensions shown (**see 1 inset B**); countersink them on the bottom face to take No 8 screws.

Hold each plinth, one at a time, in the required position against the bottom of the main assembly so there is a 19mm overhang at either side of the column (**see front elevation**) and so the back edges of both plinth and column are flush.

Mark with a bradawl through the clearance holes in the plinths onto the column and drill 2mm pilot holes at these points. Apply adhesive to the bottom of the columns and fix the two plinths in position with the 64mm long No 8 screws. Wipe off excess adhesive.

Drill four 6mm diameter

clearance holes in both front planks C and through the outside uprights A and inside uprights B at the dimensions shown (**see 4**) and countersink them to take No 12 screws; these will take the wall fixing screws.

stage 4

Hold the fireplace surround in the required position round your fireplace and mark with a pencil through the wall fixing clearance holes onto the wall. Drill holes of the required diameter and depth for the wall plugs you are using at these points. Insert the wall plugs and fix the fireplace surround firmly in position with the 100mm long No 12 screws.

Cut the half-round softwood moulding with a tenon saw into eight 1100mm lengths and rub them smooth with medium fine, then fine, glasspaper. Apply adhesive to the fixing face (flat) of each cut length, one at a time, and fix them in position on the front of both columns with the 25mm long panel pins at the dimensions shown (**see front elevation**), making sure there is an equal gap at either side of both groups of mouldings. Only three panel pins are needed to fix each length of moulding. Punch the pin heads below the surface and wipe off excess adhesive with a clean dampened cloth.

Fill all holes, cracks and abrasions with matching plastic wood or stopping and rub all surfaces smooth with fine, then flour, glasspaper. For the finish we applied two coats of clear gloss polyurethane lacquer. If you wish to darken the timber you could apply a stain first, but if you do, allow plenty of time for it to dry before applying the lacquer.

3 Fixing brace rail and front planks

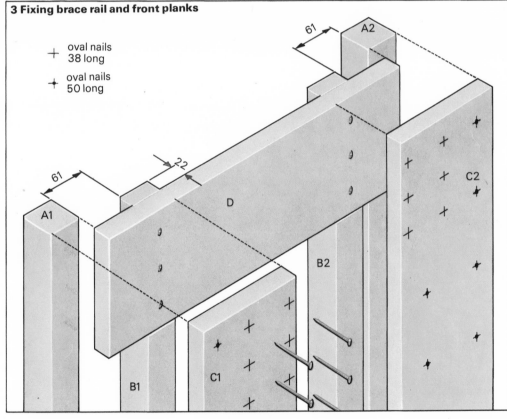

+ oval nails 38 long

+ oval nails 50 long

61 A2

22

61

A1

D

B2

C2

B1 C1

4 Drilling wall fixing holes

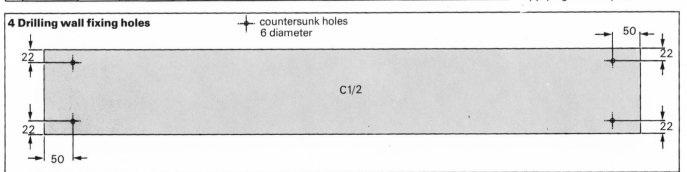

+ countersunk holes 6 diameter

50

22

22

C1/2

22

22

50

Mirror frame

This hardwood mirror frame is attractive and inexpensive to make using a simple joinery technique – the bridle joint.

Glue the remaining three battens in position; if you have cut the mitres accurately, the force exerted at each joint will hold the battens firmly in place. If they are loose, pin them to the frame at each end and in the centre with veneer pins, punching the heads slightly below the surface of the timber. The holes that remain can be filled later. Mitre the ends of all four retaining battens as before. Apply adhesive to the fixing edge of each batten and pin them in the required position **(see assembly diagram)** on the back of the frame, placing the panel pins (18mm long) at 100mm intervals.

stage 3

Fill all holes, cracks and abrasions with matching plastic wood and rub all surfaces smooth with medium fine, then fine, glasspaper.
For the finish we applied two coats of clear polyurethane lacquer. The hardwood will accept a stain or two coats of oil, applied with a lint-free rag, just as well.
Place the mirror inside the frame and pin the hardboard back in position with the veneer pins. You may need to pad between the mirror and the hardboard with newspaper for a tight fit.
To hang the mirror, screw two closed eyes into the back of the frame and tie a length of strong string or wire between them to loop over the fixing in the wall. Alternatively, fix with two mirror plates.

Materials

2100mm of 44 × 22mm hardwood for two 560mm lengths and two 407mm lengths (for frame)
1700mm of 22 × 16 × 16mm triangular batten for two 457mm lengths and two 305mm lengths
2100mm of 22 × 6mm hardwood for two 560mm lengths and two 407mm lengths (for retaining battens)
one sheet of hardboard 516 × 363 × 6mm (for backing)
one mirror 457 × 305mm

Assembly diagram
(dimensions in millimetres)

mitred ends

mitred ends

frame top

triangular batten

hardboard backing

frame side

frame side

frame bottom

mitred bridle joint

560

457

305

407

retaining batten

hardboard backing

Section

retaining batten

frame

mirror

triangular batten

22

22

44

16

stage 1

Cut all the pieces of timber to the dimensions shown **(see materials list and assembly diagram)** using a tenon saw.
Measure and mark out the bridle joint at each end of frame rails, cut each with a tenon saw and remove the waste from the slots with a 6mm bevel edge chisel. Smooth all cut edges with medium glasspaper.
To make the basic frame, apply woodworking adhesive to the fixing surfaces of all the bridle joints, bring them together and check all joints are square with a try square. Secure by pinning (with the 18mm long panel pins) from the back (unexposed) face. Place a G-clamp over each joint until the adhesive has set hard or, if you do not possess four G-clamps, place a heavy weight on top of the assembly. Wipe off all excess adhesive with a clean dampened cloth.

stage 2

Using a tenon saw and a mitre box (or guide), mitre each end of each cut length of triangular batten. Apply adhesive to the fixing edge of one of the mitred lengths and place it in the required position **(see assembly diagram)** inside the frame.

Corner cabinet

This cabinet will turn a redundant corner into a useful storage or display area. Make it with a panelled door or fit a glass one to show off crockery and ornaments. You can leave the cabinet with a natural finish or apply a stain to match your colour scheme.

Tools and materials

timber (see cutting list)
measuring tape, pencil and try square, mitre box (or guide)
sliding bevel and protractor, or combination square
fine-tooth panel saw, tenon saw, coping saw
medium fine, fine and flour glasspaper
block plane, chisel, four G-clamps, three sash cramps
screwdriver, bradawl, countersink bit
hammer and nail punch, spirit level
hand or electric drill, 2, 5, 6 and 9mm bits

For assembly

panel pins 12, 25 and 38mm long
No 10 countersunk screws 19, 32 and 38mm long
250mm of 9mm dowel, 6mm dowel (for door panel)
2.5m of 9mm quadrant moulding
2.5m of 6mm square hardwood batten
2.5m of 22 × 9mm hardwood batten
817 × 387mm of 3mm glass (cut to size)
two 75mm brass butt hinges, 25mm long brass screws to fit
one brass door knob, one lock and catch plate

For finish

matching plastic wood or stopping
wood stain (as needed), clear matt polyurethane lacquer
25 and 50mm paint brushes

Cutting list for softwood

Description	Key	Quantity	Dimensions
Uprights	A	4	1055 × 73 × 22mm
Cross rails	B	2	625 × 73 × 22mm
Brace battens	C	2	680 × 44 × 22mm
Long support battens	D	2	480 × 44 × 22mm
Short support battens	E	2	458 × 44 × 22mm
Top and base planks	F	2	666 × 225 × 22mm
Cladding	G	10	1055 × 98 × 12mm
Large main top plank	H	1	763 × 217 × 29mm
Small main top plank	J	1	450 × 225 × 29mm
Cabinet shelves	K	2	670 × 225 × 29mm
Cabinet shelf backs	L	2	220 × 63 × 29mm
Door frame uprights	M	2	907 × 44 × 22mm
Door frame cross rails	N	2	477 × 44 × 22mm
Door planks (if required)	P	4	818 × 98 × 12mm
Cabinet spine	Q	1	1011 × 66 × 66mm

stage 1

Measure and cut with a panel saw all the pieces of timber according to the dimensions and shape shown (see cutting list and cutting plan).

Measure and mark out the halving joint at both ends of uprights A2 and A3 and cross rails B according to the dimensions shown (see 1) and cut them out with a tenon saw. Apply woodworking adhesive to the

fixing edges of these joints and fix them together to form the front frame, securing each joint with a 19mm long No 10 screw. Wipe off all excess adhesive with a clean dampened cloth and allow the adhesive to set. When the adhesive has set hard, clean up the joints with medium fine glasspaper.
Mark out the 45 degree angle cutting line on the front frame uprights A2 and A3 (see 2) and cut off the waste along the length of both the uprights with a fine-tooth panel saw. Smooth the cut edges with medium fine glasspaper. Drill four 5mm diameter clearance holes in both the unfixed uprights A1 and A4 at the dimensions shown (see 2) and, instead of countersinking them, drill 9mm diameter counterbore holes to a depth of 5mm. Apply adhesive to the mitred edges of the frame and fix A1 and A4 in position with the 38mm long panel pins at the angle shown (see 3), spacing them at about 150mm intervals. Wipe off excess adhesive and punch all pin heads below the surface of the timber with a nail punch.
Drill all the 5mm diameter clearance holes in the long and short support battens D and E at the dimensions shown (see 2) and countersink them to take No 10 screws. Hold the undrilled end of each batten in turn against A1 and A4 at the dimensions shown (see 3) and mark with a bradawl through the counterbored clearance holes onto the ends of D and E. Drill 3mm pilot holes at these points, apply adhesive to this end of D and E and fix the battens firmly in position with the 38mm long No 10 screws. Wipe off excess adhesive.
Cut eight 6mm lengths of the 9mm diameter dowel, apply adhesive to these cut lengths and push them into the counterbore holes in A1 and A4. Trim flush and smooth with fine glasspaper. Fix the free ends of the battens together with the 38mm long No 10 screws and wipe off all excess adhesive.
Join the diagonals of the

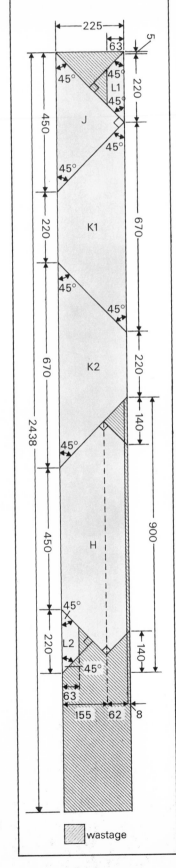

Cutting plan for main top and shelves
(dimensions in millimetres)

wastage

Assembly diagram

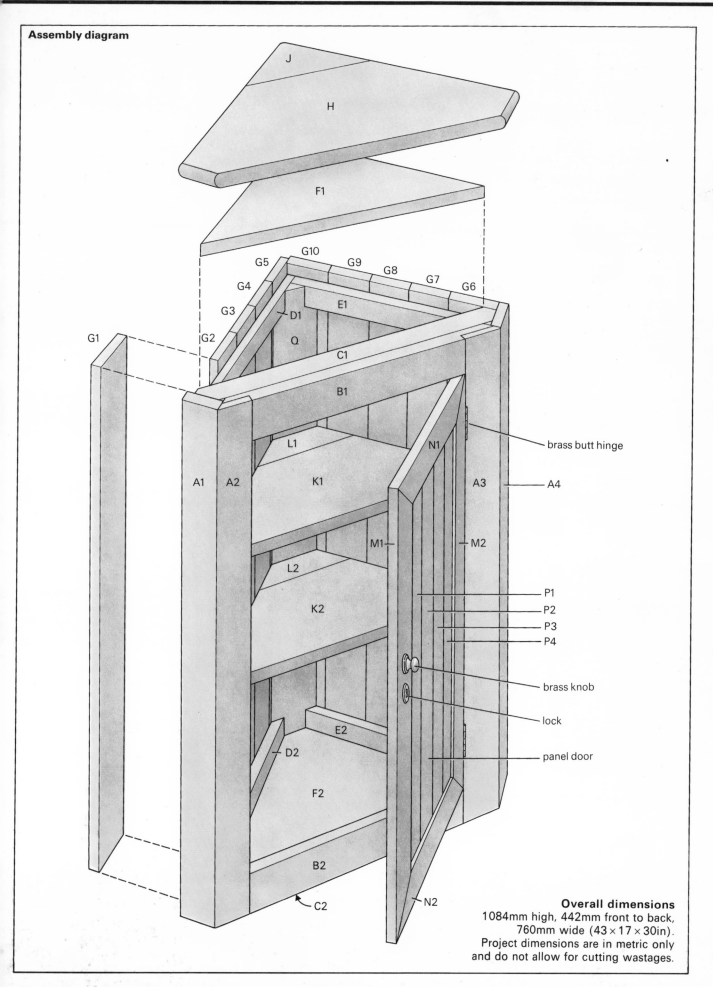

brass butt hinge

brass knob

lock

panel door

Overall dimensions
1084mm high, 442mm front to back,
760mm wide (43 × 17 × 30in).
Project dimensions are in metric only
and do not allow for cutting wastages.

1 Front frame assembly

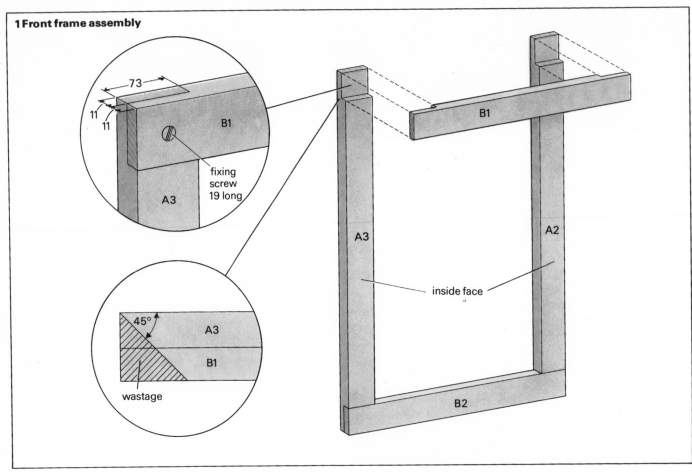

73

11
11

B1

fixing
screw
19 long

A3

45°

A3

B1

wastage

A3

inside face

A2

B1

B2

2 Drilling plans for outside uprights and support battens

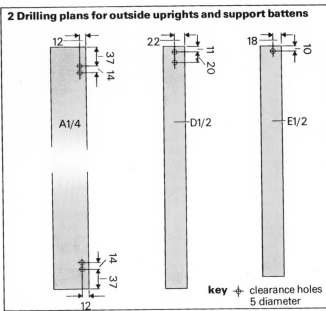

12

37 14

A1/4

14
37

12

22

11 20

D1/2

18

10

E1/2

key ⊕ clearance holes
5 diameter

cabinet spine Q and cut it diagonally in half along its length with a fine-tooth panel saw (**see 4a**). Plane smooth the cut edge.
Mark and cut with a tenon saw the recess at both ends of the cabinet spine Q according to the dimensions shown (**see 4b**). Apply adhesive to all the cut edges of both recesses and fix the

spine firmly in position with the 32mm long No 10 screws, using the previously drilled clearance holes in the support battens D and E.
Place the brace battens C in approximately the required position (**see 5**) and trace where to remove the waste from the ends, so the battens will sit neatly in position in the angles

between the uprights A and the cladding G when the cladding is fixed.
Cut the shaped ends of the brace battens C with a tenon saw, apply adhesive to the fixing edges and fix the battens firmly in position with the 38mm long panel pins, hammering the pins through the uprights A and cross rails B. Wipe off excess adhesive and punch all pin heads below the surface of the timber with a nail punch.
Place the top and base planks F in the required position (**see 6**) and mark out and cut off the waste, so the ends of the planks are flush with the outside face of the long and short battens D and E. Don't throw these pieces away.
Fix the top and base planks firmly in position with the 38mm long panel pins, applying adhesive to all fixing edges and butting the planks hard against the brace battens C. Place two of the pieces of waste (cut from F1 and F2) at the back corners of the cabinet (**see 6**) and mark out and cut them to the required size; glue and pin them in position as before.

Wipe off all excess adhesive and punch all pin heads below the surface.

stage 2

Drill a 5mm diameter clearance hole 325mm in from one end and 400mm in from the other end of all the cladding planks G and countersink them to take No 10 screws.
Apply adhesive to the outside faces of the long support battens D and fix five cladding planks to this side of the cabinet frame with the 25mm panel pins (**see 6**), starting from the front of the frame; make certain the top and bottom edges of the cladding planks are flush with the top and bottom edges of the uprights A and that the clearance hole 400mm in from one end of each cladding is nearer the bottom in every case. Butt the edges of the claddings tightly together and apply adhesive to these edges before fixing the planks to ensure a really solid structure. Wipe off all excess adhesive, remembering

3 Angle fixing detail

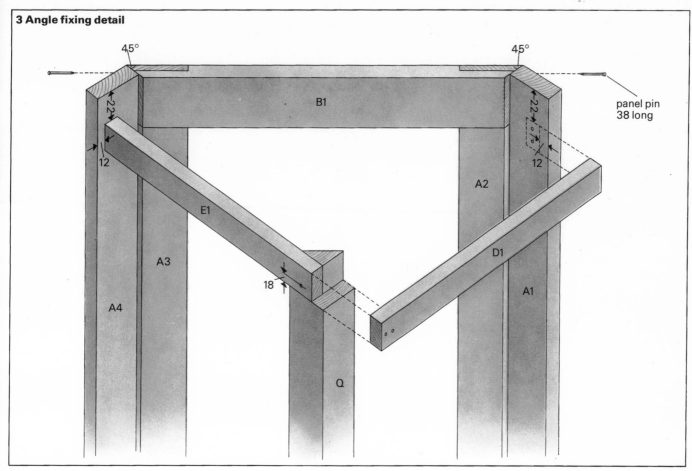

45°　　　　　　　　　　　　　　　　　　45°

22　　　　　　　　　　　　　　　　　　22

panel pin
38 long

12　　　　　　　　　　　　　　　　　　12

B1

A2

E1

A3　　　　　　　　　　　　　　　D1

A1

18　　　　　　　　　　　　　　　　A4

Q

4 Making cabinet spine

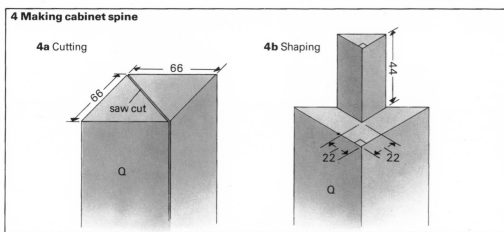

4a Cutting　　　　　　　　**4b** Shaping

66　　　　　　　　　　　　　　44

66

saw cut

Q　　　　22　　22

Q

the inside of the cabinet where a lot of adhesive will have been squeezed from the butt joints between the cladding planks.
Fix four cladding planks to the right-hand side of the cabinet in the same way, starting from the front of the frame. Before fixing the last plank, measure the distance between the back edge of the last plank fixed and the back corner of the frame; this is the required width of the remaining plank. Saw (or plane) the plank to this width and glue and pin it in

position; remove any excess from the back corner with a block plane. Wipe off all excess adhesive.
Round off the front edges of the main top plank H with a block plane then drill 5mm clearance holes (at least eight) at regular intervals through the top plank F1 and through the small plank at the back corner of the cabinet. Countersink them on the bottom (inside) face to take No 10 screws, apply adhesive to the top face of F1 and fix the small main top plank J firmly in position with the

38mm long No 10 screws so the edges of J are flush with the outside face of the cladding planks G. Glue and screw the main top plank H in position in the same way, butting it hard against J so H overlaps the four uprights A by an equal amount. Trim the main top planks flush with the cladding if necessary.
Cut six 40mm lengths of the 9mm dowel with a tenon saw and chamfer the ends of each cut length. Mark out and drill the 9mm diameter dowel holes, 20mm deep, in the

fixing edges of the cabinet shelves K and shelf backs L at the dimensions shown (**see 7**). Pour some adhesive in these holes and smear some over the fixing edge of the shelves K; fix the shelves and shelf backs firmly together with the cut lengths of 9mm dowel. Wipe off excess adhesive.
When the adhesive has set hard, smooth over both side edges of both shelves with a sharp block plane and round off the front edge. Hold the shelves inside the cabinet to coincide with the clearance holes in the cladding and check with a spirit level they are level in all directions; mark with a bradawl through the clearance holes in the cladding planks G onto the shelves. Drill 2mm pilot holes at these points, apply adhesive to the back edges of the shelves and fix both shelves with the 38mm long No 10 screws. Wipe off all excess adhesive.

stage 3

Mark out and cut the mitred bridle joint at both ends of

5 Shaping brace battens

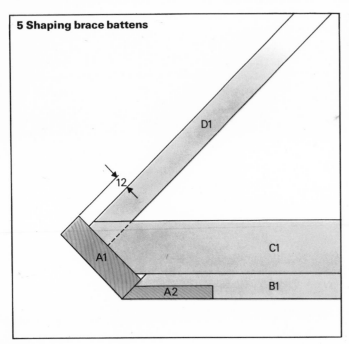

the door frame uprights M and cross rails N (**see 8**). Fit them together without adhesive to try for fit and trim any joints with a sharp chisel if necessary. Apply adhesive to all fixing faces of the joints and assemble the door frame, making absolutely certain the joints are square; tighten a G-clamp over each one until the adhesive has set. Once you have tightened the clamps, check once again all the joints are square.

When the adhesive has set hard, remove the four clamps and cut the quadrant moulding with a tenon saw into two 819mm lengths and

two 389mm lengths and mitre both ends of all the cut pieces. Glue and fix these with 12mm panel pins to the inside edges of the assembled door frame flush with what will be the front face of the frame; the mitre cuts on the bridle joints will show on the front face.

If you want a glass door, cut two 389mm lengths and two 807mm lengths of the 6mm square hardwood batten.

Place the sheet of glass inside the door frame and secure it by fixing the cut lengths of batten behind it with the 12mm panel pins; fix the two shorter lengths first. Don't use adhesive, so the securing battens can be easily removed should the glass need replacing (**see 9a**). If you want a panel door, glue and dowel the four door planks P together so all ends are flush, using 6mm diameter dowel. Wipe off all excess adhesive and cramp the planks together with three sash cramps until the adhesive has set. Make certain the planks remain flat when the cramps are tightened. When the adhesive has set hard, trim the width of the panel with a block plane, if necessary, for a snug fit in the door frame. Cut two 411mm lengths and two 841mm lengths of the 22 × 9mm hardwood batten and mitre both ends of all of them. Place the assembled panel inside the door and secure it by fixing the battens behind it with the 12mm panel pins; hammer the pins through the battens into the back faces of the door frame uprights and cross rails, fixing the shorter lengths first. Don't use

adhesive, so the panel can be easily removed if necessary (**see 9b**). Fill all holes, cracks and abrasions with matching plastic wood or stopping and rub all surfaces smooth with fine, then flour, glasspaper. We applied a stain to darken the timber and then two coats of clear matt polyurethane lacquer to seal it.

Cut the recesses for the hinges in the door frame upright M2 75mm down from the top edge and the same up from the bottom edge. Hold the door accurately in position and mark onto the upright A3 where to cut the hinge recesses. Cut these and fix the door in position with 25mm long brass screws for the hinges.

Glue and pin pieces of scrap wood to the inside of the cabinet where the upright A2 joins B1 and B2 so they protrude by about 10mm; these act as door stops. Fit a brass knob centrally to the door frame upright M1 and fix a lock (if you want one) just underneath it.

See **Dowel joints**
See **Mitre joints**
See **Halving joints**
See **Bridle joints**

6 Top plank and cladding detail

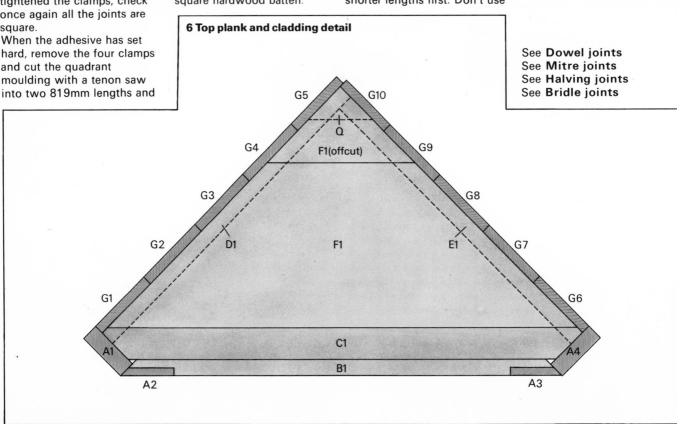

7 Shelf detail

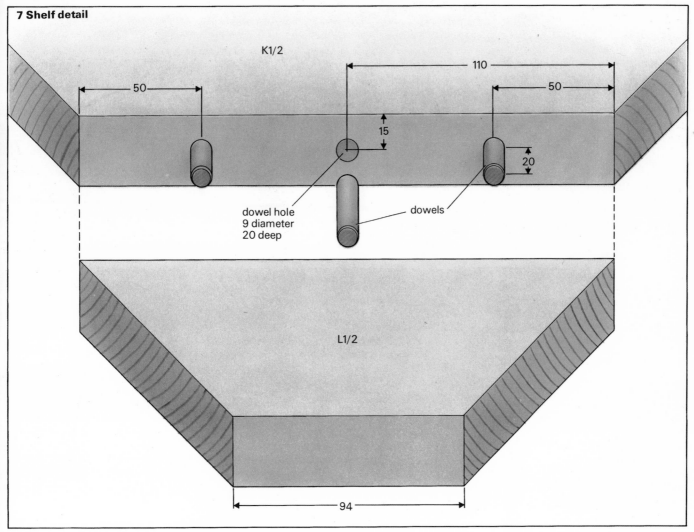

K1/2

110

50

50

15

20

dowel hole
9 diameter
20 deep

dowels

L1/2

94

8 Bridle joint detail

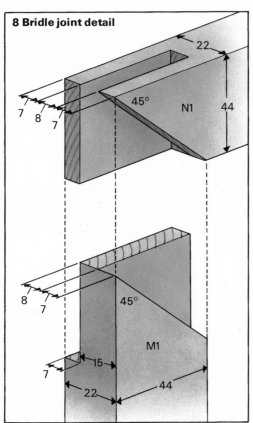

22

45°

N1

44

7 8 7

8

7

45°

M1

15

44

7

22

9 Making door

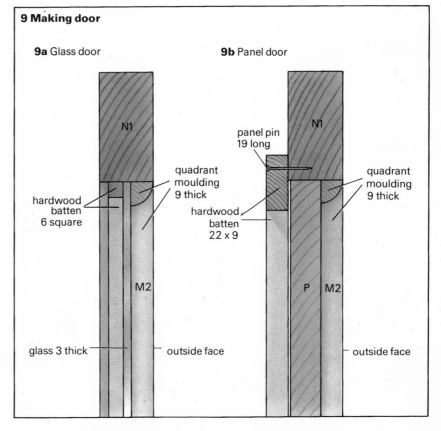

9a Glass door

9b Panel door

N1

N1

panel pin
19 long

quadrant
moulding
9 thick

hardwood
batten
6 square

quadrant
moulding
9 thick

hardwood
batten
22 x 9

M2

P   M2

glass 3 thick

outside face

outside face

Decorative screens

These beautiful screens are useful for hiding ugly areas, sectioning off part of a room or merely for decoration. We made three screens, but you can add more if you want to cover a larger area.

stage 1

Measure and cut with a tenon saw all the pieces of timber to the dimensions shown (**see cutting list**). Smooth all cut edges with medium fine, then fine, glasspaper. To avoid confusion later, label each part with the appropriate code letter.

Mark out the housings and recesses in the cross rails B at the dimensions shown (**see 1 and 2**) and remove the waste from each by making two cuts with a tenon saw and chopping out the wood from between the cut lines with a 6mm chisel.

Mark out the bridle joint at either end of the main uprights A according to the dimensions shown (**see 2**) and remove the waste with a tenon saw.

Drill a 12mm diameter hole in each upright slat C and each main upright A at the dimensions shown (**see drilling plan**) to take the reinforcing dowel. Apply woodworking adhesive to the inside edges of all the housings and recesses in the cross rails B. Push the upright slats C firmly in position in the housings, and the bridle on main uprights A into the recesses (**see assembly diagram**). Secure each bridle joint by pinning through from one side of the recess into the bridle with a 25mm long panel pin. Wipe off all excess adhesive with a clean dampened cloth.

With a tenon saw, cut a 549mm length of the 12mm diameter reinforcing dowel and push it in position. Don't apply adhesive yet.

Assembly diagram

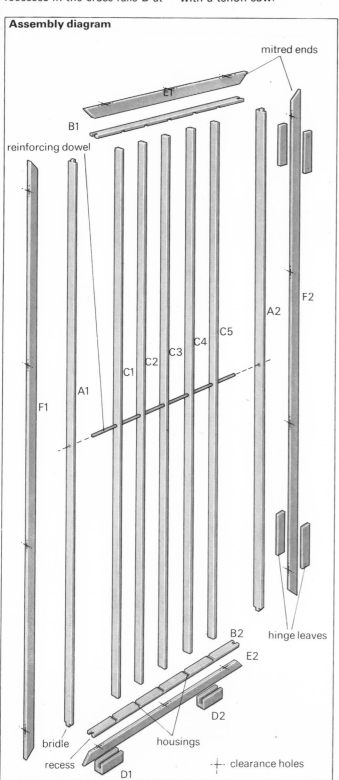

reinforcing dowel

mitred ends

E1

B1

F2

A2

C5

C4

C3

C2

C1

A1

F1

B2

E2

hinge leaves

bridle

recess

housings

D2

D1

—┼— clearance holes

Elevation and section
(dimensions in millimetres)

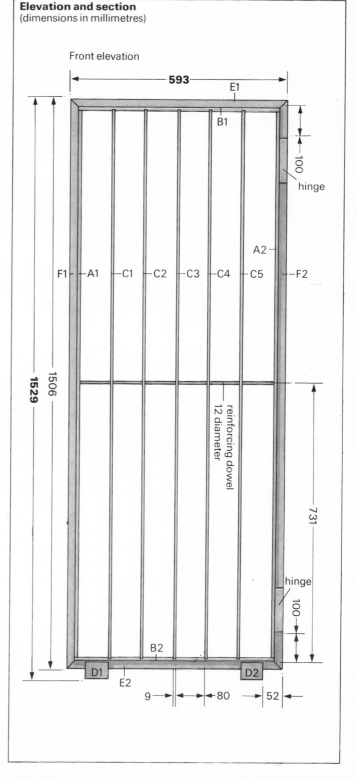

Front elevation

593

E1

B1

100

hinge

A2

F1 — A1 — C1 — C2 — C3 — C4 — C5 — F2

1506

1529

reinforcing dowel
12 diameter

731

hinge

100

B2

D1

E2

D2

9 — 80 — 52

53

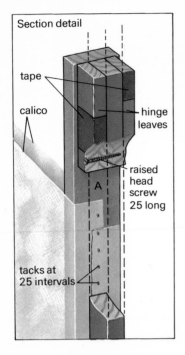

Section detail

tape

calico

hinge leaves

A

raised head screw 25 long

tacks at 25 intervals

Now move it slightly out of one of the main uprights A and apply adhesive inside this hole. Push the dowel back in position, then slightly out of the other main upright A and apply adhesive inside this hole; push the dowel back in position. This technique is used to prevent getting adhesive all over the dowel. To secure the dowel in the correct position pin through each main upright with a 25mm panel pin. Leave the frame on a flat surface to allow the adhesive to set.

stage 2

For each screen you are making cut the calico into two 152 × 60cm pieces. Lay one piece on one side of one

Overall dimensions (for each screen)
1529mm high, 593mm wide (60 × 23in).
Project dimensions are in metric only and do not allow for cutting wastages.

Tools and materials

For three screens
measuring tape, pencil and try square
tenon saw, medium fine and fine glasspaper
9 and 12mm chisels
hand or electric drill, 4 and 12mm bits
mitre box (or guide)
countersink bit, bradawl, screwdriver
scissors, woodworking adhesive and clean cloth

For assembly
2m of 12mm dowel (for reinforcing dowels)
No 6 brass raised head screws 25 and 32mm long
panel pins 25 and 38mm long, tacks 9mm long
10m of 60cm wide unbleached calico (very thin)
1.1m of 38mm wide fabric tape
2m of 22 × 9mm softwood slat (for hinge leaves)

For finish
wood stain and clear matt, or gloss, polyurethane lacquer;
  or primer, undercoat and top coat
lint-free rag, 25mm paint brush

Cutting list for softwood

Description	Key	Quantity	Dimensions
Main uprights	A	6	1462 × 32 × 12mm
Cross rails	B	6	549 × 32 × 12mm
Upright slats	C	15	1450 × 32 × 9mm
Feet	D	6	60 × 44 × 32mm
Outer frame tops and bottoms	E	6	593 × 22 × 12mm
Outer frame sides	F	6	1506 × 22 × 12mm

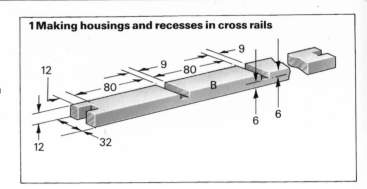

1 Making housings and recesses in cross rails

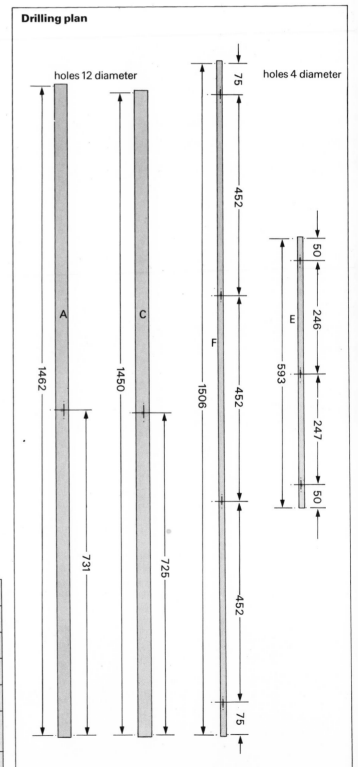

Drilling plan

holes 12 diameter

holes 4 diameter

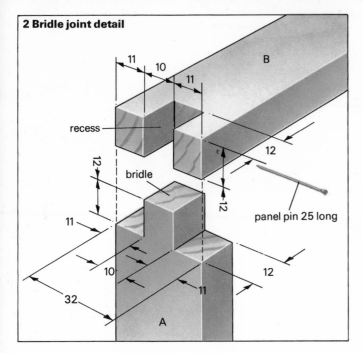

2 Bridle joint detail

recess

B

11 10

11

12

bridle

panel pin 25 long

12

11

10

11

12

32

A

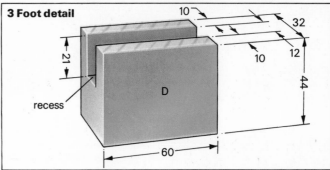

3 Foot detail

10 32

recess

21

10 12

44

D

60

of the screens and, using 9mm tacks, fix it to the two main uprights A and the two cross rails B. Working along one rail at a time, tack into the centre at 25mm intervals, avoiding the housing joints.
Warning Make sure the tension in the calico is the same all the way round to avoid wrinkles.

Trim off excess calico with a pair of scissors so it will not protrude when the outer frame is fixed (**see section detail**). Turn the frame over and fix another piece of calico to the other side in the same way.

stage 3

Mark out a recess in each foot D at the dimensions shown (**see 3**) and remove the waste by making two cuts with a tenon saw and chopping out the waste from between the cut lines with a 12mm chisel. Using a tenon

saw and mitre box (or guide), mitre each end of the outer frame tops and bottoms E and the outer frame sides F. Drill 4mm clearance holes in these rails at the dimensions shown (**see drilling plan**), countersinking them to take No 6 screws. Hold each rail, one at a time, in the required position against the frame and make pilot holes by marking with a bradawl through the clearance holes onto the cross rails B and the main uprights A.
It is best to apply a finish at this stage to avoid getting paint or stain on the calico. We applied a red stain to the

feet D, the outer frame tops and bottoms E and the sides F, then two coats of polyurethane lacquer. To do this, apply the stain with a lint-free rag; always work with the grain and allow the stain to dry thoroughly before applying the lacquer.
If you decide to paint your screens, apply a coat of primer, undercoat and top coat, allowing each to dry thoroughly before applying the next.
When the lacquer, or paint, is dry screw the outer frame tops and bottoms E and sides F firmly down with the 32mm raised head screws. Fix the feet D at the dimensions shown (**see front elevation**) by pinning centrally through the bottom of each one into the outer frame bottoms E with the 38mm panel pins.

stage 4

For the hinges cut the 22 × 9mm softwood slat into 16 pieces 120mm long. Smooth

all surfaces with medium fine, then fine, glasspaper. Drill two 4mm diameter clearance holes in eight hinge leaves, 10mm in from each end. Countersink these holes to take No 6 screws.
Apply a matching, or contrasting, finish to each hinge leaf as before.
Cut the fabric tape into eight 135mm lengths. File 2mm off the tacks to make them 7mm long so they do not protrude from the outside face of the hinge leaves when fixed. Fix the cut lengths of tape with these tacks to the hinge leaves at the dimensions shown (**see 4**), attaching one drilled and one undrilled leaf to each length of tape. Stagger the tacks so they are in different lines of grain to avoid splitting the leaves (**see 4a**). Stand two screens to be joined with outer frame sides F close together and arrange the leaves on each face of the sides F (**see 4 and 4b**) so all the clearance holes are on the same side. Screw in place at the dimensions shown (**see front elevation**) with the 25mm long No 6 raised head screws.

See **Bridle joints**
See **Housing joints**

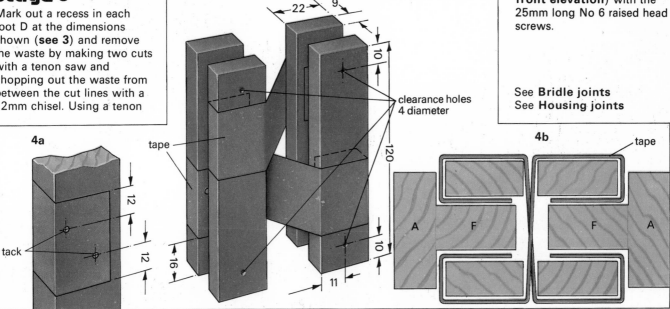

4 Making hinges

22 9

10

clearance holes
4 diameter

120

10

11

4a

tape

12

12

tack

16

4b

tape

A F

F A

Unit seating with zip-together cushions

Make as many of these simple seating units as you need and make or buy cushions to go on top. These cushions are then zipped together and a pocket flap added at the back for magazines.

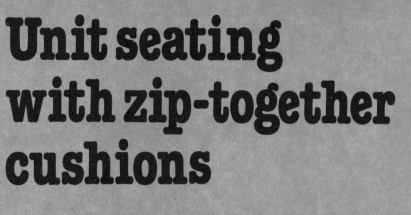

Cutting list for plywood

Description	Key	Quantity	Dimensions
Back	A	1	610 × 457 × 12mm
Seat	B	1	559 × 457 × 12mm
Sledges	C	2	610 × 184 × 18mm

Overall dimensions (chair frame)
457mm wide, 730mm front to back, 570mm high
(18 × 29 × 22in). Project dimensions are in metric only and do
not allow for cutting wastages.

We made up a two-seater
from a couple of chair frames
and four cushions – zipped
together at back and seat and
side to side. (The cushions
are held in place on the
frames with tabs of Velcro
touch-and-close tape.)
The free-hanging pocket flap
holds newspapers and
magazines and zips onto
the top of the back cushion.
If you feel in the mood you
can make an extra cushion to
zip onto the end of the base
one to make a full-length
reclining chair for lazy times.
Our firm foam cushions are
covered in hard-wearing linen
union with contrasting colour
zips, but you could make the
covers from corduroy, canvas

or any furnishing fabric to
suit your scheme, with
matching or contrasting
colour zips.

stage 1

Mark out all the pieces of
timber according to the
dimensions shown (**see
plans**). Mark these cutting
lines on both sides of
the timber and score along
them with a sharp trimming
knife held against a metal
straight-edge before making
any saw cuts. This helps stop
the surface veneer on the
plywood breaking away.
With a panel saw cut the
pieces of timber to size (**see
cutting list**), always

Tools and materials

timber (**see cutting list**)
measuring tape, pencil and try square
trimming knife and metal straight-edge
pair of compasses (if used)
panel saw, coping saw, hole-saw drill attachment (if used)
12mm chisel, medium fine and fine glasspaper
protractor or combination square
hand or electric drill, 2 and 5mm bits
fine flat file (if used), bradawl, countersink bit
screwdriver, No 8 countersunk screws 32mm long
woodworking adhesive, clean cloth

For finish
cellulose filler or plastic wood
matt polyurethane lacquer or primer, undercoat and top coat,
    lint-free rag or 50mm paintbrush

For each chair (2 cushions)
four slabs of 50mm medium density foam, 600mm square
    and two slabs, 300mm square
thixotropic impact (contact) adhesive
4.3m fabric (90cm–120cm wide)
two strong metal closed-end zips 60cm long (to match fabric)
four heavyweight nylon open-ended zips 60cm long
    (to join back and seat cushions)
paper for making patterns (optional)
cotton thread to match fabric colour
cotton thread to match open-ended zip colour

For each pocket flap
1.5m matching fabric (90cm wide or over)
one heavyweight nylon open-ended zip 60cm long
    (one half only used per flap)
3m of 40mm wide upholstery tape in contrasting colour
200mm of 30mm wide Velcro touch-and-close fastening tape,
    cut into four 50mm lengths

cutting slightly to the waste side of the line. Mark out the positions of the slots on both sides of the back A to the dimensions shown (**see plan A**). Score along these lines as before and cut down to the base line, with a panel saw, in each slot. Cut out the waste from between the cut lines with a 12mm chisel. Chop out half the thickness from one side of the board and then turn it over and work from the other side. Smooth all the cut edges and the inside surfaces of the slots with medium fine, then fine, glasspaper.

To make the curves in the top corners of the back A, draw round a can or use a pair of compasses set to 50mm, then cut off the waste with a coping saw. Smooth the curve with medium fine, then fine, glasspaper.

Next, cut the two sledges C to shape. Mark 133mm in from the back edge, place your protractor or combination square at this point and mark off a 68 degree angle; also mark out the other cutting lines to the dimensions shown (**see plan C**). Score along them with a sharp trimming knife as before and cut out all the waste in both sledges. Smooth all cut edges with medium fine, then fine, glasspaper.

Drill two 5mm clearance holes in the back A in the positions shown (**see plan A**) and countersink them to take No 8 screws. Drill six 5mm clearance holes in the seat B in the positions shown (**see plan B**) and countersink them to take No 8 screws.

stage 2

Before final assembly, smooth all surfaces with fine glasspaper and check the back A and the two sledges C fit. If the slots are too tight remove the necessary amount of wood with a fine flat file. When you have a perfectly tight fit, drill 2mm pilot holes through the clearance holes in A into the back edges of each slot in the sledges C.

Apply a layer of woodworking adhesive to all surfaces inside the slots in back A

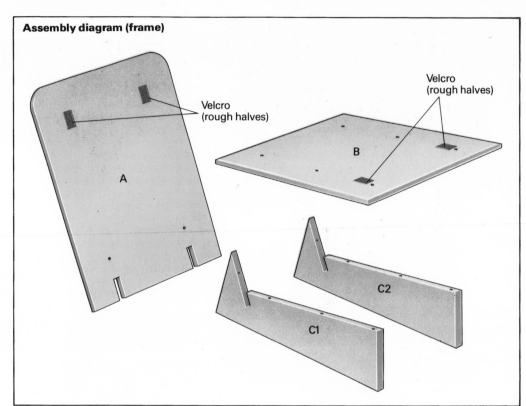

Assembly diagram (frame)

Velcro (rough halves)

Velcro (rough halves)

A

B

C2

C1

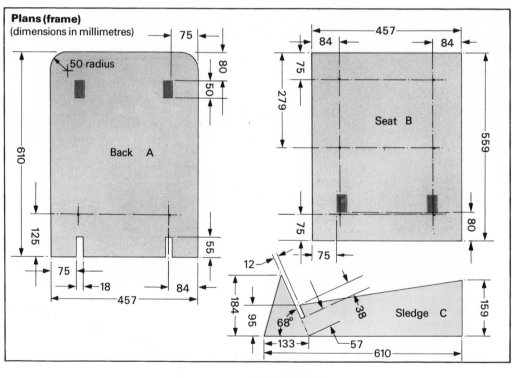

Plans (frame)
(dimensions in millimetres)

50 radius

Back A

75

80

50

610

125

55

75

18

84

457

457

84

84

75

279

Seat B

559

75

80

12

184

95

68°

133

57

38

75

Sledge C

159

610

and in the slots in both sledges C. Position A (**see frame assembly diagram**) on the two sledges and screw it firmly in place. Wipe off any excess adhesive with a clean dampened cloth.

Position the seat B (**see frame assembly diagram**) and mark with a bradawl through the clearance holes in the top edges of C1 and

C2. Remove B and drill 2mm pilot holes at these points. Apply a layer of woodworking adhesive to the top edges of C1 and C2 and then screw the seat firmly down using a G-clamp to prevent the plywood splitting. Wipe off excess adhesive with a clean dampened cloth.

Assembly diagram (upholstery)

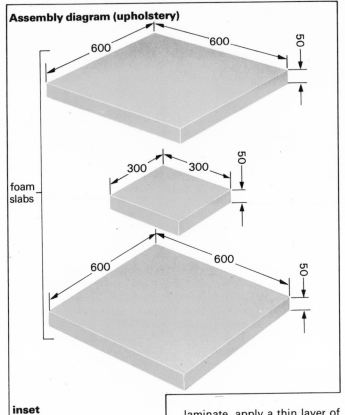

foam slabs

inset

air

50

stage 3

If finishing the seat frame with polyurethane lacquer, apply the first coat with a lint-free rag and let it dry thoroughly before applying the second.

If painting the frame, apply a coat of primer, undercoat and then top coat, allowing each coat to dry thoroughly before applying the next. When the lacquer or paint has dried, fix four 50mm long tabs of the rough half of Velcro with tacks.

Fix two of these on the back A and two on seat B at the dimensions shown (**see plans A and B**).

stage 4

Cut the upholstery foam with a serrated knife (a bread knife will do) into two 600mm squares and one 300mm square.

Using a stiff piece of card, or a piece of scrap plastic

laminate, apply a thin layer of impact adhesive to one side and two opposite edges of each 600mm square and both sides of the 300mm one. Leave the adhesive to dry (according to manufacturer's instructions) and then place the 300mm square in the centre of the glued side of one of the larger slabs; lay on the other slab to form a sandwich (**see upholstery assembly diagram**). Apply hand pressure for a few seconds. Press the outer edges of the top and bottom slabs firmly together so they meet at a point and the cushion becomes dome-shaped (**see inset**). Repeat for second cushion.

stage 5

For each chair there are two cushions, one back and one seat (both the same size) which zip together. You can make paper patterns from our cutting plans or cut straight from the fabric.

Note All seam allowances are 15mm wide unless otherwise stated. Always baste (tack) within the seam allowance and stitch on the seam line. At each stage after machine stitching remove basting stitches.

For each cushion cover, cut

Fabric cutting plans

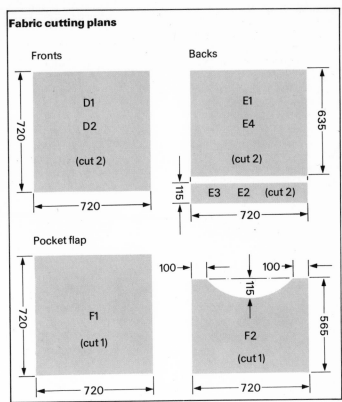

Fronts

D1
D2
(cut 2)

720

720

Backs

E1
E4
(cut 2)

635

115

E3 E2 (cut 2)

720

Pocket flap

F1
(cut 1)

720

720

100 100

115

F2
(cut 1)

565

720

1 Joining back cover pieces

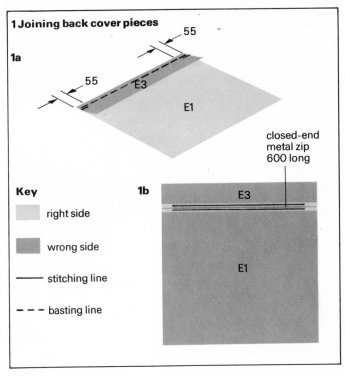

1a

55

55

E3

E1

Key

right side

wrong side

—— stitching line

- - - basting line

1b

closed-end metal zip 600 long

E3

E1

one front piece D and two back pieces E to the dimensions shown (**see cutting plans D and E**). Take back pieces E1 and E3 and, with right sides together, line up two long edges. Measure 55mm in from each side edge (and 15mm down from the top) and pin, baste and stitch these short lengths (**see 1a**). Baste across the opening,

then press the complete seam open. Neaten raw edges of seams with pinking shears or oversew if the fabric frays. On the wrong side of the fabric, place closed metal zip, right side down, centrally over the line of basting between the stitched seams. Pin, baste and machine the zip to the back piece with matching thread (**see 1b**). It will help if you use a zipper foot attachment on your machine as it enables you to stitch closer to the zip. Then press again. Repeat the process for back pieces E2 and E4. The large open-ended zips are sewn in at the same time as the front and back pieces are stitched together. Undo two zips to make four halves – two 'positives' with the zipper attached and two 'negatives' without any zipper. Note that all zips close from right to left when viewed from the front; take care when positioning them. Pin and baste one negative zip half centrally along top edge of front cover D1, right side of zip to right side of cover, with the teeth facing inwards and as close as possible to the 15mm seam allowance (**see 2a**). Pin and baste the other negative zip half in the same way along the left-hand side of D1 and the two positive zip halves on the two remaining sides, making sure all zips close from right to left.

To stitch front and back pieces together, undo the metal zip in the back piece. With right sides together, place back piece E1/3 over front piece D1, sandwiching the zips in between (**see 2b**). Pin, baste and stitch through all thicknesses round all four sides. Trim and neaten the seams, cutting off excess fabric diagonally at the corners. Turn the cover through to the right side and press. Using the contrasting colour thread, topstitch all round the outside edges of the cover, 10mm in from the seams (**see 2c**). Repeat the process for the second cover with D2 and E2/4.

To hold the double cushions in place you need to stitch two 50mm lengths of soft pad Velcro to the back of each cushion cover, to line up with their corresponding rough pad halves already attached to the chair frame. To do this accurately, insert the foam cushion slabs and zip up the covers, making sure the metal zips are at the bottom of the back cushion, and at the back of the seat cushion, or they would interfere with the placing of the Velcro tabs. Zip the back and seat cushions together and place on the chair frame.

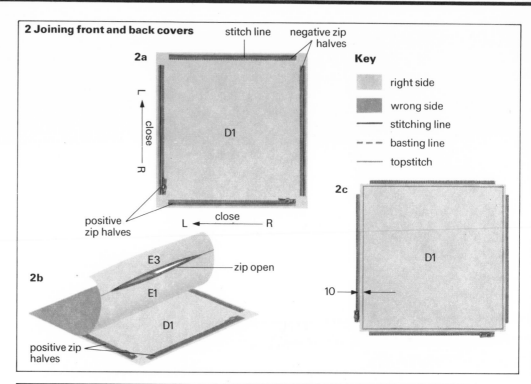

2 Joining front and back covers

Key

right side

wrong side

—— stitching line

- - - basting line

—— topstitch

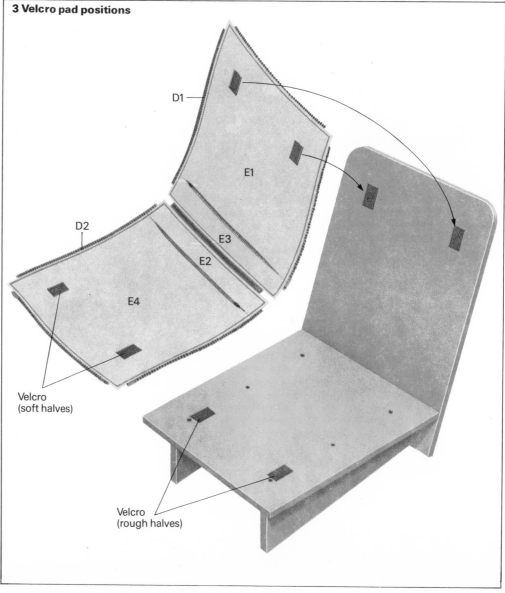

3 Velcro pad positions

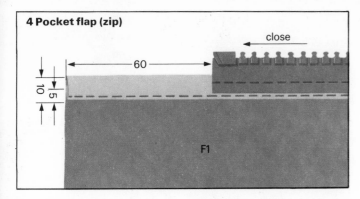

4 Pocket flap (zip)

60

10

5

close

F1

5 Pocket flap (binding)

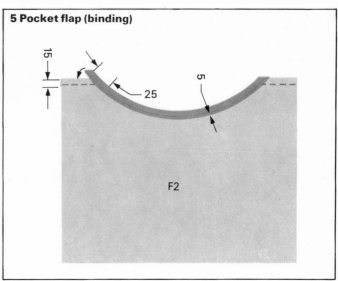

15

25

5

F2

First mark the positions for the Velcro on the back cushion cover E1.
Take off the cover, stitch the Velcro in place and reassemble the cushion. Attach the back cushion to the frame, matching the Velcro tabs, and ease the seat cushion into the angle between the frame back and seat. Then mark the correct position on the seat cushion for the remaining two Velcro tabs to line up with those on the frame seat. Remove the foam slab, stitch the Velcro and reassemble the seat cushion before fixing it in place (**see 3**).

stage 6

For the pocket flap which hangs down the back of the chair, cut one pocket flap piece F1 (to the same dimensions as cushion front D) and one pocket piece F2 (**see cutting plans F1 and 2**).
On top edge of flap piece F1 turn under 5mm to the wrong side, then a further 10mm. Pin and baste this double hem in place. Then take the positive half of an open-ended zip and, with the right side of the zip to the wrong side of flap F1, baste zip centrally along the hemmed edge, teeth facing outwards (**see 4**). When seen from the right side the zip closes from left to right here. Turn the fabric right side up and, starting at one side of the basted hemmed edge, stitch the zip in position with the contrasting colour thread to the cover fabric.
Turn under 15mm to the wrong side on the two short edges either side of the curved edge on pocket piece F2 and baste. Cut a length of upholstery tape to fit round

the curved edge, allowing an extra 50mm for turnings. Bind the curved edge with tape, pinning and basting in position and easing the tape round the curve to avoid puckering. Turn under the excess at either end of the tape and baste in place on the wrong side. Stitch the tape with matching colour thread, 5mm in from the free edge (**see 5**).
With the wrong side of pocket piece F2 to the right side of pocket flap F1, pin and baste together round the side and bottom edges.
To divide the pocket into two, mark the centre line from the base to the centre of the curve with a line of basting stitches. With contrasting colour thread, topstitch up this line to within 100mm of the curved edge. To strengthen this stitching, sew in a triangle of stitches at the top (**see 6a**). With contrasting colour thread, topstitch across the two short edges either side of the curve (including tape) through pocket piece F1, 5mm in from the fold. For extra strength, make a second line of stitches across the tape as shown (**see 6b**).
Bind the three remaining edges of the pocket flap with upholstery tape. Turn under a small hem across the tape at one end, enclosing the top corner of flap (**see 6c**). Pin and baste the tape down around the edges, neatening it at the bottom corners by folding excess tape at a diagonal and finishing off as before. Stitch tape with matching thread to the pocket flap, 5mm from free edges, through all thicknesses — then press. Zip the pocket to the complementary zip half on the top edge of the back cushion.

6 Pocket flap (finishing details)

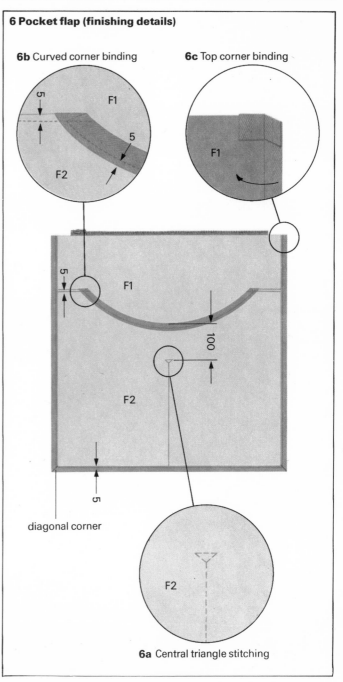

6b Curved corner binding

5

F1

5

F2

6c Top corner binding

F1

5

F1

100

F2

5

diagonal corner

F2

6a Central triangle stitching

TV cabinet

Make this simple and attractive cabinet to house your television set safely as well as provide useful shelf space for records, cassette tapes and books.

stage 1

Measure and mark the cutting lines on both sides of the sheet of plywood according to the dimensions shown (**see cutting list and cutting plan**). Score along these lines with a sharp knife held against a metal straight-edge and cut all the pieces to size with a panel saw keeping to the waste side of the line to avoid damaging the surface veneer as you cut.

Smooth all cut edges with a block plane and label each part with the appropriate letter to avoid confusion later. Place the main upright E1 in a vice with its bottom edge uppermost. Place the shelf C on top of E so E is 139mm in from the end of C. Drill five 6mm diameter dowel holes 36mm deep through C into E at the dimensions shown (**see 1**).

Insert short lengths of dowel in the first two holes as they are drilled to keep C and E accurately in position while

drilling the rest of the holes. Place the other main upright E2 in a vice and repeat the procedure to make the dowel holes in the other end of C and in the bottom edge of E2. Drill five 5mm diameter clearance holes 148mm in from each end of the base A 25mm in from the front and back edges and equally spaced between these. Countersink them on the bottom face to take No 8 screws. Hold one of the small uprights B in the required position on the base A and mark with a bradawl through the clearance holes in A onto B; drill 2mm pilot holes at these points. Apply woodworking adhesive to the bottom edge of B and fix it in position with the No 8 screws. Wipe off excess adhesive with a clean dampened cloth and fix the other small upright B in the same way.

stage 2

Hold the shelf C in the required position on top of the two small uprights B, making sure the joins between the uprights B and the base A remain square and the ends of C and A are flush.

Drill 6mm diameter holes a further 18mm deep through the previously drilled 6mm diameter holes in the shelf C

Assembly diagram

F

D1

E1

E2

B1

C

A

dowels

D2

hardwood lipping

B2

Overall dimensions
1087mm wide, 717mm high, 394mm front to back (43 × 28 × 16in). Project dimensions are in metric only and do not allow for cutting wastages.

Front elevation
(dimensions in millimetres)

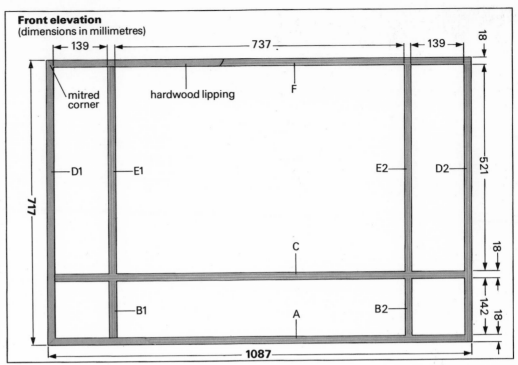

mitred corner

hardwood lipping

F

139 — 737 — 139 — 18

D1 — E1 — E2 — D2 — 521

717

C — 18 — 142 — 18

B1 — A — B2

1087

into the top edges of B1 and B2.

Cut ten 54mm lengths of the 6mm diameter dowel with a tenon saw. Apply adhesive to the fixing edges of B1 and B2 and pour adhesive in the dowel holes in B and C. Push the cut dowels firmly in position through C into B1 and B2. Wipe off excess adhesive.

Drill twelve 5mm diameter clearance holes in each side D at the dimensions shown (**see 2**) and countersink them on the outside face to take No 8 screws. Hold one of the sides D against the basic assembly so the bottom edges of D and the base A are flush. Mark with a bradawl through the clearance holes onto the ends of the shelf C and the base A. Drill 2mm pilot holes at these points, apply

Cutting plan

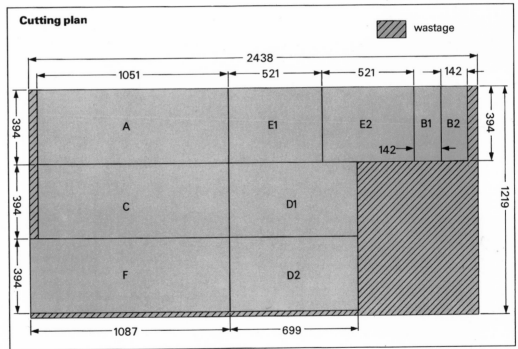

wastage

2438

1051 — 521 — 521 — 142

A — E1 — E2 — B1 B2 — 394

394

142

C — D1 — 1219

394

F — D2

1087 — 699

Tools and materials
timber (see cutting list)
measuring tape, pencil and try square, vice or Workmate
sharp trimming knife and metal straight-edge
panel saw and tenon saw, mitre box or guide
block plane, medium fine and fine glasspaper
hand or electric drill, 2, 5 and 6mm bits
screwdriver, bradawl, countersink bit
hammer, nail punch, woodworking adhesive, clean cloth
No 8 countersunk screws 38mm long, panel pins 19mm long
600mm of 6mm dowel for ten dowels 54mm long
4m of 18 × 6mm hardwood lipping

For finish
cellulose filler or plastic wood
primer, undercoat, top coat, 50mm paint brush

Cutting list for plywood

Description	Key	Quantity	Dimensions
Base	A	1	1051 × 394 × 18mm
Small uprights	B	2	394 × 142 × 18mm
Shelf	C	1	1051 × 394 × 18mm
Sides	D	2	699 × 394 × 18mm
Main uprights	E	2	521 × 394 × 18mm
Top	F	1	1087 × 394 × 18mm

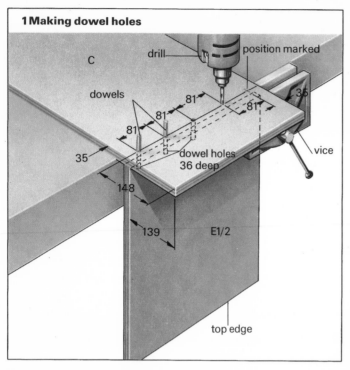

1 Making dowel holes

C

drill

position marked

dowels

81

81

81

35

81

81

35

dowel holes
36 deep

148

139

E1/2

35

vice

top edge

adhesive to these ends of C and A and fix D firmly in position with No 8 screws. Wipe off excess adhesive and fix the second side D in the the same way.

stage 3

Pour adhesive in the dowel holes in both main uprights E and smear some along the bottom edges as well. Fix the two main uprights on the dowels already glued into the shelf C. Push the uprights firmly home so there is no gap between them and the shelf C; you may need a hammer to do this so remember to protect the top edges of the uprights with a piece of scrap wood when hammering. Wipe off all excess adhesive.
Drill all the 5mm diameter clearance holes in the top F

at the dimensions shown (**see 3**) and countersink them on the top face to take No 8 screws. Lower F into the required position on the assembly so all edges are flush; mark with a bradawl through the clearance holes in F onto both sides D and both main uprights E, making sure all joints remain square while you work. Remove F and drill 2mm pilot holes at these points; apply adhesive to the top edges of both sides D and main uprights E and fix the top F firmly in position with the No 8 screws. Wipe off excess adhesive.

stage 4

Cut the hardwood lipping with a tenon saw into two 1087mm lengths and two 717mm lengths and mitre both ends of the cut lengths using a mitre box or guide. Apply adhesive to the front edges of the top, base and sides of the cabinet and fix the lippings in position with 19mm long panel pins, placing these at 50mm intervals.
Fill all holes, cracks and abrasions with cellulose filler or plastic wood, paying particular attention to the screw heads and the mitre joints in the lippings. Rub all surfaces smooth with medium fine, then fine, glasspaper. •
For the finish apply a coat of primer, an undercoat and at least two top coats, allowing plenty of time for each to dry before applying the next.

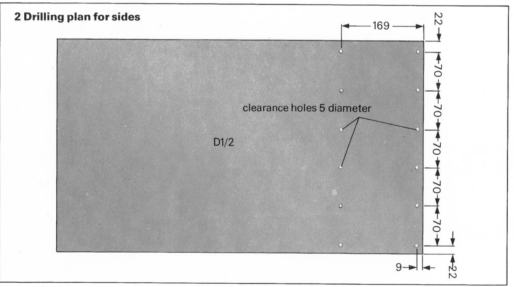

2 Drilling plan for sides

169

22

clearance holes 5 diameter

D1/2

70

70

70

70

70

70

9

22

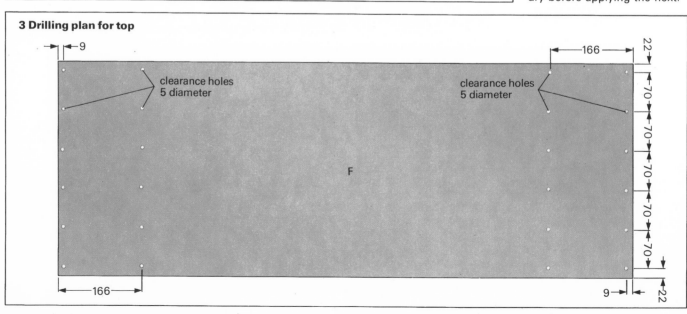

3 Drilling plan for top

9

clearance holes
5 diameter

166

22

clearance holes
5 diameter

70

70

70

70

70

F

166

9

22

The bedroom

Wardrobe

Our three-door wardrobe has ample hanging space as well as adjustable shelving on which to store clothes neatly. In the main section there is a shoe rack and full-length mirror and behind the right-hand door a make-up mirror and useful rack for jewellery and other odds and ends. The doors are opened from the top, which allows a flush front surface, and the whole wardrobe unit can be easily dismantled.

stage 1

Measure and mark out the cutting lines onto both sides of the chipboard panels according to the dimensions shown (**see cutting list**). Score along these lines through the surface veneer with a sharp knife held against a metal straight-edge. Cut all the chipboard to size with a fine-tooth panel saw, keeping slightly to the waste side of the line to avoid damaging the surface veneer. Smooth all cut edges with medium fine, then fine, glasspaper.

Cut all the hardwood and hardboard to size with a tenon saw, keeping the saw at a shallow angle to the board when cutting the hardboard. Smooth all cut edges as before and, to avoid confusion later, label each part with the appropriate code letter.

Take one of the upright panels A and lay it on a flat surface with what will be the inside face (worst face) uppermost; this is now the left-hand panel A1. Fix one half of each knock-down corner joint with the 25mm long No 6 countersunk chipboard screws at the dimensions shown (**see 1a**). Repeat this procedure for the right-hand panel A3 (**see 1b**) and for both faces of the central upright panel A2

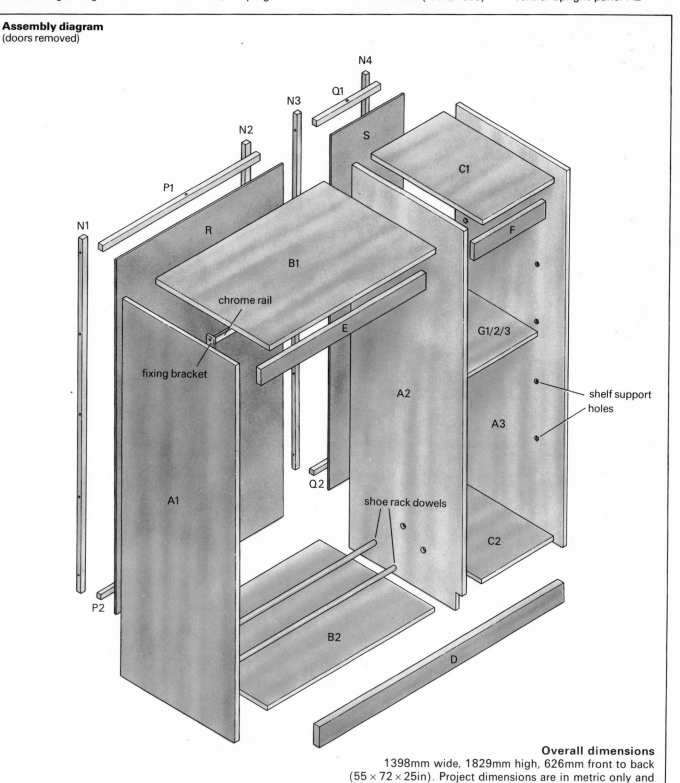

Assembly diagram
(doors removed)

N4
N3
Q1
N2
S
P1
C1
N1
R
F
B1
chrome rail
E
G1/2/3
fixing bracket
A2
shelf support holes
A3
Q2
A1
shoe rack dowels
C2
P2
B2
D

Overall dimensions
1398mm wide, 1829mm high, 626mm front to back
(55 × 72 × 25in). Project dimensions are in metric only and
do not allow for cutting wastages.

Tools and materials

timber (see cutting lists)
measuring tape, pencil and try square
fine-tooth panel saw, hacksaw, tenon saw
sharp trimming knife, metal straight-edge
medium fine, fine and flour glasspaper, block plane
screwdriver, bradawl, countersink bit
electric drill, 4, 6 and 25mm bits
hammer and nail punch, mitre box (or guide)
woodworking adhesive, clean cloth

For assembly

24 brown knock-down corner joints
20 brown shelf supports and sockets
No 6 countersunk chipboard screws 12 and 25mm long
panel pins 12, 25 and 38mm long
hardboard nails, 12mm long tacks
2m of 25mm dowel, 75mm of 6mm dowel
150mm of 16mm matching iron-on edge veneer strip
1m of 18mm diameter chrome rail and two fixing brackets
two 25mm brass backflap hinges and 12mm long brass
    countersunk screws to fit
nine lay-on hinges and 12mm long round head chipboard
    screws to fit
300mm of 50mm wide webbing tape
one 300mm square mirror (cut to size)
four double-sided sticky pads
14m of 16mm half-round moulding
matching plastic wood or stopping, clear matt polyurethane
    lacquer, coloured wood stain and 50mm and 25mm paint
    brushes (for finish)

Cutting list for veneer-faced chipboard

Description	Key	Quantity	Dimensions
Upright panels	A	3	1829 × 610 × 16mm
Large top and base panels	B	2	900 × 610 × 16mm
Small top and base panels	C	2	610 × 450 × 16mm
Plinth	D	1	1366 × 64 × 16mm
Long cross rail	E	1	900 × 64 × 16mm
Short cross rail	F	1	450 × 64 × 16mm
Shelves	G	3	480 × 450 × 16mm
Doors	H	3	1816 × 456 × 16mm
Mirror panel	J	1	300 × 300 × 16mm
Rack front	K	1	300 × 65 × 16mm
Rack base	L	1	268 × 65 × 16mm
Rack sides	M	2	65 × 65 × 16mm

Cutting list for hardwood & hardboard

Description	Key	Quantity	Dimensions
Upright battens	N	4	1733 × 18 × 18mm
Long cross battens	P	2	864 × 18 × 18mm
Short cross battens	Q	2	414 × 18 × 18mm
Large back panel (hardboard)	R	1	1733 × 900 × 3mm
Small back panel (hardboard)	S	1	1733 × 450 × 3mm

(**see 2a and 2b**). Using a tenon saw, cut the recess out of the bottom front corner of the central upright panel A2 according to the dimensions shown (**see 2a and 2b**); this is to house the plinth D.
Screw the other half of the knock-down corner joints onto those already fixed on the upright panels. Slide the large and small top and base panels B and C into the required position (**see assembly diagram**) and mark with a bradawl through the clearance holes in the corner joints onto the top and base panels.
Remove these panels, unscrew the unfixed halves of the corner joints and fix them firmly to the top and base panels as before.
Drill the 25mm diameter holes, 8mm deep, in the inside face of the left-hand upright panel A1 at the dimensions shown (**see 1a**) and in the left-hand face of the central upright panel A2 (**see 2a**); these holes are to take the dowels for the shoe rack.
Drill all the holes, of the correct diameter and depth for the shelf supports you are using, on the inside face of

the right-hand upright panel A3 at the dimensions shown (**see 1b**) and on the right-hand face of the central upright panel A2 (**see 2b**). Push the shelf support sockets in position in these holes, ramming them home with a mallet if necessary. Cut two 916mm lengths of the 25mm dowel and position these in the holes drilled in the upright panels A1 and A2 (you will need help to do this). Fix the upright panels A and the large and small top and base panels B and C together, using the previously fixed knock-down corner joints. Make sure you tighten the screw in each joint firmly. Fix the plinth D in position in the same way and stand this assembly upright.

stage 2

Drill all the 4mm diameter clearance holes in the hardwood upright battens N at the dimensions shown (**see 3a and 3b**) and the long and short cross battens P and Q (**see 4a and 4b**); countersink them to take No 6 screws. Glue and nail the upright battens N and the long and short cross

battens P and Q to the rough sides of the large and small hardboard back panels R and S, using the 12mm long hardboard nails. Make sure the countersunk holes are facing inwards in every case (**see 5**).
When the adhesive has set hard, position the back panels inside the rest of the assembly, with the smooth side of the hardboard facing inwards, so the back edges of the hardwood battens are flush with the back edges of panels A, B and C. Mark with a bradawl through the clearance holes drilled in the hardwood battens onto panels A, B and C to make pilot holes and fix the back panels firmly in position with the 25mm long No 6

countersunk chipboard screws. Don't use adhesive to fix the back panels or you will not be able to take the wardrobe apart. Cut the chrome rail with a hacksaw to 900mm long and smooth both ends with a fine flat file. Slide the chrome fixing brackets over the rail and fix them in position with the 12mm long No 6 chipboard screws at the dimensions shown (**see 6**).

stage 3

Cut six 1816mm lengths of the half-round moulding with a tenon saw and glue and pin the cut lengths to the long edges of the doors H, using the 25mm long panel pins and spacing these at about 100mm intervals. Cut three 450mm

Plan and elevation
(dimensions in millimetres)

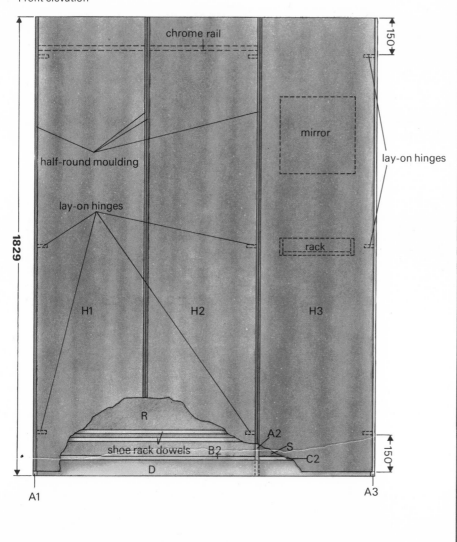

Plan

half-round moulding

Front elevation

lengths of the half-round moulding and glue and pin these to the front (450mm long) edges of the shelves G. Cut two 300mm lengths of the half-round moulding and glue and pin these to two opposite edges of the mirror panel J. Punch all pin heads below the surface with a nail punch and wipe off all excess adhesive with a clean dampened cloth.

Apply iron-on edge veneer strip to both ends of the rack front K and trim off any waste with a block plane (see 7). Apply woodworking adhesive to both ends of the rack base L and fix the rack sides M in position with the 38mm long panel pins so the front, back and bottom edges are flush.

Apply adhesive to the front edges of this assembly and fix the rack front K in position with the 38mm long panel pins, making certain all edges are flush. Punch the pin heads below the surface with a nail punch and wipe off excess adhesive.

Cut a 300mm length of the half-round moulding and mitre both ends; cut two 81mm lengths and mitre one end of both pieces (see 7). Apply adhesive to the fixing edges of these cut lengths of moulding (remembering the mitre joints) and fix the mouldings in position with the 12mm long panel pins so all edges are flush. Punch all the pin heads below the surface and wipe off excess adhesive.

Turn this rack on its front and drill a 6mm diameter hole, 25mm deep, in the middle of the back edge of both sides M. Drill two 6mm diameter holes, 8mm deep, in the inside face of the door H3 at the dimensions shown (see 7 inset) and cut two 32mm lengths of the 6mm diameter dowel. Pour adhesive inside all the dowel holes and apply some to the back edges of the sides M. Push the cut lengths of 6mm dowel into the holes and fix the rack in position on the door. Lay this door on a flat surface and place a weight on the rack until the adhesive has set. Alternatively fix the rack with two keyhole plates to

69

1 Upright panel

1a Left-hand panel

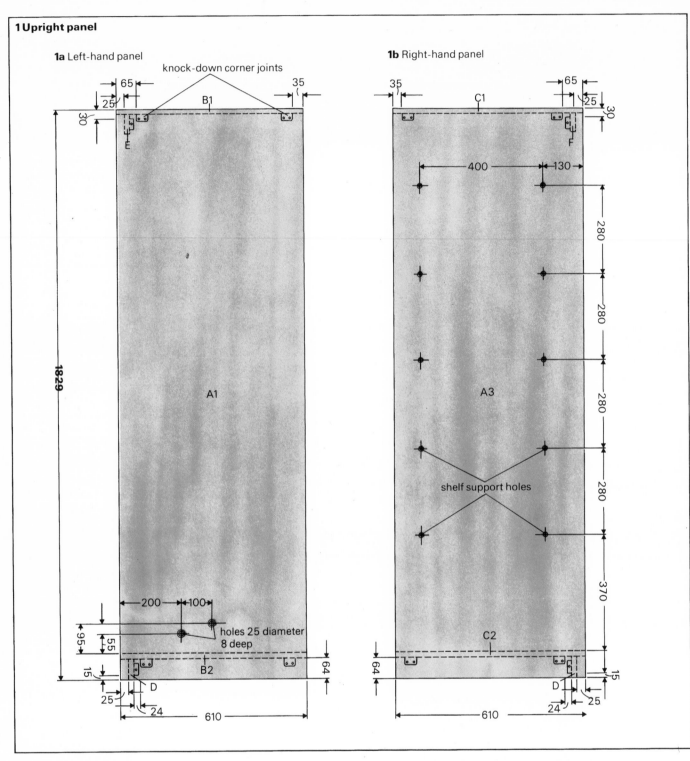

knock-down corner joints

B1

65
35
25
30
E

A1

holes 25 diameter
8 deep

200 100

95
55
15
B2
D
25
24
610
1829

1b Right-hand panel

C1

35
65
25
30
F

400 130

280
280
280
280
280
370

A3

shelf support holes

C2

64
D
15
25
24
610
64

---

enable it to be removed. Wipe off excess adhesive. Cut a 300mm length of the 50mm wide webbing and fix this to the back face of the mirror panel J with the 12mm long tacks, so you form a number of loops to take the 25mm adjusting dowel (**see 8**). Hold the two brass backflap hinges on the back face of the mirror panel 25mm in from each side edge, so the knuckle of each hinge is against the fixed edge of the half-round

moulding. Mark with a bradawl through the holes then fix the hinges firmly in position with 12mm long screws of the correct gauge to fit the hinges. Fix the mirror onto the mirror panel with four double-sided sticky pads, placing these about 25mm in from each corner (**see 8**).
Hold the mirror in the required position against the inside face of the door H3 (**see 8 inset**) and mark

with a bradawl through the holes in the unattached hinge leaves onto the door.

stage 4

Fill any holes, cracks and abrasions with matching plastic wood or stopping and rub all surfaces smooth with fine, then flour, glasspaper. Apply two coats of clear matt polyurethane lacquer to all outer surfaces of the wardrobe and doors; we

applied a light blue stain to the half-round moulding on the doors. It is not necessary to apply a finish to the inside.
Lay the wardrobe on its back ready to take the doors and place the shelves underneath to support the hardboard back. You will need help to fix the doors. Lay all three doors in position so their top edges are flush with the top edges of the wardrobe.
Remove the right-hand door,

2 Centre upright panel detail

2a Left-hand face

2b Right-hand face

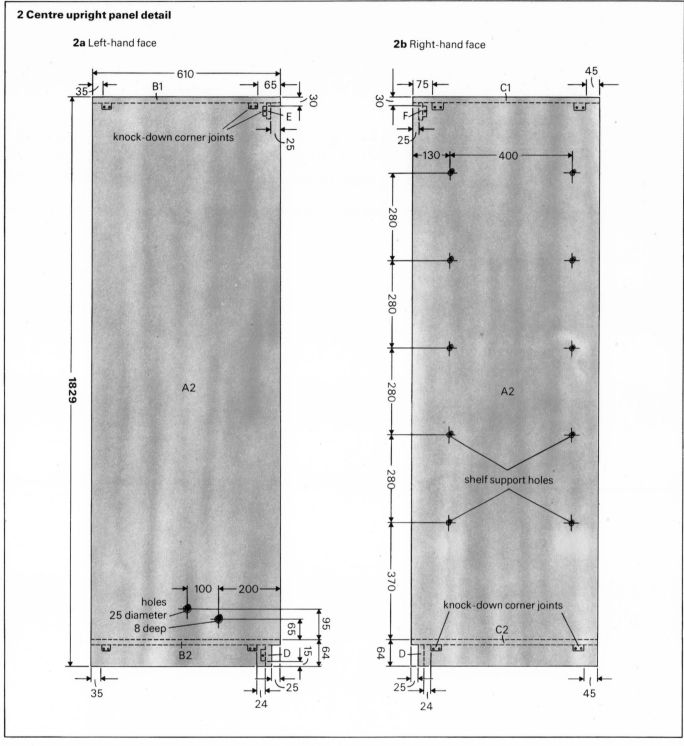

knock-down corner joints

E

A2

holes
25 diameter
8 deep

B2

D

610
B1
65
35
30
25
1829
100
200
65
95
64
15
35
24
25

75
C1
45
30
F
25
130
400
280
280
280
280
280
370
shelf support holes
knock-down corner joints
C2
64
D
25
24
45

---

3 Drilling plans for upright battens

4 Drilling plans for cross battens

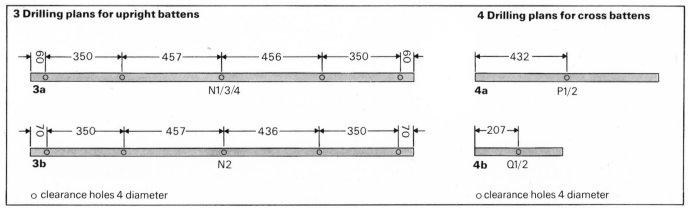

3a N1/3/4
60 350 457 456 350 60

3b N2
70 350 457 436 350 70

4a P1/2
432

4b Q1/2
207

o clearance holes 4 diameter

o clearance holes 4 diameter

5 Back assembly

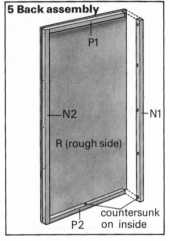

P1

N2 — — N1

R (rough side)

P2

countersunk on inside

6 Chrome rail fixing detail

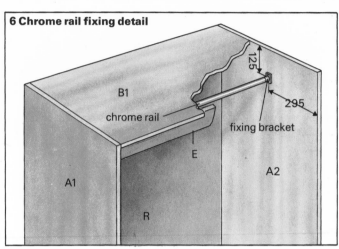

B1

chrome rail

fixing bracket

125

295

E

A1

A2

R

7 Rack assembly

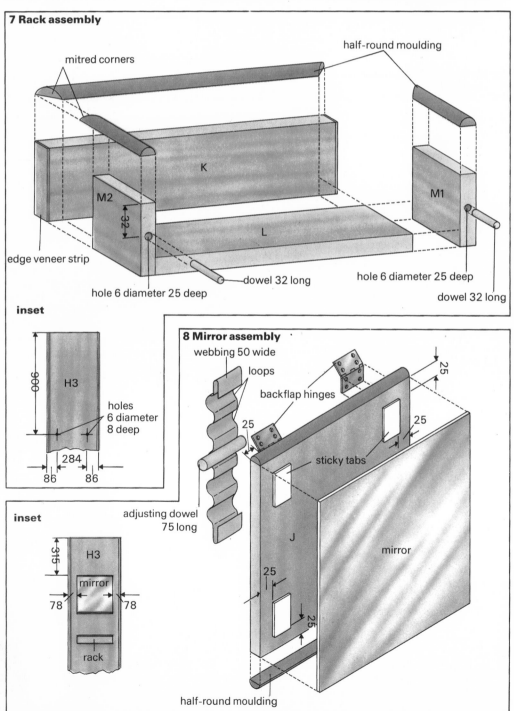

mitred corners

half-round moulding

K

M2

M1

32

edge veneer strip

hole 6 diameter 25 deep

dowel 32 long

L

hole 6 diameter 25 deep

dowel 32 long

inset

900

H3

holes 6 diameter 8 deep

284

86   86

inset

315

H3

mirror

78   78

rack

8 Mirror assembly

webbing 50 wide

loops

backflap hinges

sticky tabs

25

25

25

25

adjusting dowel 75 long

J

25

25

mirror

half-round moulding

then the centre door, taking great care not to disturb the left-hand door. Climb inside the wardrobe, taking care to step onto the area of the hardboard supported by the shelves otherwise you might break the back panel, and hold one of the lay-on hinges in the three required positions against the door and upright panel (**see 9**); mark the positions of the holes for the fixing screws with a pencil. Remove the door and make pilot holes with a bradawl at these points. Fix the hinges to the door and upright panel with the 12mm round head chipboard screws. Climb inside the wardrobe with a torch and, with help, lower the centre door into position so it lines up exactly with the left-hand door. Mark the positions of the lay-on hinges as before and fix the door in position. Fix the right-hand door with three lay-on hinges in the same way.

Stand the assembled wardrobe upright, push the shelf supports in position at the desired height and rest the shelves G on top of them. Fix the mirror in position with the 12mm long screws. Cut a 75mm length of the 25mm diameter dowel and push this through one of the loops in the webbing on the back of the mirror panel. Adjust the angle of the mirror, if necessary, by removing the adjusting dowel and trying it in some of the other loops in the webbing. Push the wardrobe into the desired position in the room. If the floor is not level, the doors will not line up correctly; to correct any discrepancy, place small wedges under each corner of the wardrobe.

9 Fixing the doors

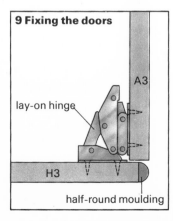

A3

lay-on hinge

H3

half-round moulding

Chest of drawers

Make this attractive chest of drawers from easy-to-use pine veneered chipboard. As well as three large drawers, it has a pull-out flap.

Assembly diagram

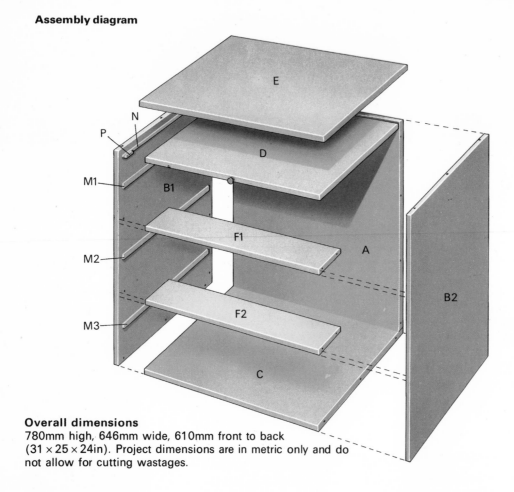

Overall dimensions
780mm high, 646mm wide, 610mm front to back
(31 × 25 × 24in). Project dimensions are in metric only and do not allow for cutting wastages.

stage 1

Measure and mark the cutting lines on both sides of the three Handiboard panels according to the dimensions shown (**see cutting list and cutting plan**). Score along these lines with a sharp knife held against a metal straight-edge and cut the various pieces to size with a fine-tooth panel saw;

keep slightly to the waste side of the line to avoid damaging the surface veneer. Smooth all cut edges with medium fine, then fine, glasspaper. Label each part with the appropriate code letter to avoid confusion later.

Measure and cut all the plywood and hardwood pieces to the dimensions shown (**see cutting list and cutting plan**), using a panel saw for the plywood and a tenon saw for the hardwood. Smooth all cut edges as before. Apply the iron-on matching edge veneer to all exposed chipboard edges that will show (**see cutting plan for Handiboard panels**).

stage 2

Drill all the 6mm diameter dowel holes in the Handiboard pieces A, B1 and B2, C, E and F1 and F2 according to the dimensions shown (**see drilling plans**). Accuracy is essential. The holes must all be 12mm deep. To ensure you do not drill too deep, insert the 6mm diameter twist bit inside the drill chuck as far as it will go and tighten up the chuck. Carefully measure the distance from the end of the chuck to the point of the twist bit, deduct 12mm from this measurement and cut a piece of scrap wood, approximately 25mm square, to exactly this length; chamfer all edges and smooth the cut ends. Drill through the centre of the piece of scrap wood until the wood touches the drill chuck; the length of protruding twist bit will now be 12mm (**see 1**).

Cut the dowel with a tenon saw into twenty 24mm lengths and chamfer the ends of each one with medium fine glasspaper.

Pour some woodworking adhesive into all the holes drilled into the edges of the panels A, B1 and B2, C and F1 and F2. Insert the cut lengths of dowel into these holes. Wipe off excess adhesive with a clean dampened cloth.

Pour some adhesive into the holes in the back surface of the base C and apply some to the bottom edge of the back A. Fix the two panels

Tools and materials

timber (see cutting lists)
measuring tape, pencil and try square
fine-tooth panel saw, tenon saw
sharp trimming knife and metal straight-edge
medium fine, fine and flour glasspaper
hand or electric drill, 2, 3, 4 and 6mm bits
screwdriver, bradawl, countersink bit
woodworking adhesive and clean cloth

For assembly

No 4 countersunk chipboard screws 12mm long
No 4 countersunk screws 19mm long
No 6 countersunk chipboard screws 19 and 25mm long
No 6 countersunk screws 12 and 38mm long
six joint blocks
500mm of 6mm dowel for 20 dowels 24mm long
six large and one small pine drawer knobs
matching plastic wood, clear matt polyurethane lacquer
    and 25 and 50mm paint brushes (for finish)

Cutting list for plywood & hardwood

Description	Key	Quantity	Dimensions
Drawer backs	H	3	573 × 213 × 12mm
Drawer sides	J	6	559 × 213 × 12mm
Drawer bases	K	3	597 × 559 × 4mm
Fixing battens	L	3	573 × 12 × 12mm
Drawer runners (hardwood)	M	12	559 × 16 × 6mm
Flap supports (hardwood)	N	2	559 × 6 × 6mm
Flap stops (hardwood)	P	4	38 × 6 × 6mm

Front elevation
(dimensions in millimetres)

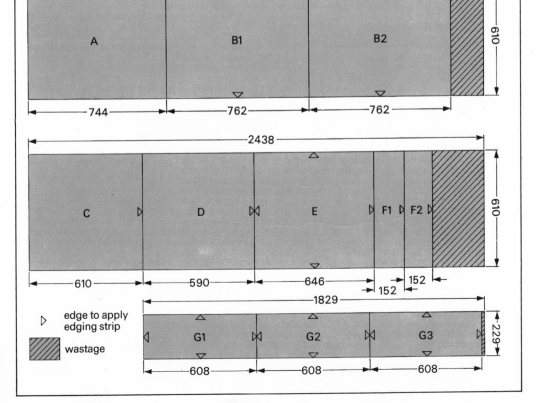

Cutting list for Handiboard panels

Description	Key	Quantity	Dimensions
Back	A	1	744 × 610 × 18mm
Sides	B	2	762 × 610 × 18mm
Base	C	1	610 × 610 × 18mm
Pull-out flap (see text)	D	1	610 × 590 × 18mm
Top	E	1	646 × 610 × 18mm
Drawer supports	F	2	610 × 152 × 18mm
Drawer fronts (see text)	G	3	608 × 229 × 18mm

together using the dowels already fixed into A. Wipe off all excess adhesive.

Pour some adhesive into the holes in the back and bottom surfaces of the side panel B1 and apply some to the fixing edge of the back A and base C (**see assembly diagram**). Fix B1 in position using the dowels already fixed in A and C; wipe off all excess adhesive. Turn the assembly carefully over so B1 is resting on the floor. Pour adhesive into the holes in B1 which will take the dowels already fixed in the drawer supports F1 and F2. Apply adhesive to one end of F1 and F2 and fix firmly to B1. Wipe off excess adhesive. Pour adhesive in all the dowel holes (there are 11) drilled in the surface of the side B2, apply adhesive to the fixing edges of A, C, F1 and F2 and fix B2 firmly down using the dowels already fixed in A, C, F1 and F2. Wipe off excess adhesive.

stage 3

Drill three 4mm diameter holes through the 16mm wide edge of six of the drawer runners M, placing one hole in the middle and the others 25mm in from each end and countersink them to take No 6 screws. Hold each runner at the required height against the inside face of both sides B (**see front elevation**) and 18mm in from the front edges of B and mark with a bradawl through the clearance holes in the runners onto the sides. Apply adhesive to the fixing edge of each runner and fix them in position with the 19mm chipboard screws. Wipe off excess adhesive. Glue and screw the remaining six drawer runners M to the drawer sides J at the required height (**see 2**), making sure the front and back edges of the runners and the drawer sides are flush and the top edges of the runners are parallel to the top edges of the drawer sides. Wipe off

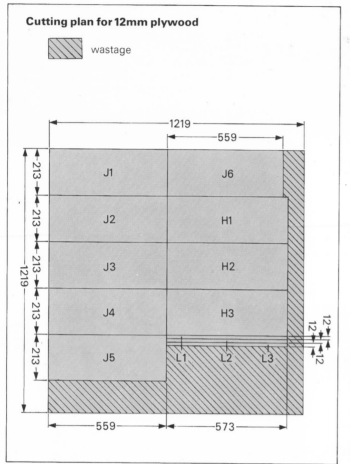

Cutting plan for 12mm plywood

▨ wastage

1219 — 559

J1 — J6
J2 — H1
J3 — H2
J4 — H3
J5 — L1 — L2 — L3

213 ×5, 1219

559 — 573

12 / 12 / 12

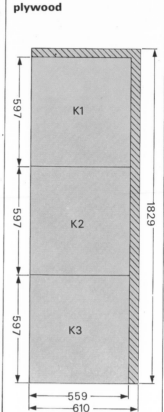

Cutting plan for 4mm plywood

K1
K2
K3

597 / 597 / 597, 1829

559
610

Drilling plans

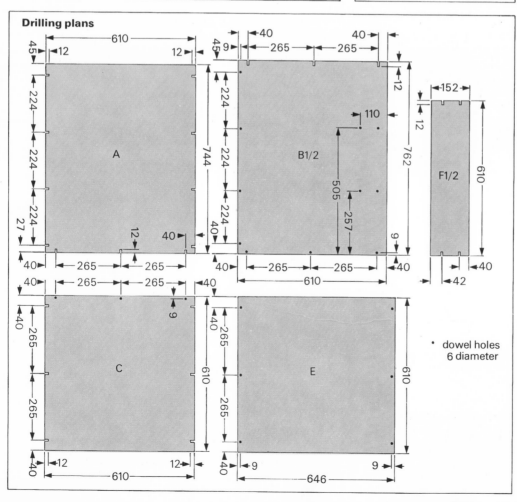

610
45 — 12 — 12
224 / 224 / 224 / 27
744
A
40 — 265 — 265 — 12 — 40
12 — 40

45 — 9 — 40 — 265 — 265 — 40
224 / 224 / 224 / 224 / 40
B1/2
12
110
505 / 257
9
40 — 265 — 265 — 40
610

152
12
762
F1/2
610
40
42

40 — 265 — 265 — 40
265 / 265
C
9
40
610
12 — 12
610

40 — 265 — 265 — 40
265 / 265
E
610
9 — 9
646

• dowel holes
6 diameter

excess adhesive.

Screw a joint block to the inside face of each of the six drawer sides J 50mm down from the top edge and flush with the front edge (**see 2**). Drill all the 4mm diameter clearance holes in the drawer bases K according to the dimensions shown (**see 2 inset**) and countersink them to take No 6 screws.

Drill three 4mm diameter clearance holes 6mm in from the back end of all drawer sides J, placing the holes 25mm in from each edge and one in the middle. Countersink them on the outside face (with the drawer runners attached) to take No 6 screws. Hold one of the drawer sides in the required position against one of the . drawer backs (**see 2**) so the top, bottom and back edges are flush. Mark through the clearance holes in the drawer sides onto the drawer back and drill 2mm pilot holes at these points. Apply adhesive to one end of the drawer back and fix one drawer side onto it with the 38mm long No 6 screws. Wipe off excess adhesive and fix the other drawer side to the drawer back. Repeat for the other two drawers.

Fix the drawer fronts G to each drawer assembly at the dimensions shown (**see 2**), using the joint blocks already fixed to the drawer sides. Make sure the joins between the drawer sides and the drawer backs remain square. Drill a 4mm diameter clearance hole 25mm in from each end of each fixing batten L and one in the middle. Countersink these to take No 6 screws. Hold each batten against the inside edge of each drawer front G so the bottom edge of the batten is flush with the bottom edges of the drawer sides J. Mark with a bradawl through the clearance holes in the batten onto the drawer front, apply adhesive to the fixing edge of the batten and fix it firmly in position with the 25mm chipboard screws.

To fix each drawer base K, turn the drawer assembly upside down and position the drawer base on it so all edges are flush. Mark with a bradawl through the clearance holes, already

drilled in the base, onto the sides J, the back H and the fixing batten L.
Drill 2mm pilot holes at these points, apply adhesive to the bottom edges of the sides, back and fixing batten and fix the base down with the 12mm countersunk screws. Wipe off excess adhesive.

stage 4

Drill 3mm diameter clearance holes in the flap supports N and stops P at the dimensions shown (**see 3 inset**) and countersink them to take No 4 screws.
Draw a line on the inside edge of both sides B exactly 19mm down from the top edge in each case, making sure the lines are parallel to the top edges. Apply adhesive to the fixing edge of N1 and N2 and fix them to the sides with the 19mm long No 4 chipboard screws. Wipe off excess adhesive.
Hold two of the four flap stops P in the required position on the flap supports (**see 3**) and mark with a bradawl through the clearance holes in the flap stops onto the flap supports. Drill 2mm pilot holes at these points, apply adhesive to the fixing edge of each flap stop and fix them in position with 12mm countersunk screws. Wipe off excess adhesive.
To provide sufficient clearance for the pull-out flap D so it will slide easily, trim 2mm off one 590mm side with a block plane and apply matching edge veneer to this side.
Glue and screw the two remaining flap stops P to the underside of the pull-out flap D at the dimensions shown (**see 4**), using the 12mm long No 4 chipboard screws. Wipe off excess adhesive.
Lay D in the required position in the chest (closed position). Pour adhesive inside the six dowel holes drilled in the underside of the top E and apply adhesive to the top edges of the back A and both sides B. Fix the top E firmly down, using the dowels already fixed in the back and sides. Wipe off excess adhesive and place a heavy weight on E until the adhesive has set.

stage 5

Fix a pair of knobs on the front of each drawer and on the pull-out flap D. Fill all holes, cracks and abrasions with matching plastic wood.
Smooth all surfaces with flour glasspaper and apply two coats of clear matt polyurethane lacquer, allowing the first to dry thoroughly.

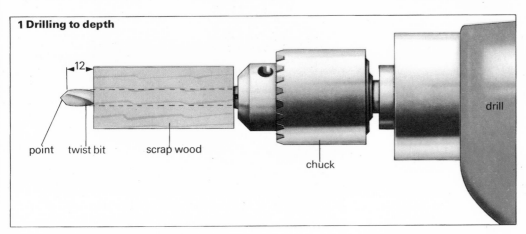

1 Drilling to depth

point   twist bit   scrap wood   chuck   drill

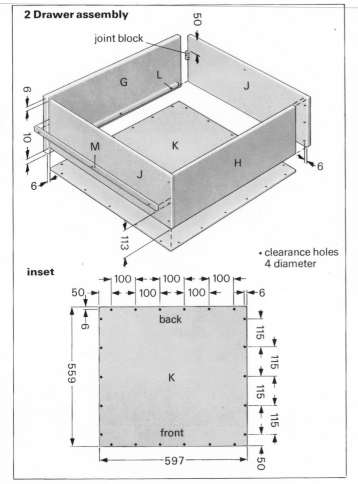

2 Drawer assembly

joint block
50
G L J
6
10
M K
6
J H
6
113
• clearance holes 4 diameter

inset
50
100 100 100
100 100 6
6
back
115
115
559
K
115
115
front
597
50

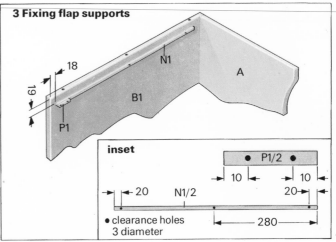

3 Fixing flap supports

N1
18
19
B1
A
P1

inset
• P1/2
10 10
20 N1/2 20
• clearance holes 3 diameter
280

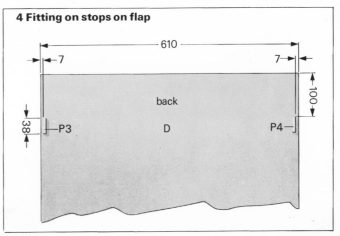

4 Fitting on stops on flap

610
7 7
100
back
38
P3 D P4

'Bed-sitter'

This bed is simple to make and a great space-saver. It has a large drawer for storage and a useful bedside trolley; both are on castors so they can be easily moved around.

Tools and materials

timber (see cutting lists)
measuring tape, pencil and try square
panel saw, tenon saw, hammer and nail punch
screwdriver, bradawl, countersink bit
hand or electric drill, 2, 5 and 12mm bits
medium fine and fine glasspaper
woodworking adhesive, clean cloth

For assembly

oval wire nails 38mm long
panel pins 38mm long, hardboard nails (if used)
No 8 countersunk chipboard screws 38mm long
No 8 countersunk screws 38mm long
10.75m of 18mm wide half-round moulding
2m of 50mm wide half-round moulding
two drawer handles
eight castors 46mm high and 18mm chipboard screws to fit
ten 19mm diameter steel furniture glides
four 150mm taper connectors and 25mm screws to fit
cellulose filler or plastic wood; primer, undercoat and top
    coat, matt polyurethane lacquer; 12 and 50mm brushes

Overall dimensions

1918mm long, 780mm wide, 351mm high (75 × 31 × 14in).
Project dimensions are in metric only.

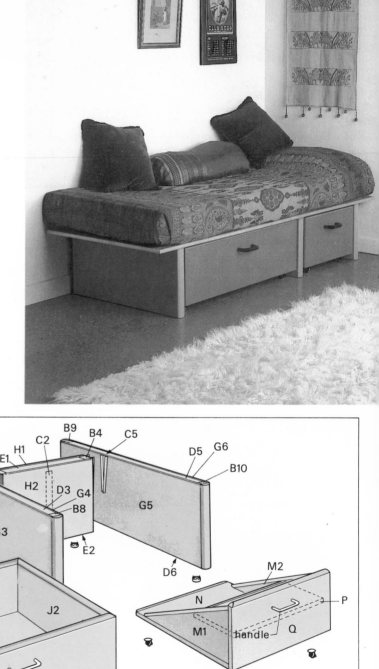

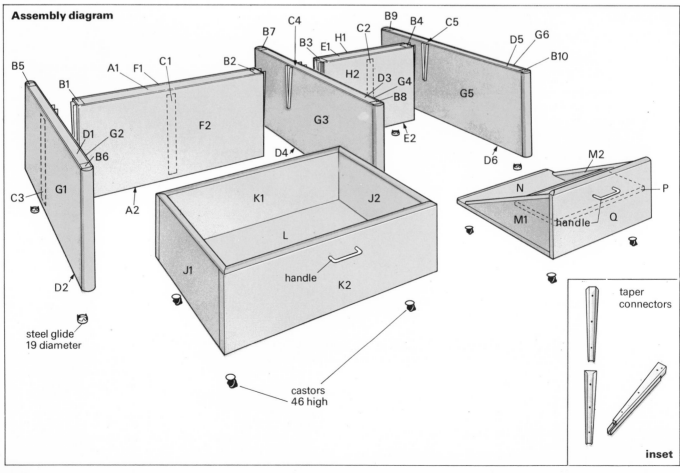

Assembly diagram

B5
B1
A1 F1
C1
B7
C4
B3 H1
B2
C2
B9 B4 C5
E1
D5 G6
B10

D1 G2
B6
F2
H2
D3 G4
B8
G5

C3
G1
G3
D4
E2
D6

J2
K1
N
M2

L
handle
P

J1
M1
handle Q

D2

K2

steel glide
19 diameter

castors
46 high

taper
connectors

inset

78

stage 1

Measure and cut with a panel saw all the pieces of timber to the dimensions shown (**see cutting lists and cutting plans**). When cutting out the two trolley sides M, cut them out as one panel and saw this in half across the diagonal (**see cutting plan for chipboard**). To avoid confusion later, label each panel with its own letter.

stage 2

To make the long support (**see assembly diagram**), apply woodworking adhesive to the end edges of long cross rail A1 then nail through uprights B1 and B2 into each end of A1 using the oval wire nails (**see 1a**). Check the joints are square and punch the nails below the surface. Wipe off excess adhesive with a clean dampened cloth.

Apply adhesive to the end edges of A2 and fix in position in the same way. Apply adhesive to the end edges of central upright C1, place it in position at the dimensions shown (**see 1a**) and pin into it through both long cross rails A using oval wire nails. Wipe off excess adhesive as before.

Fix the two long support sides F in position with the hardboard nails or panel pins, making sure all edges are flush (**see 1a**). Nail (or pin) at 100mm intervals into the edges of both rails A, uprights B1 and B2 and central upright C1 and punch the heads just below the surface of the hardboard.

To make the short support, (**see assembly diagram**) apply adhesive to both end edges of short cross rail E1 and nail through uprights B3 and B4 into E1 with oval wire nails (**see 1b**). Wipe off excess adhesive. Apply adhesive to both end edges of E2 and nail into it through both uprights B in the same way. Apply adhesive to both end edges of central upright C2, place it in position at the dimensions shown (**see 1b**) and nail into it through both short cross rails E. Wipe off excess adhesive. Fix the two short support sides H in position in the same way as you fixed the long support sides, making sure all edges are flush (**see 1b**).

There are three cross supports (**see assembly diagram**). To make each one, apply adhesive to both end edges of main cross rail D and nail into it through the uprights B using oval wire nails (**see 1c**). Check the joints are square and punch all nails below the surface as before. Wipe off excess adhesive.

Fix the other main cross rail D in position in the same way and apply adhesive to both end edges of the central upright C, hold it in position at the dimensions shown (**see 1c**) and nail into it through both main cross rails D. Wipe off excess adhesive. Fix the two cross support sides G in the same way as the other support sides, making sure all edges are flush (**see 1c**).

stage 3

To make the drawer, drill two 5mm clearance holes in each drawer side J at the

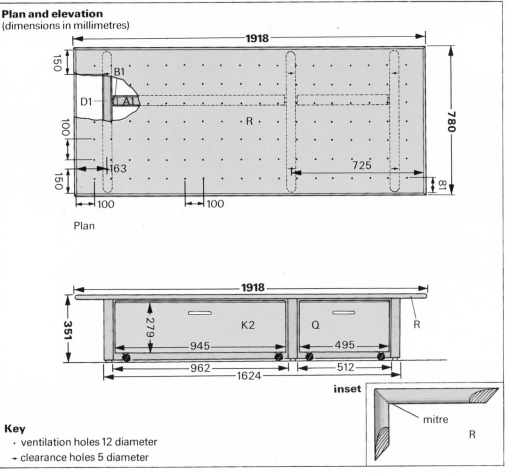

Plan and elevation
(dimensions in millimetres)

1918

150

780

B1

D1 — A1

100

R

150

163

725

81

100 — 100

Plan

351

1918

279

K2 — Q — R

945 — 495

962 — 512

1624

inset

mitre

R

Key
- ventilation holes 12 diameter
- clearance holes 5 diameter

Cutting plan for hardboard

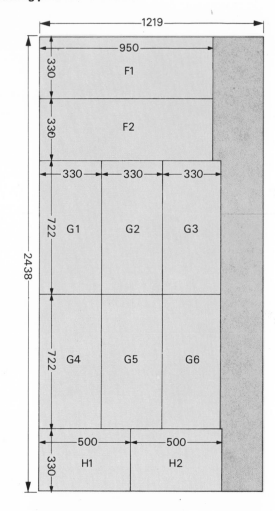

Cutting list for softwood

Description	Key	Quantity	Dimensions
Long cross rails	A	2	$906 \times 44 \times 22$mm
Uprights	B	10	$330 \times 44 \times 22$mm
Central uprights	C	5	$286 \times 44 \times 22$mm
Main cross rails	D	6	$678 \times 44 \times 22$mm
Short cross rails	E	2	$456 \times 44 \times 22$mm

Cutting list for hardboard

Description	Key	Quantity	Dimensions
Long support sides	F	2	$950 \times 330 \times 3$mm
Cross support sides	G	6	$722 \times 330 \times 3$mm
Short support sides	H	2	$500 \times 330 \times 3$mm

Cutting list for chipboard

Description	Key	Quantity	Dimensions
Drawer sides	J	2	$368 \times 270 \times 18$mm
Drawer front and back	K	2	$945 \times 270 \times 18$mm
Drawer base	L	1	$909 \times 368 \times 18$mm
Trolley side panel (to make two sides)	M	2	$359 \times 232 \times 18$mm
Trolley base	N	1	$495 \times 400 \times 18$mm
Trolley shelf	P	1	$459 \times 170 \times 18$mm
Trolley front	Q	1	$495 \times 270 \times 18$mm
Bed top	R	1	$1900 \times 762 \times 18$mm

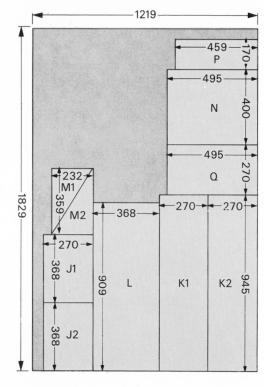

Cutting plan for chipboard

dimensions shown (**see 2**) and countersink them to take No 8 screws.

Hold J1 in the required position squarely against one side edge of the drawer base L and, using a bradawl, mark through the clearance holes in J1 onto L. Drill 2mm pilot holes at these points, apply adhesive to one side edge of L and screw J1 firmly in position. Wipe off excess adhesive. Fix J2 in the same way.

Drill all the 5mm clearance holes in the drawer back K1 and front K2 at the dimensions shown (**see 2**) and counter-sink them to take No 8 screws. Hold the back K1 in the required position squarely against L, J1 and J2 and,

using a bradawl, mark through the clearance holes onto L, J1 and J2. Drill 2mm pilot holes at these points, apply adhesive to the back edges of the base L and two sides J and screw drawer back K1 firmly in position with the chipboard screws. Wipe off excess adhesive. Fix drawer front K2 in the same way.

To make the bedside trolley, drill all the 5mm clearance holes in the trolley front Q, the base N and the two sides M at the dimensions shown (**see 3**).

Cut two 451mm lengths of the 18mm moulding and glue and pin these at 100mm intervals to the long edge of each trolley side M at the dimensions shown (**see 3 inset A**). Mitre the ends of the moulding with a tenon saw so they are flush with the other two edges of the sides M.

Hold side M1 in the required position squarely on top of base N and mark with a bradawl through the clearance holes in N onto M. Drill 2mm pilot holes at these points, apply adhesive to the bottom edge of M1 and screw the two pieces together with chipboard screws. Wipe off excess adhesive. Fix trolley side M2 in the same way.

Hold this assembly in the required position squarely against the trolley front Q and mark with a bradawl through the clearance holes in Q onto the base N and both sides M. Drill 2mm pilot holes at these points, apply adhesive to the fixing edges of N, M1 and M2 and screw the trolley front Q firmly onto the assembly with chipboard screws. Wipe off excess adhesive.

Hold the trolley shelf P in the required position squarely inside this assembly (**see 3**) and mark with a bradawl through the clearance holes in the two sides M and the front Q onto it. Drill 2mm pilot holes at these points, apply adhesive to the front and side edges of P and screw it firmly in position with chipboard screws. Wipe off excess adhesive.

stage 4

Fill all holes, cracks and abrasions on all the assemblies with cellulose filler or plastic wood. Rub all surfaces smooth with medium fine, then fine, glasspaper.

It is best to apply the finish at this stage when the individual assemblies are not yet joined together. We painted the bed (except for the chipboard top which will not show when a mattress is placed on top), the drawer and the bedside trolley as the bare chipboard and hardboard would not look attractive if given a natural finish. We gave the bed top R two coats of matt lacquer.

Apply a coat of primer to the long and short supports and

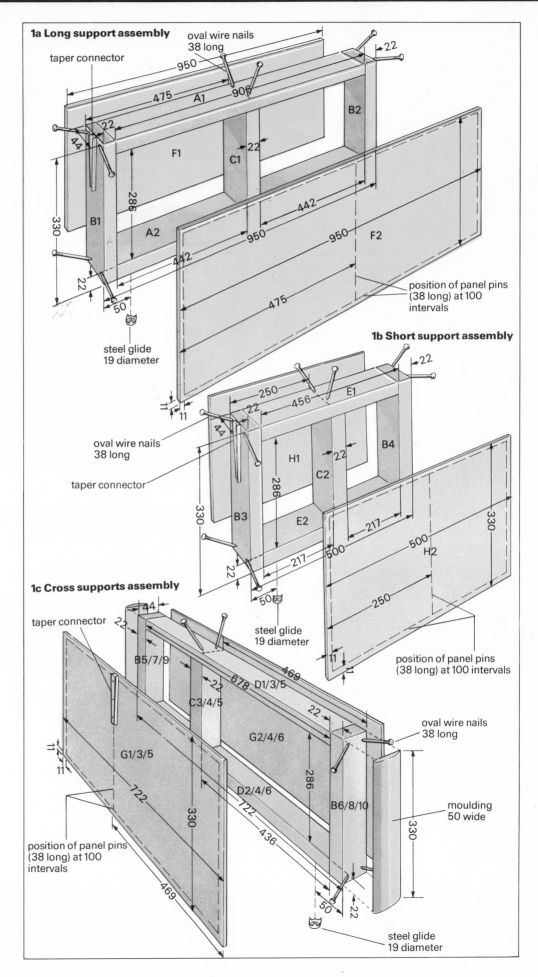

1a Long support assembly

oval wire nails 38 long

taper connector

950
475 A1
906
22
B2
22
44
F1 C1 22
286
330 B1
A2 442
950 950 F2
442
475
22
50
position of panel pins (38 long) at 100 intervals

steel glide 19 diameter

1b Short support assembly

11
11
250
456 E1 22
22
44
H1 22 B4
286
330 B3 C2
E2
217
500 500
22 217 H2 330
250 250
11
steel glide 19 diameter
oval wire nails 38 long
taper connector
position of panel pins (38 long) at 100 intervals

1c Cross supports assembly

taper connector
44
22
B5/7/9
C3/4/5 22
678 D1/3/5
469
11 G2/4/6
11 G1/3/5 286
722
D2/4/6
330 722 22
436
B6/8/10
oval wire nails 38 long
moulding 50 wide
330
position of panel pins (38 long) at 100 intervals
469
50 22
steel glide 19 diameter

81

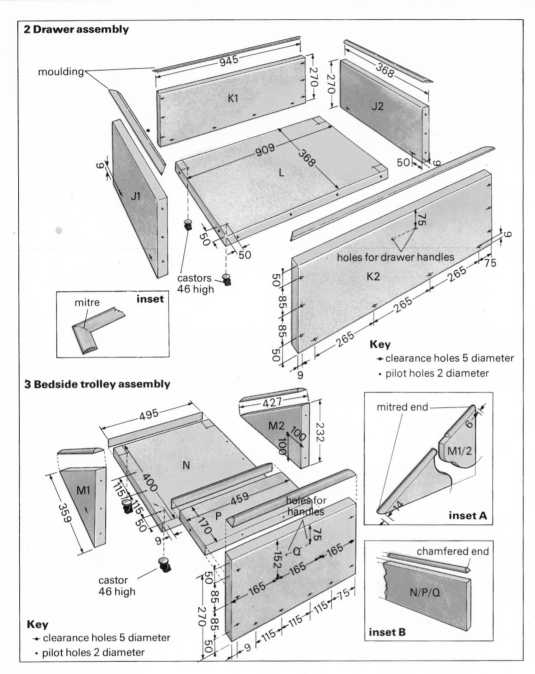

2 Drawer assembly

moulding

945

270

270

368

K1

J2

6

909

368

L

50

9

J1

50

50

castors 46 high

75

holes for drawer handles

K2

9

50

85

85

50

75

265

265

265

265

9

mitre

inset

Key
- → clearance holes 5 diameter
- • pilot holes 2 diameter

3 Bedside trolley assembly

495

427

M2

232

100

100

N

400

459

M1

359

115

115

50

9

P

170

holes for handles

75

Q

152

165

165

165

165

castor 46 high

50

85

85

270

50

9

115

115

115

75

mitred end

6

M1/2

14

inset A

chamfered end

N/P/Q

inset B

Key
- → clearance holes 5 diameter
- • pilot holes 2 diameter

the three cross supports, the drawer and the bedside trolley, and then an undercoat and a top coat, allowing each to dry thoroughly. Apply two coats of lacquer to the bed top R (both top and bottom faces) allowing plenty of time for the first coat to dry thoroughly before applying the second.

stage 5

When the lacquer on the bed top R has dried hard, drill all the 12mm ventilation holes and six 5mm clearance holes in it at the dimensions shown (**see plan**). Countersink the clearance holes to take No 8 screws.

Now glue and pin all the half-round mouldings in position. For the bed top R, cut with a tenon saw the 18mm wide moulding into two 1920mm lengths and two 782mm lengths. Mitre all the ends (**see plan inset**), apply adhesive to one edge of the bed top R and pin the relevant moulding in position, placing the panel pins at 100mm intervals. Punch all pins below the surface of the moulding and wipe off excess adhesive. Fix the other mouldings to the remaining three edges in the same way.
For the drawer, cut the 18mm wide moulding into two 947mm lengths and·two

408mm lengths. Mitre all the ends (**see 2 inset**) and fix to the relevant edges in the same way as for the bed top (**see 2**).
For the bedside trolley, cut the 18mm moulding into two 495mm lengths, and one 459mm length. Chamfer all the ends with an 18mm chisel (**see 3 inset B**) and glue and pin the mouldings in position as before (**see 3**).
With a tenon saw cut the 50mm wide moulding into six 330mm lengths and glue and pin them to each end of the cross supports (**see 1c**). Wipe off excess adhesive. Fill all the holes in the mouldings, left by the panel pins, with cellulose filler or,

preferably, matching plastic wood. Rub the mouldings smooth with medium fine, then fine, glasspaper and apply two coats of matt lacquer. Apply the lacquer very carefully with a 12mm paint brush to avoid covering any of the surfaces you have already painted.
To fix the handles on the drawer and beside trolley, drill fixing holes (of the correct diameter for the handles you are using) centrally in the front of each assembly about 75mm down from the top edge. Screw the handles firmly in position (according to manufacturer's instructions).
Screw the castors in position (according to manufacturer's instructions) at each corner of the base of both the drawer and the bedside trolley (**see 2 and 3**) far enough in from the side edges for the castors to swivel without obstruction.
Hammer a steel glide 50mm in from each end of the underside of the long and short supports and the three cross supports (**see 1a, b, c**). These glides lessen the wear and tear on carpets and other floor coverings.

stage 6

Fix a taper connector plate to one side of each cross support by screwing through the hardboard side into the central upright C (**see 1c**). One of the cross supports needs a taper connector on both sides as it is to go in the middle (**see assembly diagram**).
Screw a taper connector plate to the top of each end of the long support (**see 1a**) and to the short support (**see 1b**). Slot the taper connectors on the three cross supports to the taper connectors on the long and short supports (**see assembly diagram**), checking the joints are square. Place the bed top R centrally on top of this assembly and mark with a bradawl through the clearance holes onto the three main cross rails D at the top of each cross support. Drill 2mm pilot holes at these points and screw the bed top firmly down onto the assembly with the countersunk screws.

The children's room

Playpen

This colourful playpen folds up easily into a compact shape for storage. It is very sturdily built and has a blackboard and counting bricks.

stage 1

Measure and cut with a tenon saw all the pieces of timber according to the dimensions shown (**see cutting list**). Slightly chamfer all corners and edges of the hardwood pieces with medium fine, then fine, glasspaper.

Drill all the 12mm diameter holes 11mm deep in the 32mm wide face of the long rails A and short rails B according to the dimensions

Cutting list for hardwood & plywood

Description	Key	Quantity	Dimensions
Long rails	A	4	1200 × 32 × 22mm
Short rails	B	8	550 × 32 × 22mm
Locking pieces	C	2	66 × 16 × 6mm
Square blocks	D	18	32 × 32 × 32mm
Blackboard (plywood)	E	1	598 × 347 × 6mm

shown (**see 1a, b, c**) but don't drill holes where the slot to take the blackboard is to be cut in two of the long rails.
Smooth all surfaces of all the pieces of timber with medium fine, then fine, glasspaper and give them a

final rub over with flour glasspaper.
Cut the 12mm diameter dowel with a tenon saw into forty-seven 610mm lengths and rub them perfectly smooth with fine, then flour, glasspaper. Apply stain to these dowels. We chose four

Tools and materials

timber (see cutting list)
measuring tape, pencil and try square, pair of compasses
tenon saw, 3 and 6mm chisels, block plane
sharp knife, metal straight-edge, marking gauge
medium fine, fine and flour glasspaper, fine wire wool
hand or electric drill, 2, 3, 12 and 16mm bits
screwdriver, bradawl, countersink bit, mallet
woodworking adhesive, clean cloth

For assembly
four brass backflap hinges and 9mm long brass countersunk screws to fit
eight steel backflap hinges and 12mm long countersunk screws to fit
30m of 12mm diameter dowel and at least 50mm of 3mm dowel
nine 32mm diameter hardwood balls

For finish
coloured wood stains (as needed)
clear matt polyurethane lacquer
blackboard paint, 12 and 25mm paint brushes; beeswax

Assembly diagram

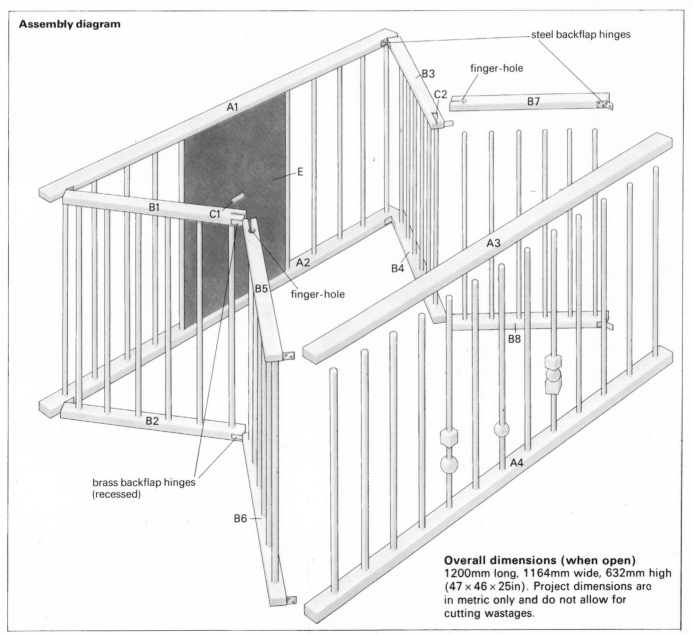

steel backflap hinges
finger-hole
B3
C2
B7
A1
E
B1
C1
A2
B5
finger-hole
B4
A3
B8
B2
A4
brass backflap hinges (recessed)
B6

Overall dimensions (when open)
1200mm long, 1164mm wide, 632mm high (47 × 46 × 25in). Project dimensions are in metric only and do not allow for cutting wastages.

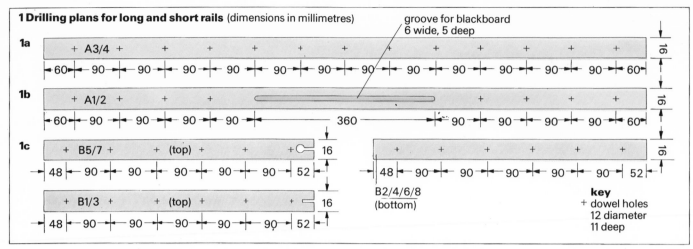

1 Drilling plans for long and short rails (dimensions in millimetres)

groove for blackboard
6 wide, 5 deep

1a + A3/4 + | 60 — 90 — 90 — 90 — 90 — 90 — 90 — 90 — 90 — 90 — 90 — 90 — 90 — 60 | 16

1b + A1/2 + | 60 — 90 — 90 — 90 — 360 — 90 — 90 — 90 — 90 — 60 | 16

1c + B5/7 + (top) | 48 — 90 — 90 — 90 — 90 — 90 — 52 | 16

B2/4/6/8 (bottom) | 48 — 90 — 90 — 90 — 90 — 52 | 16

+ B1/3 + (top) | 48 — 90 — 90 — 90 — 90 — 52 | 16

key
+ dowel holes
12 diameter
11 deep

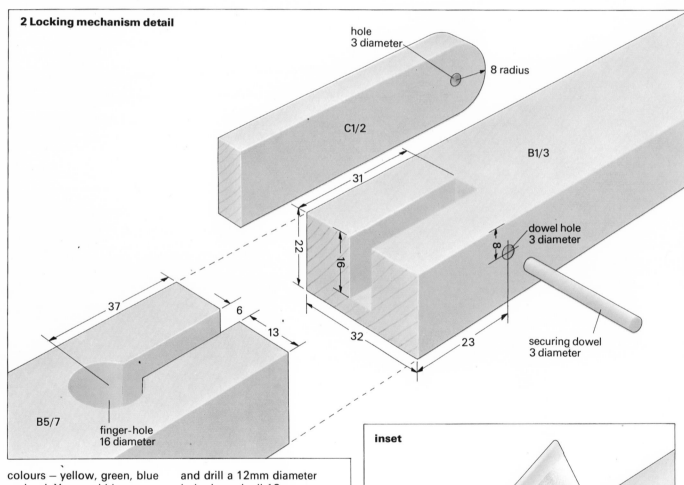

2 Locking mechanism detail

hole
3 diameter

8 radius

C1/2

B1/3

31

22

16

8

dowel hole
3 diameter

securing dowel
3 diameter

37

6

13

32

23

B5/7

finger-hole
16 diameter

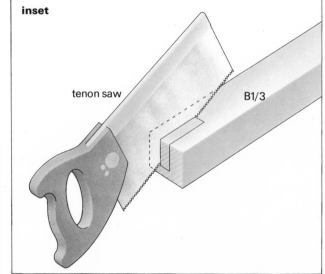

inset

tenon saw

B1/3

colours – yellow, green, blue
and red. You could leave
some of the dowels natural
as we did. When all the
stain has dried thoroughly
apply one coat of clear matt
polyurethane lacquer to all
the dowels to seal the timber
and, when all the lacquer has
dried hard, rub the dowels
over lightly with fine wire
wool.

stage 2

Mark the centre point onto
one of the end grain faces of
each of the square blocks D

and drill a 12mm diameter
hole through all 18 square
blocks D; it is important to
drill with the grain or the
blocks could split in half.
Judge the centres of the
hardwood balls and drill a
12mm diameter hole through
each one making sure to drill
with the grain as before. Rub
smooth all the blocks and
balls with fine, then flour,
glasspaper and apply a stain.
When the stain is dry apply a
coat of lacquer and, when
the lacquer has dried hard,
rub over all the blocks and
balls with fine wire wool.

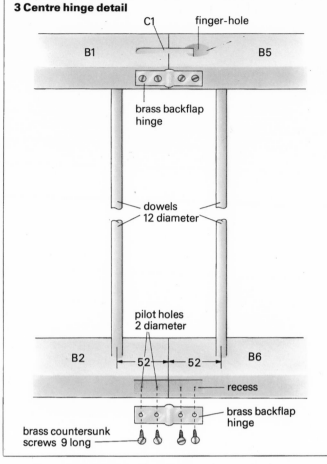

3 Centre hinge detail

finger-hole

C1

B1   B5

brass backflap hinge

dowels 12 diameter

pilot holes 2 diameter

B2   ←52→ ←52→   B6

recess

brass backflap hinge

brass countersunk screws 9 long

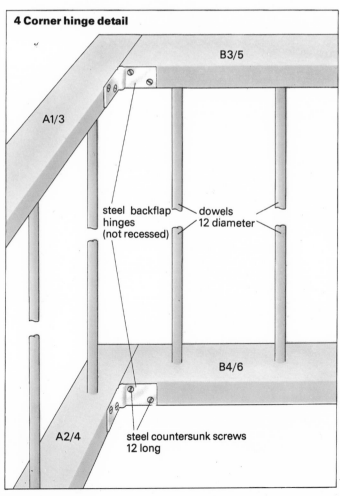

4 Corner hinge detail

B3/5

A1/3

steel backflap hinges (not recessed)

dowels 12 diameter

A2/4

steel countersunk screws 12 long

stage 3

Using a marking gauge mark out the 6mm wide groove in the two long rails A3 and A4 according to the dimensions shown (**see 1b**). Score along the lines with a sharp knife held against a metal straight-edge and chop out the waste from the grooves with a 6mm chisel to a depth of 5mm. These grooves will house the blackboard.
Give the blackboard E a final rub over with flour glasspaper and apply two coats of blackboard paint allowing plenty of time for the first to dry thoroughly before applying the second.
Draw a curve at one end of both locking pieces C with a pair of compasses set to an 8mm radius (**see 2**). Chop off the waste from each curve with a sharp chisel and rub smooth with medium fine, then fine, glasspaper.
Mark out the square-ended slots to take the locking pieces in two of the short rails B to the dimensions shown (**see 2**) and the slots with finger-holes in two other short rails. Drill the 16mm diameter holes for the finger-holes, placing a piece of scrap wood under the drilling area in both cases to stop wood breaking away from the bottom surface as the drill bit bursts through. Remove the waste from all the slots to a depth of 16mm by making two cuts to the depth line with a tenon saw held at an angle (**see 2 inset**) then chopping between the cut lines with a 3mm chisel. When making the cuts with the tenon saw be sure to cut on the waste side of the line.
Mark onto one side edge of the short rails B1 and B3 (with the square-ended slots cut in them) where to drill the 3mm diameter hole to take the securing dowel (**see 2**).
Push the curved end of the locking pieces C into these slots and drill a 3mm diameter hole through the side of the short rails at the points marked to a depth of about 25mm; but don't drill right through the rail.
Cut the 3mm diameter dowel into two lengths slightly longer than the depth of the

holes. Push these cut lengths into position in the short rails B3 and B7 to secure the locking pieces. Check the locking pieces pivot freely; when you are satisfied they do, withdraw the securing dowel a few millimetres, smear some woodworking adhesive over it and push it back in position. Wipe off excess adhesive with a clean dampened cloth. When the adhesive has set trim off any protruding dowel with a sharp chisel or block plane.

stage 4

Slide the square blocks and the balls over some of the stained dowels in the desired order and lay out the dowels to form a colour pattern of your own design – or copy ours.
Pour some woodworking adhesive in the 12mm holes in the long rails A and short rails B and push the dowels firmly in position, assembling one section at a time. Clamp each section with web-clamps until the adhesive has set and wipe off excess adhesive. When fixing the blackboard, smear some adhesive inside the slots cut in the long rails A1 and A2 to ensure the board will be held firmly in position.
When the adhesive has set lay the short rail sections flat with the locking piece engaged in the slots (**see 3**). Place a brass hinge over each join with the knuckle uppermost (**see 3**) and mark onto the short rails where to cut the recesses for the hinges. Cut a recess of the required depth for each hinge, drill 2mm pilot holes for the fixing screws and fix the hinges firmly in position in the recesses with the 9mm long brass screws.
With the brass hinges on the outside of the short rails, join the short rails to the long rails with the steel hinges and 12mm long screws (**see 4**), but this time don't cut recesses for the hinges. Open the playpen and lock it in position with the locking pieces C; check very carefully there are no splinters. Give the long and short rails a final rub over with flour glasspaper and apply two coats of beeswax.

Rocker cot

This cot, made from softwood and canvas, is ideal for the children. The framework is built with mortise and tenon joints for strength.

Description	Key	Quantity	Dimensions
End top rails	A	2	520 × 57 × 22mm
Long rails	B	2	1080 × 57 × 22mm
Uprights	C	4	520 × 57 × 22mm
Rockers (to shape)	D	2	750 × 98 × 22mm
Wedges (to shape)	E	4	57 × 27 × 8mm

Tools and materials

timber (see cutting list)
measuring tape, pencil, try square and mortise gauge
panel and tenon saws and jig, pad or coping saw
hand or electric drill, 2 and 18mm bits
fine flat file, medium fine and fine glasspaper
wood slat about 980 × 15 × 5mm, 13mm panel pin
mallet or hammer and block of wood, 6 and 19mm chisels
two G-clamps, and web-clamp or length of strong rope
woodworking adhesive, clean cloth
2.6m of 112cm wide canvas and matching thread (for sling)
3m of 18mm dowel (for canvas sling supports)
foam mattress 900 × 500 × 50mm
900 × 500mm of 6mm plywood (for mattress support)
scissors, dressmaker's pins and needle and strong thread
cellulose filler or plastic wood; oil, polyurethane lacquer or wood stain; or primer, undercoat and matt or gloss top coat; lint-free rag or 50mm paint brush (for finish)

stage 1

Measure and cut all the pieces of timber to the dimensions shown (see cutting list).

To shape the two rockers D, mark out the line of the curve to the dimensions shown (see 1).

Draw the curve for D1 with an improvised pair of compasses. Use a thin slat of wood (about 5mm thick) cut to 980mm long. Drill a 2mm hole 10mm in from one end of this piece of wood and a hole big enough to take a pencil at the other end of it exactly 950mm apart.

Clamp rocker D1 to a workbench with two G clamps and mark the centre line across its width. At one end of one long rail B, measure and mark 20mm in from one edge. Then measure and mark 852mm along from that end and 20mm in from the same edge, which will be the position of the pivot point for your compasses.

Place B on the bench square to D1, using a try square to check for accuracy, so the 20mm mark on B lines up with the centre mark on D1. Check the pivot point is 950mm in from the far edge of D1 along B and lightly hammer in a 13mm panel pin at this point. Insert a pencil through the larger hole in the slat, put the 2mm hole over the panel pin and, holding B firmly in place against D1, draw an arc from one end of

Overall dimensions

1080mm long, 750mm wide, 593mm high (43 × 30 × 23in). Project dimensions are in metric only and do not allow for cutting wastages.

Assembly diagram

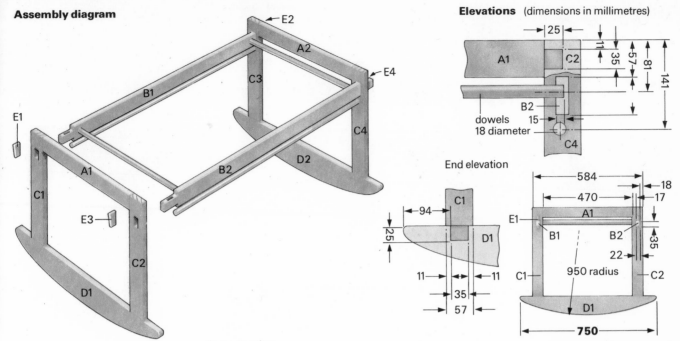

Elevations (dimensions in millimetres)

D1 to the other (**see 1**). Turn D1 over and repeat this procedure on the other face. Cut off the waste with a jig, pad or coping saw and smooth the cut edge with medium fine, then fine, glasspaper. Round off the corners with a fine flat file and smooth with fine glasspaper.
Using D1 as a template, mark the curve onto both faces of D2, remembering to turn D1 over when marking the second face in case the curve is not quite symmetrical. Mark which sides of the rockers coincide.

stage 2

Using a measuring tape, pencil and try square, measure and mark the position of the tenon at each end of the two end top rails A and the long rails B and at the bottom end of each upright C. Scribe out the position of each tenon accurately, using a mortise gauge for A and C (**see 2 and 3**).
Cut the tenons with a tenon saw and measure and mark out the position of the two mortises at the top of each upright C (**see 4a**) and at each end of the top face of both rockers D (**see 4b**).
Set the mortise gauge to the same thickness as for the tenons. Cut out the mortises with 6 and 19mm chisels.
Measure and mark out the

Side elevation

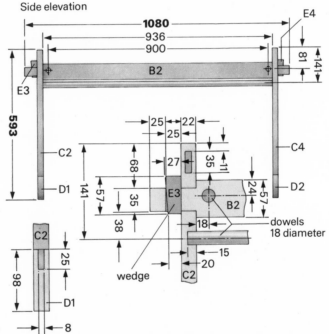

1 Rocker shaping plan

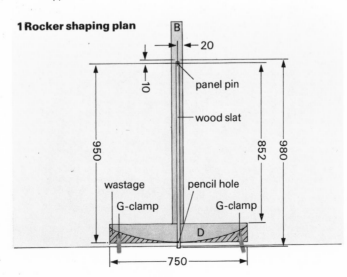

wedge recess at each end of long rail B at the dimensions shown (**see 3**).

stage 3

To make the dowel holes for the canvas sling supports, drill 18mm holes 15mm deep in the four uprights C at the dimensions shown (**see 4a**) and the two long rails B at the dimensions shown (**see 3**).
If the holes are not drilled to the correct depth the dowels will not be strong enough at each joint to support much weight in the sling. To ensure you drill to the correct depth fit a rubber collar over the drill bit (or wrap a piece of adhesive tape round it) and stop drilling when the collar (or tape) meets the surface of the wood.

stage 4

To assemble the two end frames join one end top rail A to two uprights C and one rocker D (**see assembly diagram**). Put woodworking adhesive into the stub mortises in C1 and C2 and insert the tenon at each end of end top rail A1 into these mortises. Put some adhesive into the mortises in rocker D1 and insert the tenons at the bottom of C1 and C2. Wipe off excess adhesive with a clean dampened cloth.
To ensure really strong joints

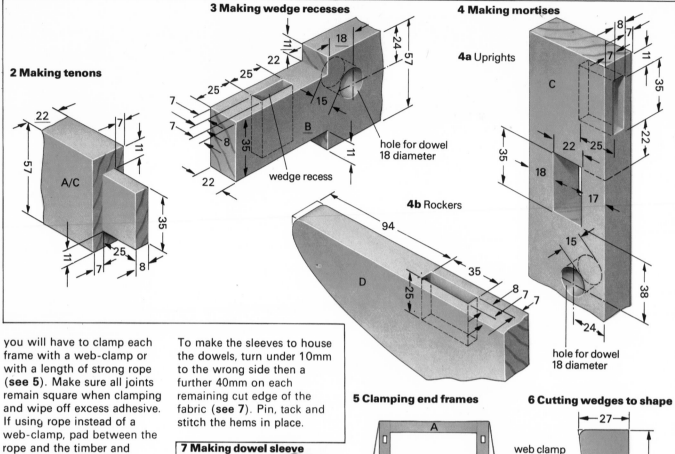

2 Making tenons

A/C

3 Making wedge recesses

B

wedge recess

hole for dowel 18 diameter

4 Making mortises

4a Uprights

C

hole for dowel 18 diameter

4b Rockers

D

5 Clamping end frames

A

C   C

D

web clamp

6 Cutting wedges to shape

E

7 Making dowel sleeve

sleeve seam

side seam

you will have to clamp each frame with a web-clamp or with a length of strong rope (**see 5**). Make sure all joints remain square when clamping and wipe off excess adhesive. If using rope instead of a web-clamp, pad between the rope and the timber and twist the rope tight with a piece of scrap wood. Once the adhesive in one frame has dried assemble the other, making sure the dowel hole will face inwards when matching up rockers on assembly.

For the dowel supports for the canvas sling cut the 18mm dowel into two 966mm lengths and two 534mm lengths. Smooth all surfaces of the dowels with fine glasspaper.

Using a tenon saw cut the four wedges E to shape to the dimensions shown (**see 6**) and round off the front edges with a fine flat file before smoothing all edges with medium fine, then fine, glasspaper.

stage 5

Cut the canvas into two pieces, one 156 × 56cm (for head to foot) and the other 104 × 96cm (side to side). Along the two long sides of the head-to-foot piece and the two short sides of the other piece, turn under 10mm to the wrong side of the fabric then a further 20mm. Pin, tack and stitch the hem.

To make the sleeves to house the dowels, turn under 10mm to the wrong side then a further 40mm on each remaining cut edge of the fabric (**see 7**). Pin, tack and stitch the hems in place.

stage 6

Fill all holes, cracks and abrasions with cellulose filler or plastic wood. It is best to use matching plastic wood if you want a natural finish. Smooth surfaces with medium fine, then fine, glasspaper. For a natural finish apply two coats of oil or lacquer allowing plenty of time for the first to dry. You could apply coloured stain. To do this, apply the stain sparingly with a clean cloth and add another coat if you wish to darken the colour. To paint the cot, apply a coat of primer, undercoat and top coat, allowing each to dry.

stage 7

Put adhesive in the 18mm dowel holes in long rail B1 and push the two shorter lengths of dowel into

position. Wipe off excess adhesive and slide the sleeves of the head to foot length of canvas over the fixed dowels. Put some adhesive in the dowel holes in long rail B2 and fix onto this assembly in the same way.

Put some adhesive in the 18mm dowel holes in uprights C1 and C2, push the two long dowels in position and wipe off excess adhesive. Slide the sleeves of the unattached piece of canvas over these dowels. Apply woodworking adhesive to the through mortises in C1 and C2 then push long rails B1 and B2 in position, arranging the canvas with the head-to-foot piece on top.

Wipe off all excess adhesive and secure the long rails temporarily with two of the wedges E. Don't apply any adhesive to them yet. Pour adhesive into the dowel

holes and through mortises in uprights C3 and C4 and push the dowels and long rails in position, securing B1 and B2 with wedges as before. Wipe off all excess adhesive.

Remove one of the wedges, spread some adhesive into the wedge recess in the long rail B and ram the wedge in position with a mallet (or hammer and block of wood). Wipe off the excess adhesive. Repeat for the other three wedges. Put the mattress support in the sling, with the foam mattress on top.

See **Dowel joints**
See **Mortise & tenon joints**

Playboard

Our ingenious board has two double-sided play surfaces — a blackboard, a pegboard on which you can make patterns or hang up drawings, a wipe-clean laminate drawing board and a baize surface for play felt.

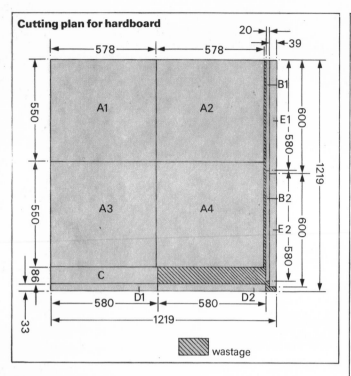

Cutting plan for hardboard

wastage

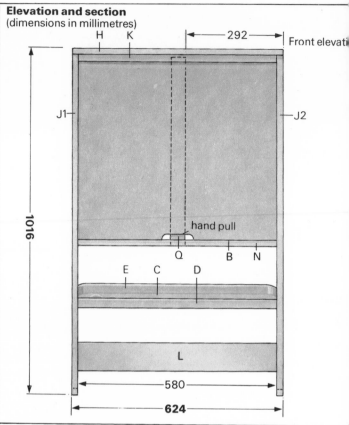

Elevation and section
(dimensions in millimetres)

hand pull

Front elevation

Overall dimensions

1016mm high, 624mm wide, 172mm thick when closed
(40 × 25 × 7in). Project dimensions are given in metric only
and do not allow for cutting wastages.

Tools and materials

timber (see cutting list)
measuring tape, pencil and try square
fine tooth panel saw, tenon saw, coping saw
coarse, medium, medium fine and fine glasspaper
hammer, nail punch, fine flat file, block plane
screwdriver, bradawl
hand or electric drill, bit same diameter as cocktail sticks
woodworking adhesive, clean cloth, impact adhesive

For assembly

panel pins 9, 12 and 25mm long
oval nails 25 and 38mm long, tacks 12mm long
self-adhesive baize at least 608 × 580mm
white plastic laminate sheet at least 582 × 554mm
two 75mm long butt hinges and 12mm long screws to fit
one large empty matchbox and yoghurt pots (if used)
150 cocktail sticks
600mm of 50mm wide upholstery webbing

For finish

cellulose filler or plastic wood; blackboard paint
primer, lead-free undercoat and top coat, 50mm paint brush

stage 1

Measure and cut with a fine-tooth panel saw all the pieces of timber to the dimensions shown (**see cutting lists and cutting plan**). To avoid confusion later, label each part with the appropriate letter. Smooth all surfaces with medium fine, then fine, glasspaper.
Mark out the halving joints at both ends of the board tops and bottoms F and sides

G (**see 1**) and cut off the waste from each one with a tenon saw. Apply woodworking adhesive to the fixing surfaces of each joint and bring them together, securing the joints with the 12mm long panel pins; hammer the pins into the timber at an angle so they do not protrude at the other side (**see 1**). Wipe off excess adhesive with a clean dampened cloth and smooth flush all the joint edges with

Cutting list for hardboard

Description	Key	Quantity	Dimensions
Board panels	A	4	578 × 550 × 3mm
Location pieces	B	2	580 × 20 × 3mm
Shelf top	C	1	580 × 86 × 3mm
Shelf fronts	D	2	580 × 33 × 3mm
Shelf backs	E	2	600 × 39 × 3mm

Cutting list for softwood

Description	Key	Quantity	Dimensions
Board tops/bottoms	F	4	578 × 44 × 12mm
Board sides	G	4	550 × 44 × 12mm
Tops	H	2	624 × 86 × 16mm
Sides	J	4	1000 × 44 × 22mm
Top supports	K	2	580 × 19 × 19mm
Lower stiffeners	L	2	624 × 86 × 16mm
Cross battens	M	4	624 × 39 × 12mm
Board supports	N	2	580 × 39 × 12mm
Shelves	P	2	580 × 86 × 16mm
Inside stiffeners	Q	2	550 × 39 × 12mm

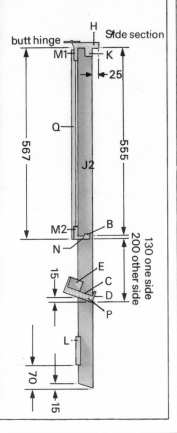

Side section

butt hinge

H
M1
K
← 25 →
Q
J2
567
555
M2
B
N
130 one side
200 other side
E
15
C
D
P
L
70
15

Assembly diagram

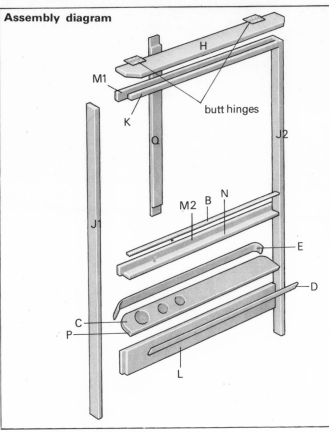

H
M1
K
butt hinges
Q
J2
J1
M2 B N
E
D
C
P
L

1 Board assembly

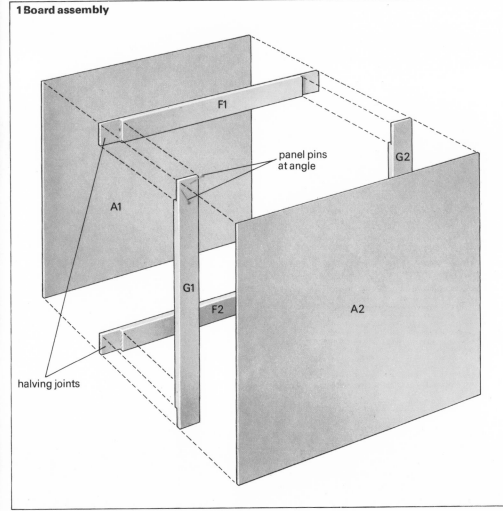

F1
panel pins at angle
G2
A1
G1
F2
A2
halving joints

medium glasspaper. Make the second board frame in the same way.

Apply adhesive to one side of both frames and fix the board panels A in position on each one with 9mm panel pins keeping the pins clear of the hand pull area (see 2). Make sure the smooth side of the hardboard is outermost and all edges are flush. Punch all pins below the surface with a nail punch; the holes that remain can be filled later. Wipe off excess adhesive.

stage 2

Glue and pin another board panel A onto one of the boards as before. Mark out the hand pull area in the board bottom F2 at the dimensions shown (see 2), cut out the waste with a coping saw and smooth the cut edges with medium fine, then fine, glasspaper.

On one side of the board carefully mark out a grid of 15mm squares, leaving a 50mm border round the edges. Select a drill bit of the same diameter as the cocktail sticks (to be used as pegs) and drill holes through both board panels where the grid lines cross. Use coarse glasspaper to smooth the side where the drill bit has come through and caused burrs on the surface of the hardboard. Coat this side with impact adhesive – and the rear of the laminate sheet – and leave until touch-dry. Fix the laminate in position on the board so it overhangs all edges and rub it over with a dry cloth to ensure a firm bond. Trim all edges flush with a fine flat file.

Fill all holes, cracks and abrasions with cellulose filler or plastic wood and rub all surfaces (except the laminate) smooth with medium fine, then fine, glasspaper. For a finish, apply a coat of primer, an undercoat then a top coat to all surfaces (except the laminate) allowing plenty of time for each to dry.

stage 3

For the second board (partially made up in **Stage 1**) mark out and cut the hand pull area with a coping saw according to the dimensions shown (**see 2**) and smooth the cut edges with medium fine, then fine, glasspaper. Place the remaining unfixed board panel A in a vice and plane off 1mm from all four edges with a block plane. Make the hand pull area in this panel in exactly the same place as for the other board. Rub over the smooth side of the unfixed board panel A with fine glasspaper and seal it with a coat of primer. When the paint is thoroughly dry, cut a 608 × 580mm piece of the self-adhesive baize and stick this to the painted side of the unfixed board panel A so it overlaps the hardboard by 15mm all round.

Fold this over to the back of the panel, mitre the baize in the corners and press firmly down (**see 3**). Apply impact adhesive to the board tops and bottoms F and sides G and lay the hardboard panel in position so all edges are flush. Place the frame on a flat surface and put weights on top of it round all edges until the adhesive has set. Fill all holes, rub smooth and apply a finish as before, taking care not to get paint on the baize. This time apply two coats of blackboard paint to the other side.

stage 4

For each frame, cut off two corners on the top H with a tenon saw at the dimensions shown (**see 4**), mark the shaping lines for the chamfer on the back edge (**see 4 inset**) and remove the waste with a block plane. The chamfer prevents fingers being pinched when the playboard is folded. Smooth the cut and planed edges with medium fine, then fine, glasspaper.

Apply adhesive to the top edge of the cross batten M1 and top support K1 and nail them in position to the underside of the top H1 at the dimensions shown (**see side section**) using the 25mm oval nails. The chamfer on H should line up with M. Wipe off excess adhesive. Mark out the rebate at either end of the lower stiffener L to the dimensions shown (**see 5**) and cut off the waste with a tenon saw. On the inside

edge of both sides J mark the required fixing position of the board support N to the dimensions shown (**see side section**). Apply adhesive to both end edges of N and to the inside edges of the rebates on L and nail these in the required position to the two sides J using 38mm oval nails.

Apply adhesive to the inside face of the cross batten M2 (only a 20mm wide strip at each end) and along the back of N and fix through M2, with 38mm oval nails, into the back edges of the two sides J and the board support N, so the bottom edges of M and N are flush. Wipe off excess adhesive. Mark out the rebate at either end of the inside stiffener Q to the dimensions shown (**see 6**) and cut off the waste with a tenon saw. Apply adhesive to the inside edges of the rebates and fix Q centrally between sides J to the two cross battens M with the 12mm panel pins. Wipe off excess adhesive.

Place one of the two assembled boards in position hard up against the cross batten M2 and glue and pin the location piece B in position with 12mm panel pins so there is 2mm clearance between the board and the back edge of B. Plane B flush with the front edge of N. Wipe off excess adhesive. Make the second frame in the same way.

stage 5

Make a gentle curve on one edge at either end of both shelves P at the dimensions shown (**see 7**). Use a large

dinner plate, saucepan or other large round object as a template and cut off the waste with a coping saw. Whatever template you use it must be greater than 100mm diameter since hardboard cannot easily be bent round a tight curve.

Make holes in the shelf top C of the correct diameter to take empty yoghurt pots, apply adhesive to the bottom face (rough side) of C and fix it on top of one of the shelves with the 9mm panel pins. Wipe off excess adhesive and trim flush any protruding hardboard with a block plane.

Apply adhesive to the curved edge of both shelves and fix the shelf backs in position with the 25mm panel pins

spacing the pins at 20mm intervals. It is best to start at one end and work round to the other. Apply adhesive to the front edge of both shelves and fix the shelf fronts D in position with 25mm panel pins so the bottom and both side edges are flush. Wipe off excess adhesive.

Apply adhesive to both side edges of both shelves and nail them in position at the correct angle (**see side section**). The bottom edge of one of the shelves should be 130mm down from the bottom edge of the board support N and the other shelf should be 200mm down. This is so the two shelves do not meet and prevent the playboard closing right up.

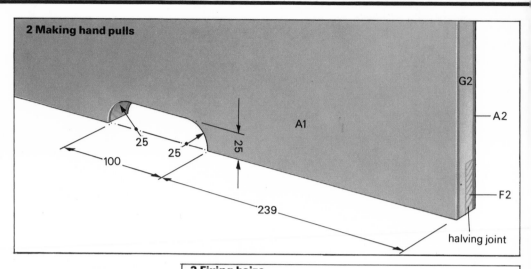

2 Making hand pulls

100   25   25   25

A1

239

G2

A2

F2

halving joint

3 Fixing baize

mitred corner   overlap

A

hand pull

4 Shaping top

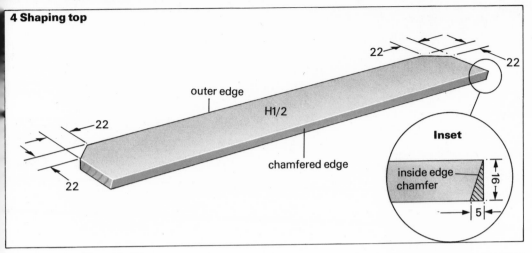

outer edge

22   22   22

H1/2

22

22

chamfered edge

Inset

inside edge chamfer

16

5

5 Lower stiffener rebates

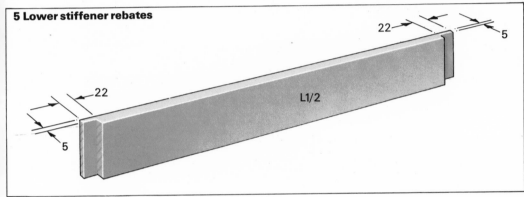

22

22

5

L1/2

5

6 Inside stiffener rebates

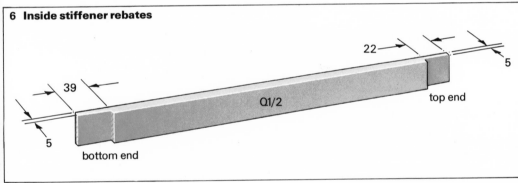

39

22

5

Q1/2

5

top end

bottom end

7 Shaping shelves

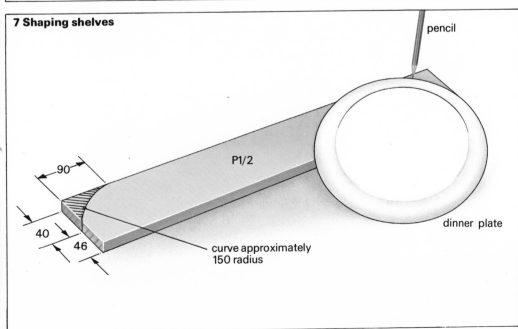

pencil

90

P1/2

40

46

curve approximately
150 radius

dinner plate

Chamfer the outside edge of all four sides J and make a mark 15mm up from the bottom edge; draw a line squarely across the leg at this height. Cut off the waste by sawing at diagonals to make the inside edge of the leg the shorter in each case (**see side section**).

stage 6

Fill all holes, cracks and abrasions with cellulose filler or plastic wood and rub all surfaces smooth with medium fine, then fine, glasspaper. For the finish, apply a coat of primer, undercoat and two top coats (we chose gloss yellow), allowing plenty of time for each to dry before applying the next. When all painted surfaces have dried hard, turn over 40mm at each end of the webbing and nail through the double thickness centrally to the underside of the two board supports N using six 12mm tacks at each end. To join the two frames together fix one leaf of each hinge, knuckle uppermost, to the top face of one of the tops H 70mm in from either end using the 12 mm long screws. Screw the other leaf of each hinge to the other top H in the same way. To make pegs for the pegboard, cut off the sharp ends of cocktail sticks (about 150 should be enough) then cut them in half. You can paint or stain the sticks easily with the help of potatoes. Divide the sticks into several quantities and stick them in potatoes so about 15mm of each stick protrudes. Apply paint or stain to the 'porcupines', leave them to dry and pull them out of the potatoes. Use as many different colours as you want.

We painted a large match box and stuck it to one of the shelves to house these pegs (when they are not in use) and placed empty yoghurt pots in the previously made holes in one of the shelves to take chalk or paints.

See **Rebate joints**
See **Halving joints**

Pet hutch

Our hutch houses six guinea-pigs but can be used for other pets. Make it from exterior grade plywood for outdoor use or from blockboard for indoors. The floor is in fact the base of two drawers, which can be pulled out completely for easy cleaning or just far enough for the animals to play on the grass but not escape. The connecting door can be shut to separate the animals, if necessary.

Cutting list for exterior grade plywood

Description	Key	Quantity	Dimensions
Side panels	A	2	1000 × 400 × 16mm
End panels	B	2	468 × 330 × 16mm
Divider	C	1	468 × 400 × 16mm
Drawer fronts	D	2	466 × 68 × 16mm
Grille frame	E	1	515 × 466 × 16mm
Sliding top	F	1	504 × 500 × 16mm
Sliding top sides	G	2	500 × 30 × 16mm
Bedroom drawer base	H	1	434 × 360 × 16mm
Bedroom drawer back	J	1	434 × 47 × 16mm
Bedroom drawer sides	K	2	376 × 47 × 16mm
Main drawer base	L	1	560 × 434 × 16mm
Main drawer back	M	1	434 × 47 × 16mm
Main drawer sides	N	2	576 × 47 × 16mm

Cutting list for softwood

Description	Key	Quantity	Dimensions
Bedroom drawer runners	P	2	376 × 22 × 22mm
Main drawer runners	Q	2	576 × 22 × 22mm
Grille supports	R	2	576 × 22 × 22mm

Overall dimensions
1000mm long, 536mm wide, 416mm high (39 × 21 × 16in). Project dimensions are in metric only and do not allow for cutting wastages.

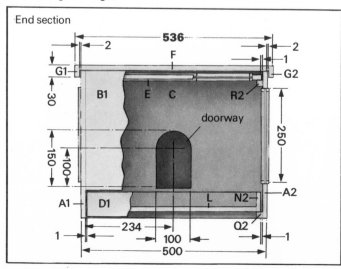

End section

Assembly diagram

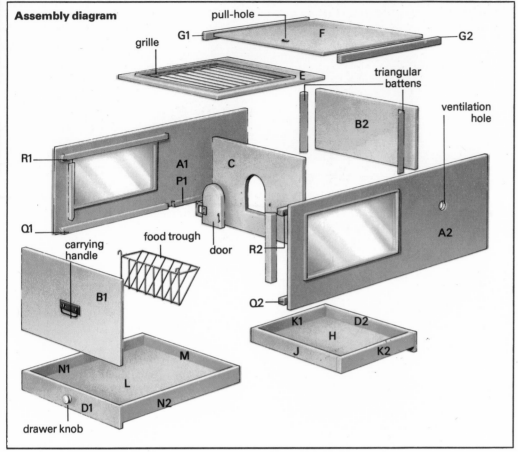

pull-hole

grille

G1

F

G2

triangular battens

B2

ventilation hole

R1

A1

C

P1

Q1

carrying handle

food trough

door

R2

A2

Q2

B1

K1

D2

H

J

K2

N1

M

L

D1

N2

drawer knob

Tools and materials

timber (see cutting lists)
measuring tape, pencil
try square, trimming knife
panel saw, pad saw, tenon
    saw
metal straight-edge
mitre box or guide
medium fine, fine glasspaper
hammer, nail punch
bradawl, countersink bit
electric or hand drill
2, 5 and 25mm bits
hacksaw, fine flat file,
pliers, screwdriver
soldering iron and solder
water-resistant woodworking
    adhesive

For assembly
panel pins 12, 32, 50mm long
two 3mm glass panes
    480 × 250mm
6800mm of 12 × 6mm
    hardwood beading
1300mm of 31 × 22 × 22mm
    triangular batten
one flush hinge 50mm long
    and 16mm screws to fit
one hook and eye (for door)
two closed eyes (for trough)
10m of 3mm rustproof
    metal rod
two small knobs (for drawers)
two large carrying handles
    and 16mm screws to fit

For finish
cellulose filler or matching
    plastic wood
clear matt polyurethane
    lacquer or primer,
    undercoat and top coat
lint-free rag or 9 and 50mm
    paint brushes

Plan and section (dimensions in millimetres)

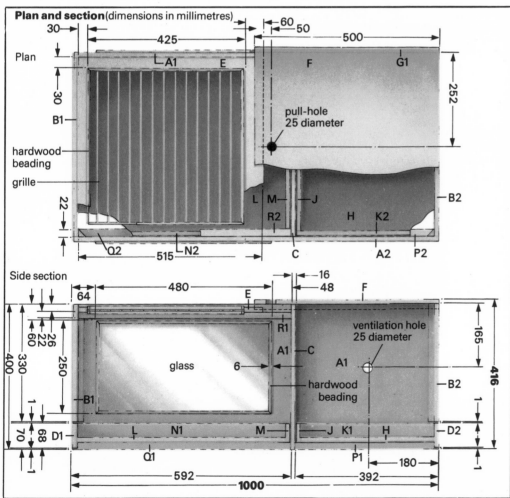

30

425

60

50

500

Plan

30

A1

E

F

G1

252

B1

pull-hole 25 diameter

hardwood beading

grille

22

L

M

J

B2

R2

H

K2

Q2

515

N2

C

A2

P2

Side section

16

48

480

F

64

E

R1

ventilation hole 25 diameter

26
60
22

250

glass

6

A1 C

A1

B2

400
330
70

1
68

B1

hardwood beading

D1

L

N1

M

J

K1

H

D2

165

1

1

Q1

P1

180

592

1000

392

stage 1

Mark lightly with a pencil all
the cutting lines on both
sides of the boards **(see
cutting lists)**. Score along
these lines with a sharp knife
and metal straight-edge to
prevent the surface veneer
breaking away as you saw.
Cut all the pieces of timber to
size with a panel saw, cutting
slightly to the waste side of
the line. Label each panel
with the appropriate code
letter. Smooth all cut edges
with medium fine glasspaper.

stage 2

Cut the apertures for the
windows in the two side
panels A. Mark the cutting
lines with a pencil **(see side
section)** and drill a 5mm
diameter hole in each corner

of the sections to be cut out to take your pad saw blade. Saw along the cutting line until you have enough room to change over to a panel saw. Don't try to cut too far with the pad saw as the small blade tends to wander off the line which will give you an inaccurate finish.

Drill a 25mm diameter ventilation hole in side panel A2 (see side section). Mark out the cutting lines for the doorway aperture in the divider C, tracing round a saucer or similar circular object, or using a pair of compasses set to a 50mm radius, to get an accurate curve. Drill a series of 2mm holes (see 1); with a 6mm chisel, cut through between them. Cut out the waste with a pad saw and keep this piece of wood for the door (see Stage 6).

Glue and pin the bedroom drawer runners P to the bottom inside face of side panels A at the bedroom end and the main drawer runners Q at the other end (see assembly diagram). To do this, apply a layer of water-resistant woodworking adhesive to the fixing edges of the runners and pin each into position with 32mm panel pins while the adhesive is still wet. Punch all pins below the surface of the wood with a nail punch – the resulting holes can be filled later with cellulose filler or plastic wood. Wipe off any excess adhesive with a clean dampened cloth.

Glue and pin in the same way the two grill supports R to the side panels A, 16mm in from the end and 26mm down from the top of each panel (see assembly diagram and side section).

stage 3

Glue and pin the two end panels B squarely to the sides A so the top edge of each end is flush with the top of the sides (see assembly diagram). To do this, apply water-resistant woodworking adhesive to the side edges of the end panels and fix with the 50mm panel pins through the sides into the end panels, punching all pins below the surface. To make the joints really strong, fix a triangular

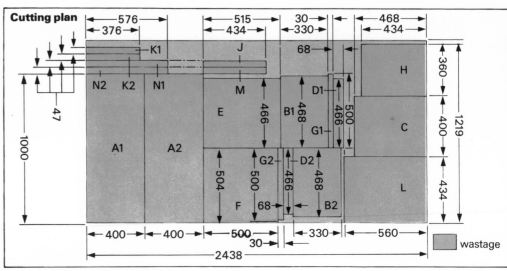

Cutting plan ... wastage

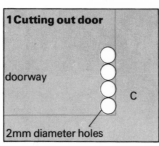

1 Cutting out door

doorway

C

2mm diameter holes

batten to each corner. Cut with a tenon saw two 282mm lengths for the window end and two 330mm lengths for the bedroom end. Apply water-resistant woodworking adhesive to the 22mm edges and pin (using 12mm panel pins) the shorter battens to the window end so they rest firmly against the bottom edges of the grill supports. Fix in the same way the two longer battens to the bedroom end so the top of each batten is flush with the top edges of the end panel and sides. Wipe off excess adhesive with a clean dampened cloth.

Apply water-resistant woodworking adhesive to both side edges of the divider C and slide it into position between the two side panels A (see plan). Check with your try square that the divider is squarely in position and fix with 50mm panel pins through each side panel into the divider, punching all pins below the surface as before. Wipe off excess adhesive.

stage 4

Cut the beading into eight 480mm lengths and eight 250mm lengths and mitre all the ends with a tenon saw

and mitre box (or mitre guide). Apply water-resistant woodworking adhesive to all surfaces in each window aperture in turn. With 12mm panel pins first fix the cut lengths of the beading to the inner edge, leaving an overhang (see 2). Push the glass into position

and then pin the beading to the outer edges so the glass is sandwiched firmly in place. Drill a 25mm diameter pull-hole in the sliding top F, 50mm in from one end (see plan). Glue and fix with 50mm panel pins the sliding top sides G squarely to the top F, making sure all edges

Making grille

To make the metal grille and food trough you need a soldering iron.

Plug in the iron and allow it to get really hot. Put the metal rods (one at a time) into a vice and cut with a hacksaw into two 423mm lengths and fifteen 404mm lengths. Smooth all cut edges with a fine flat file.

Place the four outside rods of the grille squarely together on a flat surface so the ends of the two shorter rods are on top of the longer ones. Keeping the soldering-iron

and the solder wire as close as you can to the work, apply a little solder to the iron and allow this molten metal to drop over the join (see 5). Apply plenty of solder to each join to make the structure secure. When you have made the outside frame complete the rest of the grille in the same way, spacing the shorter rods at 30mm centres. With a tenon saw, cut the beading into four 425mm and four 406mm lengths and mitre all the ends as before. Fix the grille into position in frame E in the same way as for the windows.

5 Applying solder

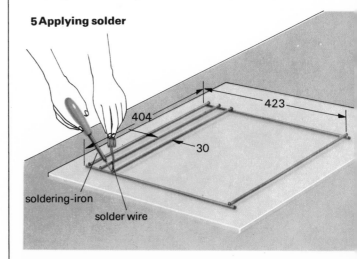

423

404

30

soldering-iron

solder wire

2 Fixing glass in windows

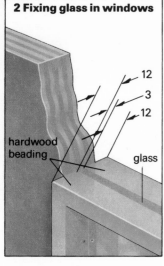

12
3
12

hardwood beading

glass

are flush. Wipe off excess adhesive with a clean dampened cloth.
Cut out the aperture in the grille frame E to the dimensions shown (see plan) in the same way as before. Smooth these cut surfaces with medium fine glasspaper.

3 Drawer construction

376

J
K1
H
K2
D2
466

drawer knob

stage 5

Glue and pin the bedroom drawer back J to the drawer base H (see 3). Fix the two sides K and the drawer front D2 onto this assembly in exactly the same way. When fixing D2, the top of which must be flush with the top of the two sides K, there will be an overhang at the bottom (see 3). This hides the drawer runners when the drawer is closed. Assemble the other drawer in the same way.

stage 6

Fill all holes, cracks and abrasions with cellulose filler or plastic wood and smooth all surfaces with fine glasspaper.
We gave our hutch four coats of polyurethane lacquer for weather-protection and painted the drawers in white gloss for easy cleaning.
Apply the lacquer with a lint-free rag and allow plenty of time for the first coat to dry thoroughly before putting on the second. Be sure to cover all surfaces, even those that will not show, as this will protect them from the weather, if the hutch is kept outdoors.
If you decide to paint rather than lacquer your hutch,

apply a coat of primer and then undercoat, allowing each to dry thoroughly. Apply the top coat, covering all surfaces as before. Use gloss paint for the drawers.
When all the lacquer (and paint) is thoroughly dry, screw the two eyes into end panel B1 (make pilot holes with a bradawl), 210mm up from the bottom edge and 109mm from the sides of the panel, and hook the turned up ends on the food trough through them. The trough will remain firmly in place but can be easily removed when necessary.
The small door in the divider C must be inserted the same way round as it was cut out; this will ensure a neat fit. Screw on the smaller leaf of the hinge halfway down the straight left side of the door and screw in a hook to the other side, making sure it will reach the eye when that is fixed into the divider (see 4).
Place the door in position, open the hinge and mark with a bradawl through the holes in the unattached leaf where the fixing screws are to go in the divider.
Screw the hinge firmly into position and, with the door in the closed position, mark where the eye will take the hook. Screw the eye into the divider (see 4).
Screw each of the two small drawer handles in the centre of each drawer front and the larger handles (for carrying the hutch) to each end panel.

Making food trough

To make the food trough, first cut with a hacksaw eight 250mm and two 150mm lengths of metal rod. Make the basic frame of the trough by soldering the ends of two of the 250mm long rods to the ends of the 150mm rods (see 6a).

Food trough

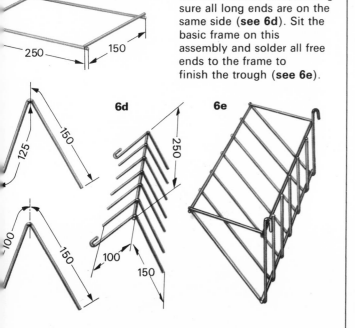

250
150

125
150

100
150

6d
250
100
150

6e

Cut two 300mm lengths of metal rod, bend each in half and then bend over 25mm at one end of each rod with a pair of pliers to the shape shown (see 6b). Bend five of the 250mm long rods to the shape shown (see 6c). Solder the seven rods to the remaining unbent 250mm rod, fixing the two 300mm rods at either end and spacing at 41mm centres the five 250mm rods, making sure all long ends are on the same side (see 6d). Sit the basic frame on this assembly and solder all free ends to the frame to finish the trough (see 6e).

See **Mitre joints**

4 Fixing door

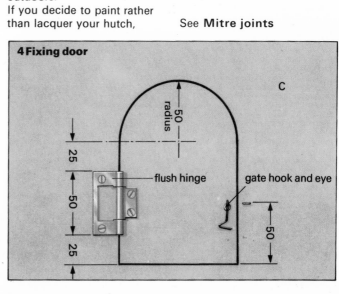

C
50 radius
25
50 — flush hinge
gate hook and eye
50
25

Dressing table

This dressing table and storage system is ideal for a teenager's bedroom. Not only will it house clothes and cosmetics, but also a lot of other personal odds and ends to help keep the room looking tidy.

Tools and materials

timber (see cutting lists)
measuring tape, pencil and try square
panel saw, coping or jig saw
pair of compasses
medium fine and fine glasspaper
hand or electric drill, 2, 5 and 38mm bits
hole saw drill attachment (if used)
countersink bit, bradawl, screwdriver
hammer and nail punch
woodworking adhesive, clean cloth

For assembly

No 8 countersunk chipboard screws 9 and 38mm long
No 8 countersunk screws 25 and 38mm long
panel pins 32mm long
four castors 46mm high, magnetic catch
two 50mm long cabinet hinges (uncranked) and 6mm long
    screws
one round mirror not more than 400mm diameter
four double-sided sticky pads (for fixing mirror)

For finish

cellulose filler or plastic wood
primer, undercoat and semi-gloss paint
clear matt polyurethane lacquer
masking tape, 50 and 100mm paint brushes

Overall dimensions

Trolley – 400mm high, 366mm wide, 366mm front to back
(16 × 14 × 14in). Box – 400 × 400 × 400mm (16 × 16 × 16in).
Dressing table – 1200mm high, 400mm wide, 400mm front to
back (47 × 16 × 16in). Project dimensions are in metric.

stage 1

Measure and mark out all the pieces of timber according to the dimensions shown (**see cutting lists and cutting plans**). Using a panel saw cut all the pieces squarely to size and smooth all cut edges with medium fine, then fine, glasspaper.

To cut the curve on the main back L (**see cutting plan for 12mm chipboard**) draw a line centrally down the length of the panel, set your compasses to a 200mm radius and place the point on the centre line 200mm in from one end of the panel. Draw the curve and cut off the waste with a coping saw or jig saw. Smooth the cut edges with medium fine, then fine, glasspaper.

Drill all the 5mm clearance holes in the two trolley tray bases K at the dimensions shown (**see 1**) and countersink them to take No 8 screws. Place a piece of scrap wood under the drilling area to prevent wood breaking from the surface. Hold D1 against K1 flush with one shorter edge and mark with a bradawl through the clearance holes in K1 onto D1. Drill 2mm pilot holes in D1 at these points, apply a layer of woodworking adhesive to the fixing edge of D1 and screw the trolley tray front D1 firmly in position with the 38mm long countersunk screws. Wipe off excess adhesive with a clean dampened cloth. Fix the trolley tray back D2 and the trolley tray sides C1 and C2 in the same way; assemble the other trolley tray following the same techniques.

Drill all the 5mm clearance holes in the trolley sides J1 and J2 at the dimensions shown (**see 1**) and countersink them to take No 8 screws. Hold J1 in the required position (**see 1**) against C1 (the top tray is fixed upside down so it can be used as a seat) and mark with a bradawl through the clearance holes in J1 onto C1. Drill 2mm pilot holes at these points, apply adhesive to the fixing edge of C1 and screw J1 firmly onto it with the 25mm long countersunk

screws. Wipe off excess adhesive. Fix trolley side J1 to trolley tray side C3 in the same way in the required position (**see 1**) then J2 to C2 and C4. Wipe off all excess adhesive.

Fix four castors to the underside of trolley tray base K2 (according to maker's instructions) far enough away from the trolley sides J to allow the castors to swivel without obstruction.

stage 2

Drill all the 5mm clearance holes in one of the tray bases G at the dimensions shown (**see 2**) and countersink them to take No 8 screws. Place a piece of scrap wood under the drilling area as before. Hold the tray front B1 in the required position against G so all edges are flush (**see 2**) and mark with a bradawl through the clearance holes in G onto B1. Drill 2mm pilot holes at these points. Apply adhesive to the fixing edge of B1 and screw through G into B1 using the 38mm long countersunk screws. Wipe off excess adhesive. Fix B2 to G in the same way and then the tray sides A1 and A2 between B1 and B2, again following the same techniques. Wipe off all excess adhesive. Assemble the remaining six trays in the same way – they are all identical.

stage 3

There are two box assemblies and the following instructions apply to both, except that one of the boxes has a door (**see 3**).

Drill all the 5mm clearance holes in the four box sides H at the dimensions shown (**see 3**) and countersink them to take No 8 screws. Place a piece of scrap wood under the drilling area as before. Hold one of the trays (assembled in **Stage 2**) in the required position against box side H3 (**see 3**) so all edges are flush and mark with a bradawl through the clearance holes in H onto the tray side A5. Drill 2mm pilot holes at these points, apply adhesive to the fixing edge of tray side A5 and screw H3 firmly in position with the

25mm long countersunk screws. Wipe off excess adhesive.

Glue and screw tray side A7 to H3 (see 3) in the same way then fix H4 onto this assembly. Wipe off excess adhesive.

The other box is made in exactly the same way.

On one of the box assemblies drill a 38mm diameter pull hole in the box door R at the dimensions shown (see 3) and smooth the inside of the hole with medium fine, then fine, glasspaper. Hold one leaf of each cabinet hinge on the front face of the box door R at the dimensions shown (see 3) and mark with a bradawl through the holes onto the door. Screw the hinges firmly down with 9mm long chipboard screws.

Hold the door on the front of the box and mark with a bradawl through the holes in the unattached hinge leaves onto the box side H4. Screw the hinges firmly in position to secure the door.

To fix the catch, screw the magnetic part to the underside of the tray base G3 and the metal plate to the inside face of the door R at the dimensions shown (see 3).

stage 4

There are two drawer assemblies and the following instructions apply to both. Drill 5mm clearance holes in the drawer sides N and the drawer back P 6mm up from the bottom edge of each (50mm in from each end and one half way between) and countersink them to take No 8 screws.

Hold the drawer back P in the required position against the drawer base Q and mark with a bradawl through the clearance holes in P onto Q. Drill 2mm pilot holes at these points, apply adhesive to the fixing edge of Q and screw P firmly in position with the 38mm long chipboard screws. Wipe off excess adhesive. Fix the drawer sides N to the drawer base Q in the same way and wipe off all excess adhesive.

Apply adhesive to the fixing edge of long drawer reinforcer E and pin it in position flush with the top edge of the drawer side N1 (see 4).

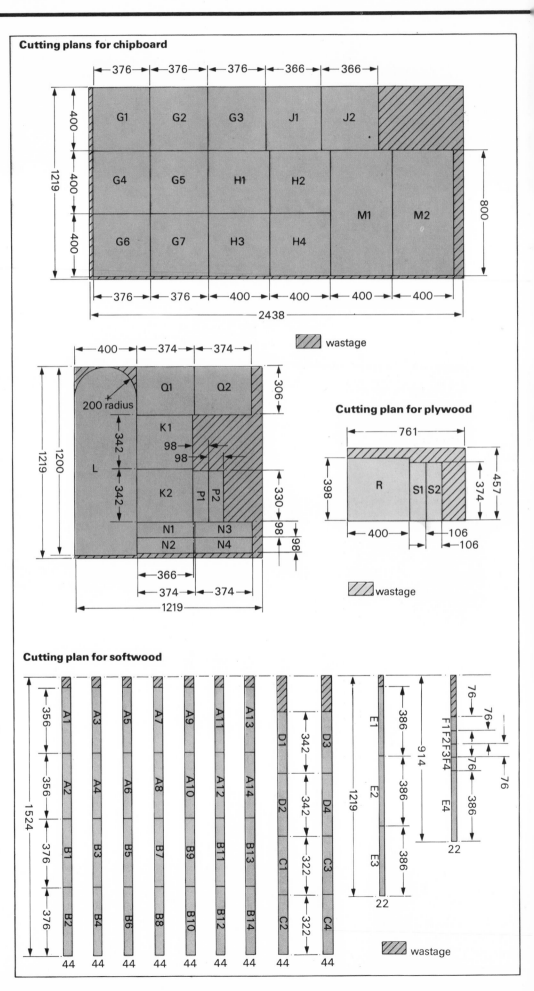

Cutting plans for chipboard

wastage

Cutting plan for plywood

wastage

Cutting plan for softwood

wastage

Cutting list for softwood

Description	Key	Quantity	Dimensions
Tray sides	A	14	356 × 44 × 22mm
Tray fronts and backs	B	14	376 × 44 × 22mm
Trolley tray sides	C	4	322 × 44 × 22mm
Trolley tray fronts and backs	D	4	342 × 44 × 22mm
Long drawer reinforcers	E	4	386 × 22 × 22mm
Short drawer reinforcers	F	4	76 × 22 × 22mm

Cutting list for chipboard & plywood

Description	Key	Quantity	Dimensions
Tray bases	G	7	400 × 376 × 12mm
Box sides	H	4	400 × 400 × 12mm
Trolley sides	J	2	400 × 366 × 12mm
Trolley tray bases	K	2	366 × 342 × 12mm
Main back	L	1	1200 × 400 × 12mm
Main sides	M	2	800 × 400 × 12mm
Drawer sides	N	4	374 × 98 × 12mm
Drawer backs	P	2	330 × 98 × 12mm
Drawer bases	Q	2	374 × 306 × 12mm
Box door (plywood)	R	1	400 × 398 × 9mm
Drawer fronts (plywood)	S	2	374 × 106 × 9mm

1 Trolley assembly
(dimensions in millimetres)

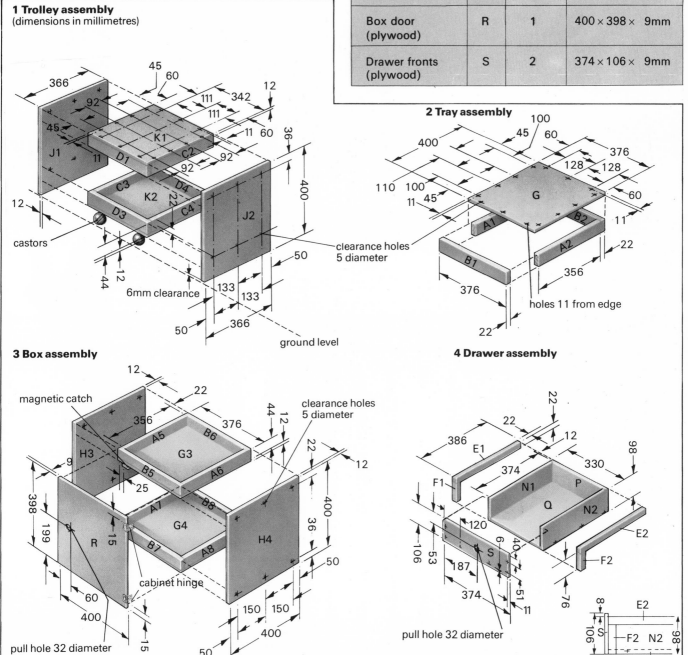

2 Tray assembly

3 Box assembly

4 Drawer assembly

Hammer the panel pins in very carefully to avoid weakening the joint between N and Q and sink all pins below the surface of the timber with a nail punch.

Glue and pin the short drawer reinforcer F1 to N1 so it is flush with the front edge of N1 (see 4) and wipe off all excess adhesive. Fix long and short drawer reinforcers E2 and F2 to the drawer side N2 in the same way.

Drill a 38mm diameter pull hole in the drawer front S at the dimensions shown (see 4), placing a piece of scrap wood under the drilling area as before. Smooth the inside of the hole with medium fine, then fine, glasspaper.

Drill 5mm clearance holes in the drawer front S at the dimensions shown (see 4) and countersink them to take No 8 screws. Hold the drawer front S in the required position against the front edge of the drawer assembly, mark with a bradawl through the clearance holes in S onto the front edges of the two short drawer reinforcers F and drill 2mm pilot holes at these points.

Apply adhesive to the front edges of the two drawer sides N, the two short drawer reinforcers F and drawer base Q and screw the drawer front S firmly in position with 25mm countersunk screws to F1 and F2, and with 38mm chipboard screws to Q. Wipe off all excess adhesive. Assemble the other drawer following the same techniques.

stage 5

Drill the 5mm clearance holes in the main back L and the two main sides M at the dimensions shown (see 5) and countersink them to take No 8 screws. Hold L and M1 squarely together in the required position and mark with a bradawl through the clearance holes in L onto M1. Drill 2mm pilot holes at these points, apply adhesive to the back fixing edge of M1 and screw the main back L firmly onto it with the 38mm long chipboard screws. Wipe off excess adhesive. Fix M2 to L in the same way.

Hold one of the trays (assembled in Stage 2) between the two main sides M so all top edges are flush and mark with a bradawl through the clearance holes in M1 and M2 onto the tray sides A. Drill 2mm pilot holes at these points, apply adhesive to both tray sides A and screw the tray firmly in position with the 25mm long countersunk screws. Wipe off excess adhesive. Fix the other two trays upside down in the required position (see 5).

stage 6

Fill all holes, cracks and abrasions with cellulose filler or plastic wood paying particular attention to ragged chipboard edges. Rub all surfaces smooth with medium fine, then fine, glasspaper. We painted all the chipboard in semi-gloss and gave the softwood two coats of polyurethane lacquer. To do this, place masking tape over all the softwood components and over the hinges and magnetic catch. Also place masking tape over the castors or, depending on the type of fixing, remove them completely before painting. Apply a coat of primer, an undercoat and then a top coat to all chipboard surfaces, leaving each to dry. Lift the masking tape and apply two coats of lacquer to the softwood, taking care not to get any lacquer on the paint. Fix a mirror centrally to the top part of the main back L with four double-sided sticky pads. Stick these to the back of the mirror and push the mirror firmly in position.

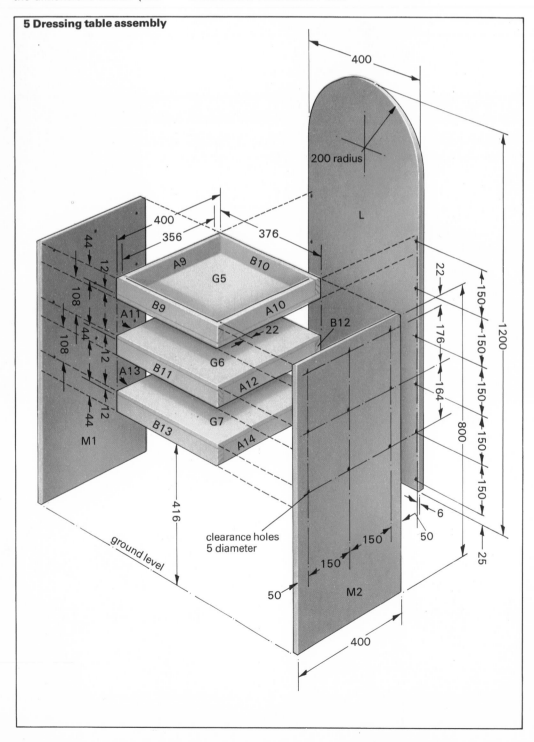

5 Dressing table assembly

The bathroom

Bathroom storage unit

This free-standing unit goes neatly at the end of your bath and has adjustable shelves, a linen bin and a cupboard with a mirror

Overall dimensions

1837mm high, 748mm front to back, 457mm wide (72 × 29 × 18in). Project dimensions are in metric only and do not allow for cutting wastages.

Tools and materials

Timesaver panels (see cutting list)
measuring tape, pencil and try square
sharp trimming knife and metal straight-edge
panel saw, block plane
domestic iron and brown paper
hand or electric drill, 2 and 5mm bits
screwdriver, bradawl, countersink bit
vice, hacksaw, fine flat file
600 × 300mm self-adhesive mirror

For assembly

No 8 Pozidriv countersunk chipboard screws 38mm long
No 6 round head chipboard screws 12mm long
15 joint blocks
280mm of 25mm continuous (piano) hinge
two spring-loaded lay-on hinges
16 white shelf supports
12 white plastic Pozi tops

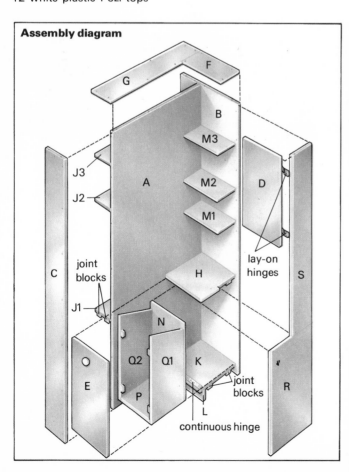

stage 1

Mark lightly with a pencil all the cutting lines on both sides of the Timesaver panels according to the dimensions shown (**see cutting list and cutting plan**). To avoid confusion later, label each panel with the appropriate code letter. Score along the cutting lines, using a sharp knife held against a metal straight-edge, to prevent damaging the melamine surface when sawing. With a panel saw cut all the panels to size, keeping slightly to the waste side of the line. Smooth all the cut edges with a block plane. Cut each top edge of the two linen bin sides Q to the required shape (**see cutting plan**). Place the two sides together and smooth the cut edges as before, making sure they are identical.

stage 2

Drill three 5mm clearance holes in the divider A at the dimensions shown (**see 1**) and countersink them to take No 8 screws. Then drill holes, of the correct diameter and depth for the shelf supports you are using, in A at the dimensions shown (**see 1**). Drill all the 5mm clearance holes and the holes for the shelf supports in the back panel B in the same way (**see 2**).

Mark on the panels which way round they will be fixed – there are no holes for shelf supports on the bath side of the divider A and none on the back face of the back panel B as this face will rest against the bathroom wall.

Hold the divider A in the required position against the back panel B (**see plan**) and, using a bradawl, mark through the 5mm clearance holes in B onto the side edge of A. Drill 2mm pilot holes at these points and screw A and B squarely and firmly together with the chipboard screws.

Warning Don't overtighten the screws as this would cause them to work loose inside the board and give you a weak joint.

Drill all the 5mm clearance holes in the main upright C at the dimensions shown (**see 3**) and countersink them

Cutting list for Timesaver panels

Description	Key	Quantity	Dimensions
Divider	A	1	1822 × 718 × 15mm
Back	B	1	1822 × 457 × 15mm
Main upright	C	1	1822 × 152 × 15mm
Cupboard door	D	1	610 × 305 × 15mm
Linen bin front	E	1	614 × 287 × 15mm
Small top	F	1	312 × 167 × 15mm
Main top	G	1	748 × 152 × 15mm
Linen bin cover	H	1	305 × 305 × 15mm
Bath shelves	J	3	718 × 137 × 15mm
Base	K	1	305 × 290 × 15mm
Plinth	L	1	290 × 39 × 15mm
Cupboard shelves	M	3	290 × 152 × 15mm
Linen bin back	N	1	540 × 287 × 15mm
Linen bin base	P	1	263 × 257 × 15mm
Linen bin sides	Q	2	585 × 263 × 15mm
Bottom side panel	R	1	672 × 305 × 15mm
Top side panel	S	1	1150 × 152 × 15mm

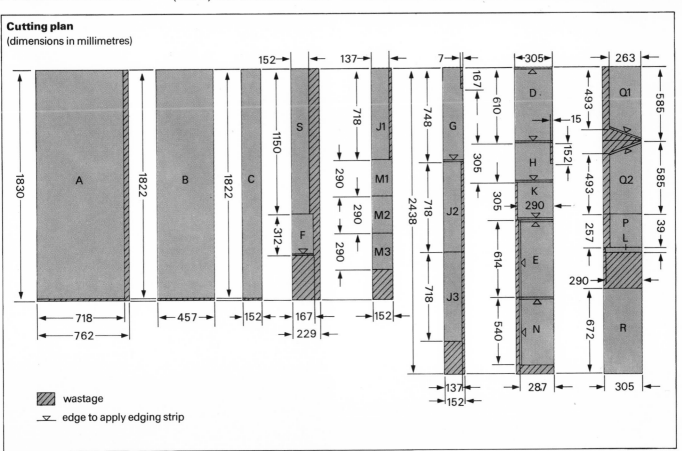

Cutting plan
(dimensions in millimetres)

▨ wastage

▽ edge to apply edging strip

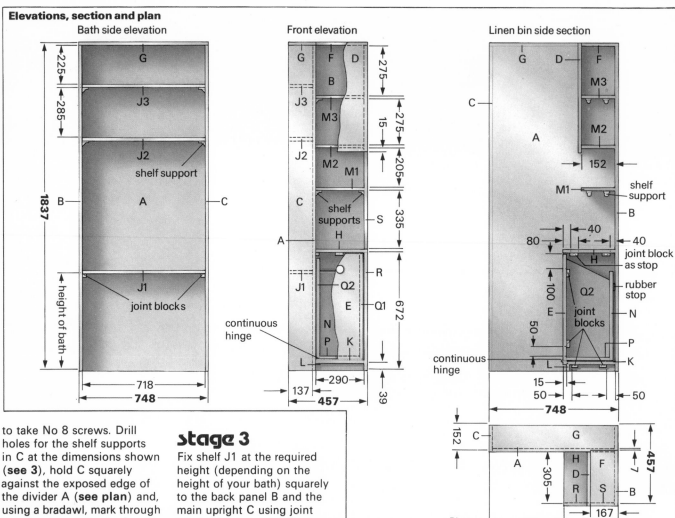

Elevations, section and plan

Bath side elevation

G

J3

J2

shelf support

B — A — C

J1

joint blocks

225

285

1837

height of bath

718

748

Front elevation

G F D

B

J3

M3

J2

M2 M1

C

shelf supports

S

A

H

J1

Q2

R

E

Q1

N

P K

continuous hinge

L

275

15

275

205

335

672

290

137

457

39

Linen bin side section

G D F

M3

C

M2

A

152

M1

shelf support

B

80 40

40

100

joint block as stop

H

rubber stop

Q2

E

joint blocks

N

50

P

L K

continuous hinge

15
50

50

748

152

C G

457

A

H
D
R

F

S

B

305

Plan

428

167

320

7

to take No 8 screws. Drill holes for the shelf supports in C at the dimensions shown (**see 3**), hold C squarely against the exposed edge of the divider A (**see plan**) and, using a bradawl, mark through the clearance holes in C onto A. Drill 2mm pilot holes at these points and screw main upright C firmly and squarely to A with chipboard screws.
Drill all the 5mm clearance holes in the main top G at the dimensions shown (**see 4**).
Lay G on the top edges of A, B and C so edges are flush and joints square. Using a bradawl, mark through the clearance holes in G onto the top edges of A, B and C and drill 2mm pilot holes at these points before fixing G firmly in position with chipboard screws.
Drill four 5mm clearance holes in the small top F at the dimensions shown (**see 5**), make pilot holes as before in the top edges of A and B to correspond with the clearance holes in F and fix F firmly in position with chipboard screws so one end of it fits snugly inside the rebate in G (**see plan**). Angle the screw within the rebate in towards the centre of A.

stage 3

Fix shelf J1 at the required height (depending on the height of your bath) squarely to the back panel B and the main upright C using joint blocks. Fix two joint blocks at each end of the shelf and flush with each end, one 25mm in from the front edge the other 25mm in from the back. Hold the shelf squarely in position and, using a bradawl, mark through the holes in the joint blocks onto the back panel B and the main upright C before screwing the shelf firmly in position with chipboard screws.
Drill three 5mm clearance holes in the base K at the dimensions shown (**see 6**) and countersink them to take No 8 screws. Hold K in the required position on top of the plinth L (**see linen bin side section**) and, using a bradawl, mark through the clearance holes in K onto the top edge of L. Drill 2mm pilot holes at these points and fix K squarely and firmly to L with chipboard screws.
Fix this base and plinth assembly squarely to the bottom side panel R with two joint blocks. Fix the joint blocks 50mm in from the

front and back edges of K flush with the side edge; mark with a bradawl through the holes in the joint blocks into R and fix the base and plinth assembly to R with chipboard screws.
Hold the base, plinth and bottom side assembly in the required position against the divider A and the back panel B (**see front elevation and linen bin side section**). Using a bradawl mark through the clearance holes in A and B onto the edges of the base K and then through the clearance holes in B onto the back edge of R. Drill 2mm pilot holes at these points and fix the base and side panel firmly in position with chipboard screws.
Drill three 5mm clearance holes in the top side panel S at the dimensions shown (**see 7**) and countersink them to take No 8 screws. Drill all the holes for the shelf supports at the dimensions

shown (**see 7**) and hold S in the required position (**see plan and front elevation**).
Using a bradawl, mark through the clearance holes in the back panel B and the small top F onto the back and top edges of S and fix S firmly in position with chipboard screws.

stage 4

The linen bin cover is fixed with four joint blocks. Screw two of these to the divider A at the dimensions shown (**see 1**) and the other two on the inside face, and flush with the top edge, of the bottom side panel R, one 40mm in from the back edge and the other 40mm in from the front edge. Screw through these joint blocks into H in the same way as before, check the joints are square and remove H so the linen bin can be made up and inserted.

Fix a joint block centrally to the underside of H so the distance from the front edge of the panel to the back edge of the joint block is 80mm (**see 8**). This will act as a stop so the linen bin cannot open too far. Remove this joint block; having already made a threaded screw hole, it will be easier to fix it permanently after the assembled linen bin is hinged in position.

stage 5

The linen bin front E is fixed to the two linen bin sides Q with four joint blocks and the linen bin back N and base P are then screwed onto this assembly.
Screw two joint blocks to the inside, flush with the front edges, of linen bin side Q1, one of them 50mm up from the bottom and the other 100mm down from the top. Screw two joint

- countersunk hole 5 diameter (facing side)
- countersunk hole 5 diameter (reverse side)

shelf support hole

1 Drilling plan for divider

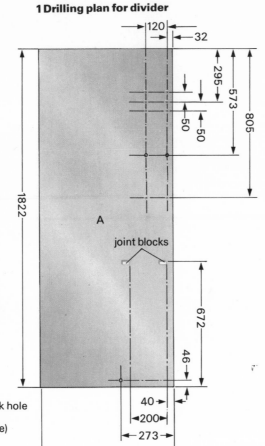

joint blocks

2 Drilling plan for back panel

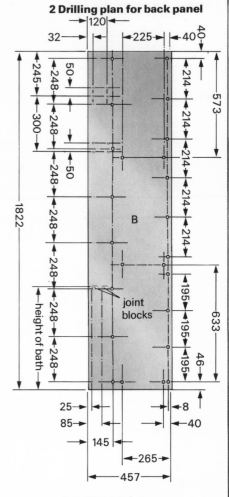

joint blocks

height of bath

3 Drilling plan for main upright

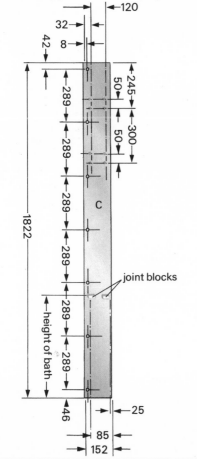

joint blocks

height of bath

4 Drilling plan for main top

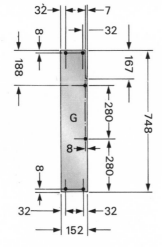

5 Drilling plan for small top

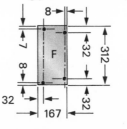

6 Drilling plan for base

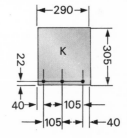

7 Drilling plan for top side panel

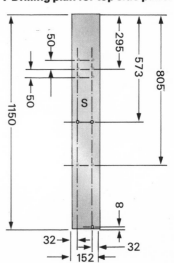

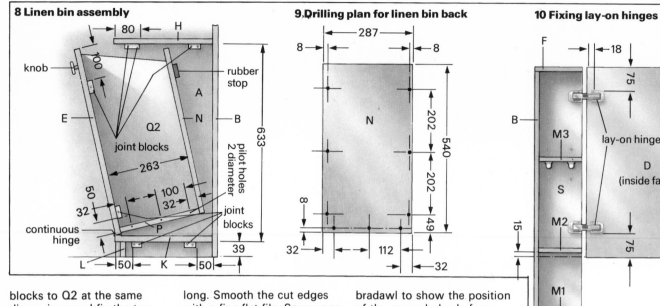

8 Linen bin assembly

80 — H
knob
100
rubber stop
A
E
Q2
N
B
joint blocks
263
pilot holes 2 diameter
633
50
100
32
32
32
joint blocks
continuous hinge
P
L — 50 — K — 50
39

9 Drilling plan for linen bin back

287
8
8
N
202
540
202
8
49
32
112
32

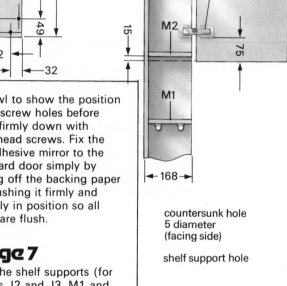

10 Fixing lay-on hinges

F
18
75
B
M3
lay-on hinges
S
D (inside face)
M2
15
75
M1
168

countersunk hole 5 diameter (facing side)

shelf support hole

blocks to Q2 at the same dimensions and fix the two sides Q to the front E, screwing through the remaining holes in the joint blocks (**see 8**).

Drill all the 5mm clearance holes in the linen bin back N at the dimensions shown (**see 9**) and countersink them to take No 8 screws. Hold N in the required position against the back edges of the two linen bin sides Q so all the bottom edges are flush and, using a bradawl, mark through the clearance holes in N onto Q1 and Q2. Drill 2mm pilot holes at these points and fix N firmly in position with chipboard screws.

Drill three 5mm clearance holes at the bottom of both sides Q at the dimensions shown (**see 8**).

Slip the linen bin base P in the correct position (**see 8**) and, using a bradawl, mark through the clearance holes in the sides Q and the back N onto the edges of the base P. Remove P, drill 2mm pilot holes at these points, replace P and fix it firmly in position with chipboard screws.

Screw a knob centrally onto the linen bin front E about 50mm down from the top edge of the panel and a rubber door stop to the linen bin back N to the same dimensions (**see 8**).

The linen bin assembly can now be fixed in position with a length of continuous hinge. Place the hinge (in the closed position) in a vice and trim, from the knuckle down, with a hacksaw to 280mm

long. Smooth the cut edges with a fine flat file. Screw one leaf of the hinge along the bottom edge of the linen bin front E so the knuckle lies just clear in front and the other leaf along the front of the top face of the base K (**see 8**).

Using the previously placed joint blocks (**see Stage 4**) fix the linen bin cover H back in position. Close the linen bin enough so its back N lies just behind where the stop is to be fixed in the underside of the linen bin cover M and screw the stop (joint block) into the previously made holes.

stage 6

Fix shelf M2 at the dimensions shown (**see front elevation and linen bin side section**). To do this, hold the shelf in the required position and mark with a bradawl through the clearance holes in the divider A, the top side panel S and the back panel B onto the side and back edges of M2. Drill 2mm pilot holes at these points and fix the shelf firmly in position with chipboard screws.

Mark the position of the two lay-on hinges on the back of the inside face of the cupboard door D and the front of the inside face of the top side panel S at the dimensions shown (**see 10**). There is no need to cut recesses for the hinges as they are fixed directly onto the melamine surface. Mark through the hinges with a

bradawl to show the position of the screw holes before fixing firmly down with roundhead screws. Fix the self-adhesive mirror to the cupboard door simply by peeling off the backing paper and pushing it firmly and squarely in position so all edges are flush.

stage 7

Push the shelf supports (for shelves J2 and J3, M1 and M3) into position at the desired height in the holes already drilled.

Push the plastic Pozi tops in any screw heads that will show and press on the self-adhesive edging strip with a 'warm' iron over brown paper to all exposed chipboard edges that will show.

Wipe off all pencil marks with soapy water before standing the unit in the required position in the bathroom. Rest the four unattached shelves on the fixed shelf supports.

Patio
and garden

Picnic table

This attractive picnic table folds away like a brief case and can be put up in seconds simply by clipping the legs in position. It is light and easy to carry and there is enough room inside for a few plates, serviettes and cutlery. Just the job for the summer.

stage 1

Measure and cut with a tenon saw all the pieces of timber to the dimensions shown (**see cutting list**) and label each part with the appropriate code letter.
Using a tenon saw and mitre box (or guide) mitre each end of the frame sides A and ends B, apply woodworking adhesive to the fixing edge of each mitre and assemble each frame clamping with web-clamps until the adhesive has set. Check each frame is square and wipe off all excess adhesive with a clean dampened cloth.
When the adhesive has set,

remove the clamps and reinforce the mitre joints with the 3mm diameter dowels which are inserted into holes drilled at right-angles to each mitre. To do this, mark out the hole centres on the outside face of the frame sides A 22mm in from each end and 22mm in from the top and bottom edges. Drill a 3mm diameter hole right through the mitre joint at each of these points.
Cut the 3mm dowel into eight 36mm lengths, apply adhesive to each one and push them in position. Wipe off excess adhesive with a clean dampened cloth and remove the protruding

Tools and materials

timber (see cutting list)
measuring tape, pencil and try square
tenon saw, coping or jig saw, mitre box or guide
hammer and nail punch, two web-clamps, vice
screwdriver and countersink bit
medium fine and fine glasspaper
combination square or sliding bevel or protractor
pair of compasses, piece of scrap hardboard (for template)
hand or electric drill, 3, 5, 6 and 12mm bits
15 and 18mm chisels, block plane
water-resistant woodworking adhesive, clean cloth

For assembly

1600mm of 12mm dowel for two 410 and two 366mm lengths
400mm of 3mm dowel for eight 40mm and four 16mm lengths
one 6mm round head bolt 75mm long with wing nut and washer
panel pins 18, 25, 32 and 38mm long
No 8 countersunk rustproof screws 45mm long
No 6 rustproof countersunk screws 32mm long
one 6mm and four 12mm wide Terry clips
two 50mm long brass butt hinges and 38mm long rustproof
    screws to fit
two small brass toggle catches

For finish

wood stain and lint-free rag, clear matt polyurethane
    lacquer or primer, undercoat and top coat
50mm paint brush

Cutting list for softwood & plywood

Description	Key	Quantity	Dimensions
Frame sides	A	4	564 × 44 × 22mm
Frame ends	B	4	486 × 44 × 22mm
Cross slats	C	22	442 × 32 × 9mm
Supporting battens	D	4	520 × 32 × 16mm
Legs	E	8	500 × 32 × 22mm
Handles (plywood)	G	2	486 × 75 × 6mm

Overall dimensions (when folded)
608mm long, 486mm wide, 88mm thick (24 × 19 × 3in).
Project dimensions are in metric only and do not allow for
cutting wastages.

dowel with a chisel.
Mark out the shaping lines on
all four frame sides A and
two of the four frame ends B
according to the dimensions
shown (**see end section**).
Place each frame in a vice
and plane down to these
lines. Smooth all surfaces
with medium fine, then fine,
glasspaper. The two unshaped
frame ends B will be hinged
together to form the centre of

the table.
Mark the slots for the toggle
catches 90mm in from each
end of both shaped frame
ends B (**see plan**), make
two cuts with a tenon saw to
a depth of 5mm (**see 1**) and
spaced according to the width
of your catches and
remove the waste from
between the cut lines with a
chisel. The catches should
fit flush with the timber when

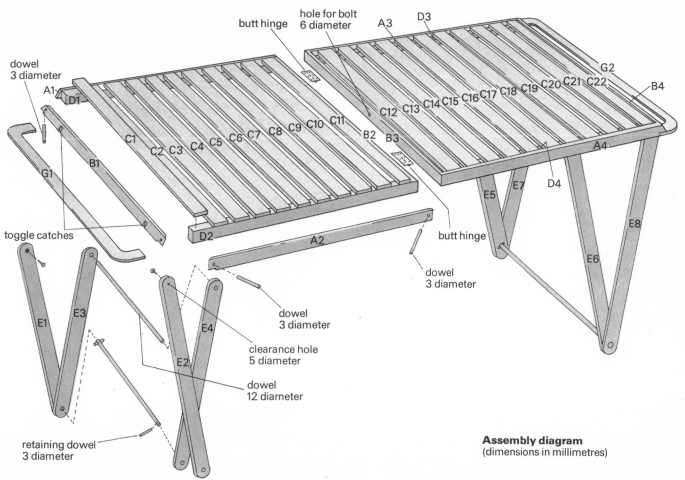

Assembly diagram
(dimensions in millimetres)

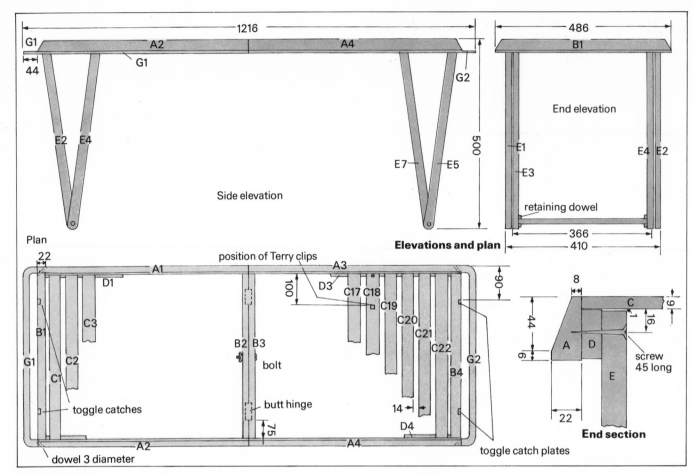

1216   486

G1   A2   A4   B1

G1

44

G2

E2 E4   E7   E5   500   End elevation

E1

Side elevation   E3

Plan   366   E4 E2

Elevations and plan   410   retaining dowel

22   position of Terry clips   A3

A1   D3   90

D1   C17 C18   8

100   C19   C

B1   C3   C20   44   16

C2   C21   1

G1   C22   A   D   6

C1   B2 B3   G2   screw 45 long

toggle catches   bolt   B4   E

butt hinge   22

75   End section

A2   14   A4

dowel 3 diameter   D4   toggle catch plates

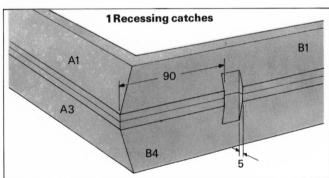

1 Recessing catches

A1   B1

90

A3

B4

5

screwed in place so try them for fit and make the slots deeper if necessary.

stage 2

For the handles, mark on the cutting lines at the dimensions shown (**see 2**). Set your compass to a radius of 44mm, place the compass point at X (**see 2**) and draw the outside curve. Place the point at Y to draw the other outside curve and draw the inside curves by placing the compass point at X and Y, with the radius set at 22mm. Remove the waste with a coping or jig saw and smooth all cut edges with medium fine, then fine, glasspaper.

Use this finished handle as a template to mark out the second handle. This ensures both handles are identical. Make the slots on the underside of the corners of the frame where the handles are to be (**see 2 inset**). These slots must be 22mm square and 6mm deep to house the thickness of the plywood. Remove the waste from the slots with an 18mm chisel, apply a layer of adhesive to all four slots and pin the handles in position using the 25mm long panel pins. Wipe off excess adhesive.

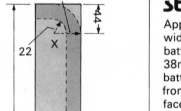

44

44

22   X

486   G

22   wastage

44

22   Y

75

stage 3

Apply adhesive to one 32mm wide face of each supporting batten D and, using the 38mm long panel pins, fix the battens in position 9mm down from the top on the inside face of the frame sides A (**see end section**). Wipe off excess adhesive with a clean dampened cloth.

Apply adhesive to the top edge of all four supporting battens D and to each end of all the cross slats C and pin the slats in position at the dimensions shown (**see plan**), using two 18mm long panel pins for each end of each slat. Punch all pin heads

2 Making handles

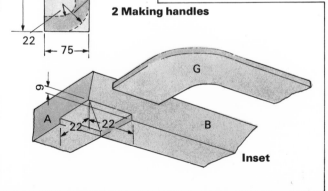

6

A   22   22   B

G

Inset

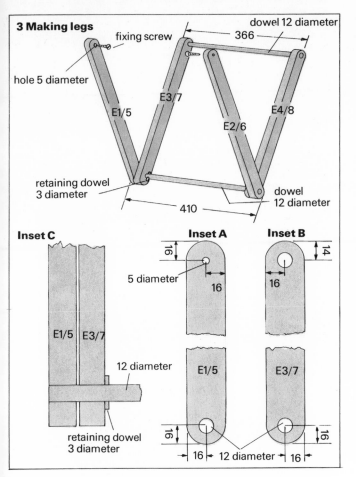

3 Making legs

dowel 12 diameter
366
fixing screw
hole 5 diameter
E3/7
E1/5
E2/6
E4/8
retaining dowel
3 diameter
410
dowel
12 diameter

Inset C

E1/5 E3/7

12 diameter

retaining dowel
3 diameter

Inset A

16
5 diameter
16
E1/5
16
16 12 diameter 16

Inset B

14
16
E3/7

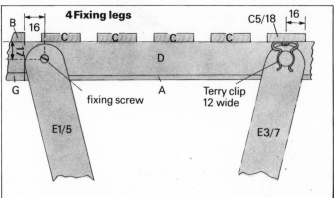

4 Fixing legs

B
16
C
C
C
C
C5/18
16

17
D
G
fixing screw
A
Terry clip
12 wide
E1/5
E3/7

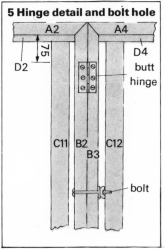

5 Hinge detail and bolt hole

A2
A4
D2
75
D4
butt
hinge
C11 B2 C12
B3
bolt

below the surface of the timber with a nail punch. Wipe off excess adhesive. Drill a 4mm diameter clearance hole 8mm in from each end of the fifth slat in from the handle end of both frames and countersink them to take No 6 screws. Mark through these holes with a bradawl and drive the No 6 screws firmly home. These slats will take some of the pressure exerted by the legs when weight is put on the table and they therefore require a stronger fixing.

stage 4

To make the curve at both ends of each leg E first make a hardboard template. This ensures all 16 curves will be identical. Mark a 32mm square onto a piece of scrap hardboard, place the point of your compass at the centre of this square (where the diagonals cross) and draw a semicircle of 16mm radius. Remove the waste with a coping saw and smooth the cut edge with fine glasspaper. Place this template at each end of each leg and trace

round it with a pencil. Cut off the waste from the ends of the legs with a coping saw and smooth the curves with medium fine, then fine, glasspaper.
Drill a 12mm diameter hole at both ends of four of the legs but only at one end of the other four at the dimensions shown (**see 3a and b**).
With a tenon saw cut the 12mm dowel into two 410mm lengths and two 366mm lengths. To assemble each leg, apply adhesive to the inside of the hole at one end of two of the legs with holes drilled at both ends and insert the 366mm length of dowel (**see 3**). Make sure these legs are parallel by laying them on a perfectly flat surface and pin through them into the dowel with 25mm long panel pins, making sure the ends of the dowel are flush with the outside faces of the legs. Push the 410mm dowel in position (**see 3**) and pin into it through the outer legs only, making sure its ends are flush with the outside faces of the outer legs.

Drill a 3mm diameter hole through the 410mm dowel just inside each inner leg (**see 3c**), cut the 3mm dowel into two 16mm lengths, apply adhesive to each one and push them in position so 2mm protrudes at either side of the dowel. These small retaining dowels prevent the inner leg sliding out of position. Wipe off all excess adhesive and assemble the other leg in the same way.
To fix the legs in position, drill a 5mm diameter clearance hole at the unattached end of all four outer legs (**see 3b**) at the dimensions shown. Countersink these holes to take No 8 screws and fix the legs in place (loosely enough for them to pivot easily) at the dimensions shown (**see 4**) with No 8 screws 45mm long.

stage 5

Fill all holes, cracks and abrasions with plastic wood and rub all surfaces smooth with medium fine, then fine, glasspaper.
For a finish we applied a

dark green stain with a lint-free rag and four coats of clear matt polyurethane lacquer for weather protection. Allow plenty of time for each coat to dry before applying the next.
To paint the table apply a coat of primer, an undercoat and at least two top coats, allowing time for each to dry before applying the next.
On the underside of the fifth slat from the handle end of each frame screw two 12mm Terry clips in position with the 6mm long rustproof screws. These clips should be about 100mm in from each end of the cross slats C5 and 18 (**see** 4); they hold the legs in position when the table is in use.
To fix the two frames together, mark and cut a recess for the hinges 75mm in from each end of the unshaped frame ends B (**see 5**). Make these recesses the same depth as the thickness of the hinge leaves and screw the hinges firmly in position with the 38mm long countersunk rustproof screws.
Drill a 6mm diameter hole in the centre of each hinged frame end B (**see 5**) so, when the table is in use, a bolt can be inserted for extra strength and stability. Screw the 6mm wide Terry clip in position as before to the underside of one of the cross slats near the middle; this houses the stabilizing bolt so you do not lose it when the table is not being used.
Screw the body of each catch in position inside the slots in one frame end B using 25mm long screws to fit and screw the catch-plates inside the slots in the other frame end B in the same way.

'Recliner'

Just right for the garden, this reclining seat is easily wheeled to wherever the sun is shining and, with a simple adjustment, you can sit up or stretch out. The backrest fits neatly underneath the assembly for storage when not in use.

Tools and materials

timber (see cutting list)
measuring tape, pencil and try square, mortise gauge
panel saw, tenon saw, coping saw
block or bench plane
electric or hand drill, 2 and 5mm bits
pair of compasses, protractor
screwdriver, bradawl, countersink bit
hammer and nail punch, mallet, vice, round file
6 and 18mm chisels
medium and fine glasspaper
web-clamp or length of strong rope
water-resistant woodworking adhesive

For assembly
panel pins 19 and 38mm long
two wheels and fixing bolts (with wing nuts and washers)
No 8 rustproof countersunk screws 38mm long
No 10 rustproof countersunk screws 50mm long

For finish
cellulose filler or plastic wood
clear matt polyurethane lacquer, 50mm paint brush

Overall dimensions (when stored)
2000mm long, 800mm wide, 322mm deep without wheels (79 × 31 × 13in). Project dimensions are given in metric only and do not allow for cutting wastages.

stage 1

Measure and mark out, then cut with a panel saw, all the pieces of timber according to the dimensions shown (**see cutting list and plan**).
Mark out with a mortise gauge the tenon at each end of each backrest cross slat E according to the dimensions shown (**see 1b**) and cut to size with a tenon saw.
To make the wedged stub tenons, saw out two slits in each tenon and make wedges (**see 1b**) out of scrap pieces of wood. Mark out mortises (**see 1a**) on the inside edge of both backrest uprights F (there are four on each) at the dimensions shown then chop out the waste with a 6mm chisel. Cut a recess at one end of both rails according to the dimensions shown (**see 1**).
Mark out the shape of the halving joint at either end of

the backrest top G and both backrest uprights F at the dimensions shown (**see 1c**).
Pour some water-resistant woodworking adhesive inside all the mortises in the two uprights F and insert the tenons on the backrest cross slats E (**see 1**), ramming them firmly home with a mallet. Apply adhesive to the halving joints on the backrest top G and on the two backrest uprights F, and pin them together with the 19mm panel pins. Punch the heads below the surface. Wipe off all excess adhesive with a clean dampened cloth and place a G-clamp over both halving joints and a web-clamp round the edges of the assembly; tighten the clamps making sure all joints are square.
When clamped more adhesive will be squeezed out — wipe off immediately.
If you do not have a web-

clamp you can improvise with a length of strong rope. Put newspaper or cloth padding between the rope and the frame to prevent bruising the wood, tie the rope round the backrest assembly and tighten it with a screwdriver.

stage 2

For the handles, draw a circle at one end of one of the main side rails A at the dimensions shown (**see 2**) with your compass set to a radius of 30mm. Draw the

Cutting list for softwood

Description	Key	Quantity	Dimensions
Main side rails	A	2	2000 × 124 × 22mm
Main end rails	B	2	800 × 124 × 22mm
Cross slats	C	16	800 × 72 × 22mm
Shaped cross slat	D	1	800 × 44 × 22mm
Backrest cross slats	E	4	736 × 72 × 22mm
Backrest uprights	F	2	750 × 72 × 22mm
Backrest top	G	1	800 × 72 × 22mm
Legs	H	2	300 × 44 × 44mm

curved cutting lines approximately to the dimensions shown (**see 2**) and cut off the waste with a coping saw; smooth the cut edges with medium fine, then fine, glasspaper. Trace the shape of the handle onto one end of the other main side rail A and cut off the waste as before. This ensures both handles will be identical.

Assembly diagram

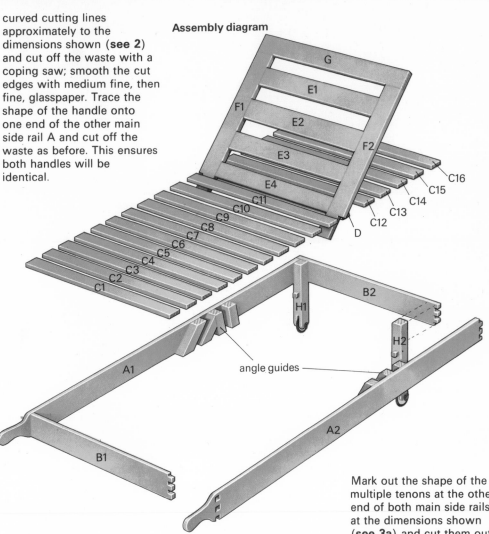

Mark out the shape of the multiple tenons at the other end of both main side rails A at the dimensions shown (**see 3a**) and cut them out with a tenon saw and an 18mm chisel.

Mark out and cut the tenons at either end of the main end rails B in the same way (**see 3c**). Mark out the required positions of the multiple mortises near the handles in both main side rails A at the dimensions shown (**see 3b**); chop out the waste with an 18mm chisel.

Cut with a tenon saw the backrest angle guides out of pieces of scrap wood to the dimensions shown (**see 4a**). To do this, use a protractor to mark the cutting lines on the timber; place each piece in a vice and cut very carefully along the cutting lines with a tenon saw. These angle guides must be cut very accurately or the backrest will not slide easily and squarely in position. Don't forget there are four angle guides to make for each main side rail A. Drill 5mm clearance holes in each backrest angle guide

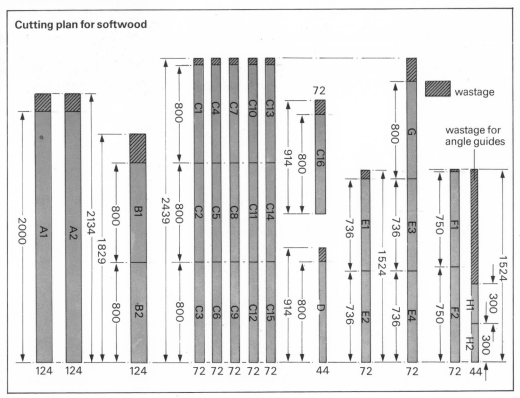

Cutting plan for softwood

30mm centrally in from each end and countersink them to take No 8 screws. Hold each guide at the required position on the inside face of main side rail A1 (**see 4**) and mark through the clearance holes onto A with a long-bladed bradawl. Drill 2mm pilot holes at these points, apply adhesive to the fixing edge of each angle guide and screw the four guides firmly in position with the No 8 screws. Fix the other four angle guides to A2 in the same way.

Apply adhesive to the fixing edges of all the box joints and join main end rail B1 to the handle end of the two main side rails A (**see assembly diagram**). Wipe off excess adhesive. Slide the main end rail B2 into position at the leg end of the main side rails A and secure all joints with 38mm long panel pins (**see assembly diagram**), sinking the heads below the surface of the timber with a nail punch. The holes that remain can be filled later. Wipe off excess adhesive and make

absolutely sure all box joints are square and will remain so until the adhesive has set hard.

Cut a slot with a tenon saw in the bottom end of both legs H (**see 5**) by making two cuts with a tenon saw and chopping out the waste from between the cut lines with a chisel. Make the slot big enough to house the wheel with about 10mm clearance between the top of the wheel and the top of the slot. Make the arch shape at the top of the slot with a round file. Drill holes in each side of the slot of the same diameter as the fixing bolt for the wheel (**see 5**). Hold the wheel in position and slide the bolt through the holes and the wheel; tighten up with a wing nut, placing a washer between the nut and the wood.

Using a tenon saw, cut a 22mm square out of a piece of scrap wood, apply adhesive to one edge of it and fix it in position with 38mm long panel pins on the back face of the leg H so the top edge of the block is 150mm down

from top edge of H (**see 5**). Sink the pin heads below the surface of the timber with a nail punch. These small blocks stop the backrest falling out when it is strapped to the underside of the recliner while it is not being used.

stage 3

Shape cross slat D by marking the cutting lines at each end and 100mm along the length of the slat (**see 6a**) using a protractor to mark the angles accurately. Remove the waste with a sharp chisel.

Drill two 5mm clearance holes 11mm in from each end and 20mm in from each edge (**see plan**) of all 16 cross slats C and one 5mm clearance hole 11mm in from each end of shaped cross slat D 12mm in from one edge. Lay these slats in the required position over the two main side rails A at the dimensions shown (**see side elevation**) and mark with a bradawl through the clearance holes in the slats onto the top edge of A1 and A2. When positioning the cross slats, don't forget to place the shaped cross slat D and mark through it with a bradawl in the same way. Remove the slats and drill 2mm pilot holes at these points, apply adhesive to the top edge of both main side rails A and screw all the cross slats C and the shaped cross slat D firmly down with the No 8 screws. Wipe off excess adhesive.

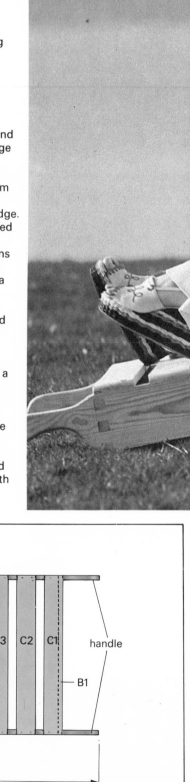

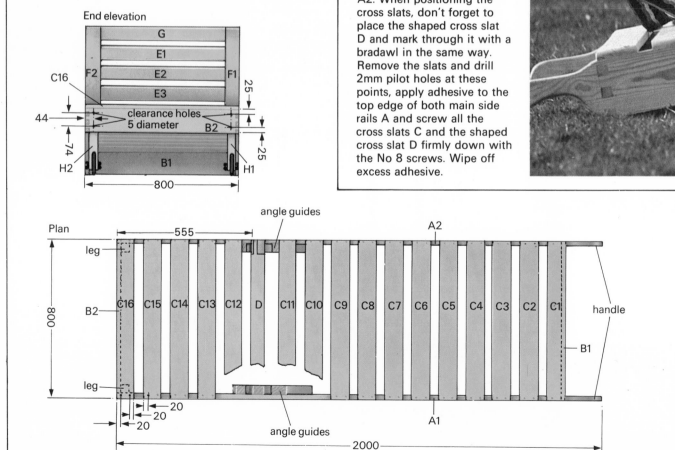

End elevation

C16

F2   F1

44

74

H2   H1

G
E1
E2
E3
clearance holes
5 diameter
B2
B1

25
25

800

Plan

555

angle guides

A2

leg

B2

C16 C15 C14 C13 C12 D C11 C10 C9 C8 C7 C6 C5 C4 C3 C2 C1

handle

B1

leg

20
20
20

angle guides

A1

800

2000

stage 4

To fix the legs drill two 5mm clearance holes at each end of the main end rail B2 at the dimensions shown (**see end elevation**) and one 5mm clearance hole at the square end of each main side rail A at the dimensions shown (**see side elevation**) and countersink them to take No 10 screws.

Hold one of the legs in the required position and mark with a bradawl through these clearance holes onto the leg. Drill 2mm pilot holes at these points, apply adhesive to the fixing edges of H, spreading the adhesive no more than 124mm down from the top, then screw the leg firmly in position with the No 10 screws. Fix the second leg to the other main end rail

Elevations and plan
(dimensions in millimetres)

Side elevation

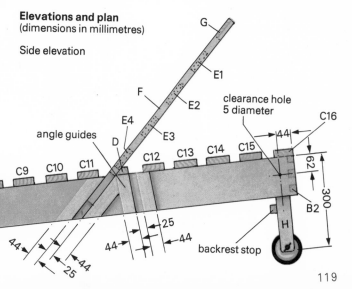

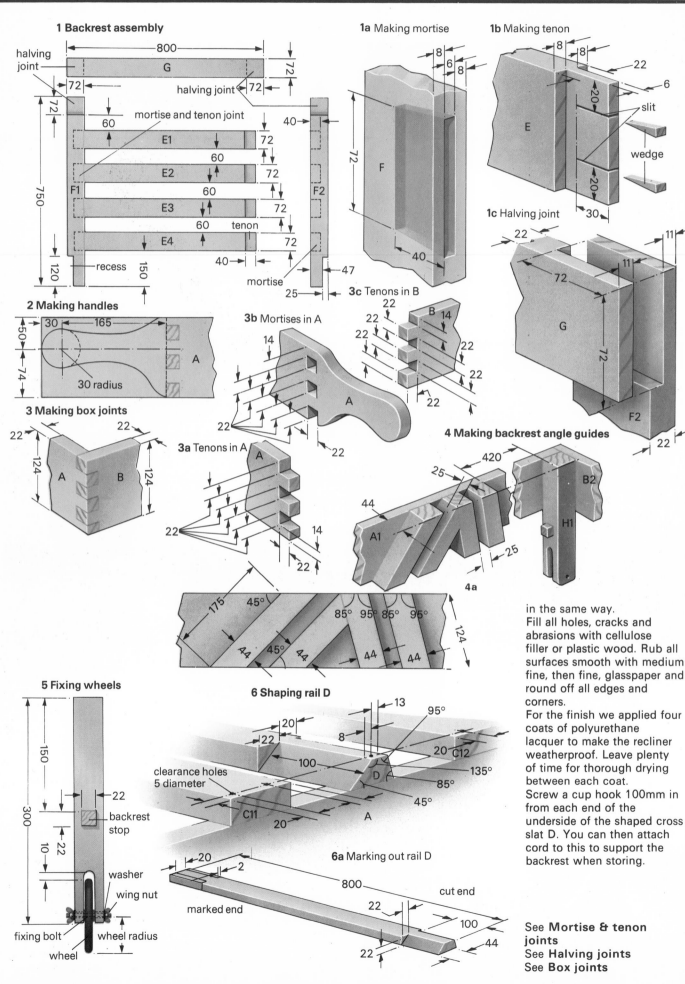

1 Backrest assembly

halving joint

800

72

72

halving joint

72

72

40

72

60

mortise and tenon joint

E1

72

60

E2

72

F1

60

F2

E3

72

750

60

tenon

E4

72

120

recess

150

40

47

mortise

25

2 Making handles

30

165

50

A

74

30 radius

3 Making box joints

22

22

124

A

B

124

1a Making mortise

8

6

8

72

F

40

1b Making tenon

8

8

22

20

E

slit

wedge

20

30

1c Halving joint

22

11

11

72

G

72

F2

22

3a Tenons in A

14

22

14

3b Mortises in A

14

A

22

22

22

3c Tenons in B

22

B

14

22

22

22

22

22

4 Making backrest angle guides

420

25

44

25

A1

B2

H1

4a

175

45°

85° 95° 85° 95°

124

44

45°

44

44

44

5 Fixing wheels

150

22

backrest stop

300

22

10

washer

wing nut

fixing bolt

wheel

wheel radius

6 Shaping rail D

13

20

95°

22

8

100

20

C12

clearance holes 5 diameter

D

135°

85°

C11

20

A

45°

6a Marking out rail D

20

2

800

cut end

marked end

22

100

22

44

in the same way.
Fill all holes, cracks and abrasions with cellulose filler or plastic wood. Rub all surfaces smooth with medium fine, then fine, glasspaper and round off all edges and corners.
For the finish we applied four coats of polyurethane lacquer to make the recliner weatherproof. Leave plenty of time for thorough drying between each coat.
Screw a cup hook 100mm in from each end of the underside of the shaped cross slat D. You can then attach cord to this to support the backrest when storing.

See **Mortise & tenon joints**
See **Halving joints**
See **Box joints**

Canopy deck-chair

Laze in the warm sunshine in this deck-chair. Its height is adjustable so you can sit up in it or lie back and go to sleep.

Cutting list for softwood and plywood

Description	Key	Quantity	Dimensions
Main frame sides	A	2	1530 × 98 × 22mm
Seating frame sides	B	2	1480 × 98 × 22mm
Back support arms	C	2	700 × 98 × 22mm
Canopy sides	D	2	1300 × 98 × 22mm
Notch covers (plywood)	E	2	350 × 98 × 16mm

Overall dimensions (folded)
1880mm long (minimum), 750mm wide (70 × 30in).
Project dimensions are in metric only and do not allow for
cutting wastages.

Tools and materials
timber (see cutting list)
measuring tape, pencil and try square
panel, tenon and coping saws
pair of compasses, piece of scrap hardboard
vice, hand or electric drill, and 2, 5, 12 and 38mm bits
medium fine and fine glasspaper
hole saw drill attachment (if used)
bradawl, screwdriver, countersink bit
mitre box or guide (as needed)
12mm chisel, block plane, hammer, half-round file
3m of 84cm wide deck-chair canvas and 1.2m cotton fringing
sewing thread (to match canvas colour)
dressmaker's scissors, needle and pins, domestic iron
water-resistant woodworking adhesive, clean cloth

For assembly
4500mm of 38mm dowel for six dowels 750mm long
1800mm of 12mm dowel for 12 dowels 64mm long and
  12 dowels 80mm long
No 8 countersunk rustproof screws 25mm long
four 12mm diameter rustproof bolts 60mm long and
  eight flat washers and four wing nuts to fit bolts
galvanized or brass tacks 6mm long

For finish
cellulose filler or matching plastic wood
clear matt polyurethane lacquer or primer, undercoat
  and gloss paint
lint-free rag or 50mm paint brush

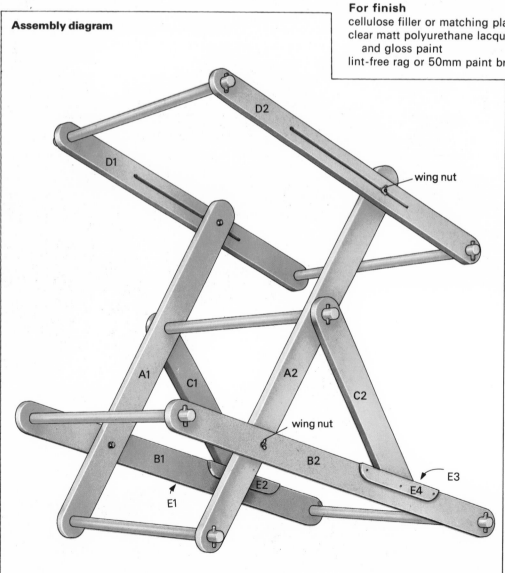

Assembly diagram

stage 1
Measure and cut with a
panel saw all the pieces of
timber squarely to size to the
dimensions shown (see
cutting list and cutting
plan).
Both ends of the main frame
sides A, the seating frame
sides B, the canopy sides D
and the plywood notch
covers E and only one end of
the back support arms C
are curved (see assembly
diagram). To form these
curves you must first make
a hardboard template.
Cut a 98mm square out of a
piece of hardboard and mark
on the diagonals (see 1).
Set your compass to a 49mm
radius and place the point in
the centre of the square
(where the diagonals cross)
and draw on the curve. Cut
off the waste with a coping
saw and smooth with fine
glasspaper. Using this
template mark the curves on
the various pieces of timber
(see assembly diagram)
and cut off all the waste with
a coping saw. Before cutting
the notch covers, score along
the cutting lines on both
sides of the timber with a
sharp knife to prevent the
surface veneer breaking away
when sawing.

Side section
(dimensions in millimetres)

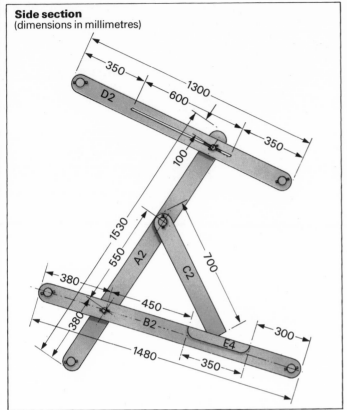

stage 2

With a tenon saw cut the 38mm diameter dowel into six 750mm lengths, and the 12mm diameter dowel into twelve 64mm and twelve 80mm lengths. With medium fine glasspaper chamfer both ends of all the dowels.
Drill two 38mm diameter holes on both main frame sides A for the dowels and two 12mm holes for the bolts at the dimensions shown **(see 2a)**. Then drill holes in B, C and D at the dimensions shown **(see 2b, c, d)**. Smooth the holes in C with medium fine, then fine, glasspaper or with a half-round file.
When drilling, place a piece of scrap wood under the drilling area to prevent the surface wood on the bottom face breaking away as the bit drills through.
Drill 12mm diameter holes 24mm in from each end of five of the 38mm dowels and 46mm in from both ends of the remaining one. This one will be used to fix the bottom ends of the two main frame sides A so label the dowel accordingly.
Place one of the seating frame sides B in a vice, mark on the cutting lines for the

notches and then cut them out with a tenon saw to the dimensions shown **(see 3)**. Cut the notches in the other seating frame side B.
With a panel saw cut the two notch covers E in half (to make four pieces) by cutting centrally along their length, again scoring the cutting lines. Drill three 5mm clearance holes in each piece at the dimensions shown **(see 3)** and countersink them to take No 8 screws. Hold one of these notch covers in the required position **(see 3)** so its top edge is flush with the top edge of the seating frame side B and, with a bradawl, mark through these clearance holes onto B. Drill 2mm pilot holes at these points, apply a layer of woodworking adhesive to the fixing edge of the notch cover and screw it firmly in position with 25mm long screws. Wipe off excess adhesive with a clean dampened cloth. Fix the remaining three notch covers in the same way.
To make the slots for the bolts in the canopy sides D drill a series of 12mm holes at the dimensions shown **(see 4)**, placing a piece of scrap wood under the drilling area as before, and cut out the remaining waste with a

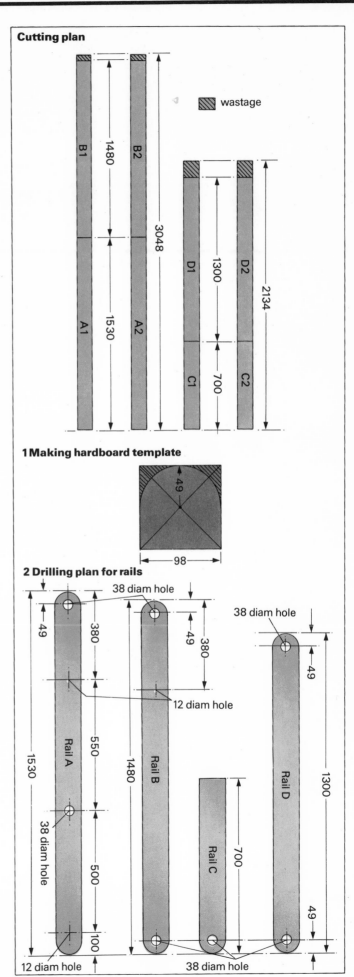

Cutting plan

wastage

1 Making hardboard template

2 Drilling plan for rails

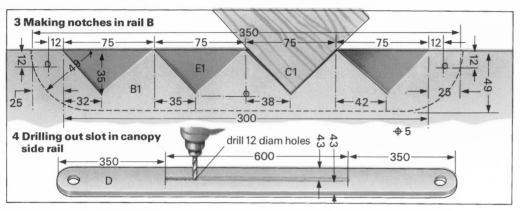

3 Making notches in rail B

12 | 12 | 75 | 350 | 75 | 75 | 75 | 12 | 12 | 49

E1 C1 B1

25 | 32 | 35 | 38 | 42 | 25

300

⊕ 5

4 Drilling out slot in canopy side rail

drill 12 diam holes

350 | 600 | 350

43 | 43 | 43

D

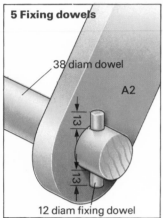

5 Fixing dowels

38 diam dowel

A2

13

13

12 diam fixing dowel

12mm chisel. Alternatively, drill a 12mm hole at either end of the slot and cut out the waste with a pad saw. Smooth the inside of the slot with a half-round file or a piece of medium fine glasspaper wrapped round a length of dowel of no more than 9mm diameter.

stage 3

Fill all holes, cracks and abrasions with cellulose filler or plastic wood. Matching plastic wood is better if you are applying a natural finish. Rub all surfaces smooth with medium fine, then fine, glasspaper, rounding off all sharp corners and edges. Apply a finish before assembling the chair. We applied four coats of matt lacquer for a durable, natural finish. Be sure to apply at least three coats so the deck-chair can be left outdoors even if it rains. Allow each coat to dry before applying the next. If painting, apply a coat of primer, two undercoats and then gloss, leaving each coat to dry.

stage 4

Apply adhesive to the inside edges of the 38mm holes in the canopy sides D and to four of the 64mm long 12mm dowels. Push two 38mm dowels in position in D1 and D2 (see assembly diagram) and secure them with the 64mm long 12mm dowels so they protrude 13mm at either side (see 5). Wipe off excess adhesive. Check the joints are square, and that D1 and D2 are close against the 12mm dowels, place the structure on a flat surface and leave for the adhesive to set thoroughly. Fix two 38mm dowels in the seating frame sides B in the same way and leave on a flat surface as before for the adhesive to set thoroughly. When the adhesive has set hard, fix the main frame sides A to the seating frame sides B with the 12mm bolts, placing a washer between the bolt head (and the wing nut) and the timber (see assembly diagram).
Apply adhesive to the 38mm holes in main frame sides A and position A1 and A2 so they are not parallel. Slide the previously marked 38mm dowel into the bottom hole in A1 and another 38mm dowel into the other hole in A1 so they protrude 90mm. Then position A2 parallel to A1 and push the dowels back through into A2 to the required position. Wipe off excess adhesive.
Push the back support arms C over the top dowel (see assembly diagram), making sure there is no adhesive on the dowel as C must pivot freely for adjusting height. Apply adhesive to four 64mm long 12mm dowels and push these in position as before.

stage 5

When all the adhesive has set, drill a 12mm hole, 80mm deep, in the underside (so as not to be easily seen) of rails A, B and D through the 38mm dowels so that small (12mm diameter) stabilizing dowels can be inserted (see 6). Again, don't drill through the back support arms C as they must be able to move freely. Apply adhesive to the 80mm long stabilizing dowels (two at a time) and push them firmly into position in these holes. Wipe off excess adhesive and trim any protruding dowels with a block plane. Patch up these areas with whatever finish you used for the chair.

stage 6

For the seat cut a piece of deck-chair canvas 1.6m long

and 66cm wide. Turn 1cm of the canvas to the underside on both long edges and press the folds with a domestic iron. Turn these a further 2cm, pin in position then baste and stitch them down. Turn under 2cm to the underside across both width edges. With the right side of the canvas uppermost, and the length of it lying away from you, fix the canvas with tacks to the back side of the front dowel, placing the tacks at 25mm intervals.
Bring the canvas round under the front dowel and loop it round the back dowel, taking it round far enough so the tacks will not show (see 7). For the canopy cut the canvas to 1.4m long and 66cm wide. Turn all hems as before and place the canvas over the canopy frame, marking on the required position of the cotton fringing. Remove the canvas and stitch on the fringing. Fix the canvas to the back and front dowels of the canopy frame as before, pulling it taught enough between them to prevent it flapping.
Screw the canopy frame in position with the wing nuts and bolts, placing a washer between the wing nuts (and bolt heads) and the timber.

See **Dowel joints**

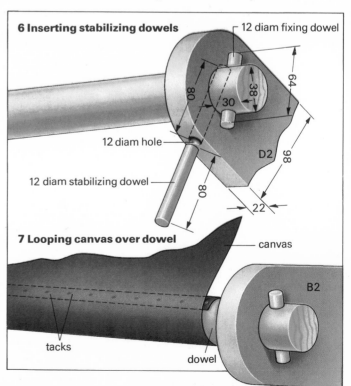

6 Inserting stabilizing dowels

12 diam fixing dowel

80 | 38 | 64

30

12 diam hole

D2

12 diam stabilizing dowel

98

80

22

7 Looping canvas over dowel

canvas

B2

tacks

dowel

Window box

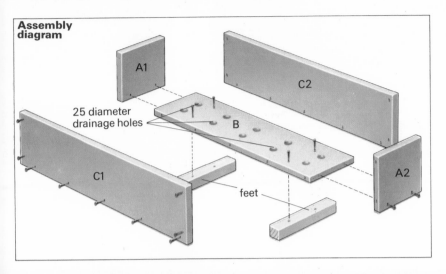

Assembly diagram

A1

C2

25 diameter drainage holes

B

C1

A2

feet

Tools and materials

measuring tape, pencil and try square
panel and tenon saw
hand or electric drill
2, 5 and 25mm drill bits
medium fine and fine glasspaper
vice, countersink bit
bradawl, screwdriver
water-resistant woodworking adhesive
600mm of 50mm square softwood batten
No 8 countersunk screws 50mm long

For finish

clear matt polyurethane lacquer or
   horticultural clear wood preservative,
   or primer, undercoat and gloss paint
lint-free rag or 50mm paint brush

Overall dimensions

915mm long, 300mm wide, 280mm high
(36 × 12 × 11 in). Project dimensions are
in metric only and do not allow for
cutting wastages.

This timber window box is very easy to make and will brighten up the outside of your home. You can fill it with soil or stand pots in it.

stage 1

Measure and cut with a panel saw all the pieces of timber to the dimensions shown (**see cutting list and cutting plan**).

If you are going to use your box outdoors, drill ten 25mm drainage holes in the base B at the dimensions shown (**see plan**).

When drilling, place a piece of scrap wood under the drilling area to prevent surface wood on the bottom face breaking away as the bit drills through. Smooth the inside of the holes with medium fine, then fine, glasspaper.

For the feet, place the softwood batten in a vice and cut with a tenon saw into two 300mm lengths. Drill 5mm clearance holes in B at the dimensions shown (**see plan**) and countersink them to take No 8 screws. Stand the base B on top of the two feet in the correct place (**see side elevation**), so the feet protrude the same amount at each side. With a bradawl mark through the base B onto the two feet, remove the base and then drill 2mm pilot holes at these points. Apply a layer of woodworking adhesive to the top face of one of the feet and then screw through B into it with the 50mm long screws. Wipe off excess adhesive with a clean dampened cloth. Fix the base to the other foot in the same way.

stage 2

Drill two 5mm holes in A1 11mm up from the bottom edge and 40mm in from each side. Place scrap wood under the drilling area as before. Hold A1 against B and mark with a bradawl through these holes onto B. Drill 2mm pilot holes at these points, apply a layer of woodworking adhesive to this edge of B and screw the end A1 firmly into position with the 50mm long screws. Wipe off excess adhesive. Fix the end A2 onto the base B in the same way. Place a piece of scrap wood under the drilling area as before and drill 5mm holes in side C1 at the dimensions shown (**see side elevation**).

Hold C1 against the base and ends and, using a bradawl, mark through these clearance holes onto the base B and both ends A. Apply a layer of adhesive to the edges of A1, A2 and B to be joined to C1, then screw the side C1 firmly in position with the 50mm long screws. Wipe off excess adhesive. Fix the other side C2 in the same way.

Fill all holes, cracks and abrasions with cellulose filler or matching plastic wood and rub smooth with medium fine, then fine, glasspaper. Slightly round all edges and corners with fine glasspaper to prevent splintering.

stage 3

For a natural finish apply matt lacquer or horticultural clear wood preservative.

If using lacquer, apply three coats for an indoor box and at least four for an outdoor one. Allow each coat to dry thoroughly before applying the next. With an outdoor box be sure to lacquer or paint the inside of the drainage holes as well for complete weather protection. If using wood preservative, apply two generous coats with a paint brush and then leave the box for at least two weeks for the preservative to soak in before putting in any plants.

To paint the box, apply a coat of primer, two undercoats and then a gloss top coat allowing each coat to dry thoroughly before applying the next.

As an indoor box has no drainage holes drilled in the base it is a good idea to line it with a sheet of plastic or aluminium kitchen foil to ensure the box is waterproof.

Cutting list for softwood

Description	Key	Quantity	Dimensions
Ends	A	2	230 × 230 × 22mm
Base	B	1	871 × 230 × 22mm
Sides	C	2	915 × 230 × 22mm

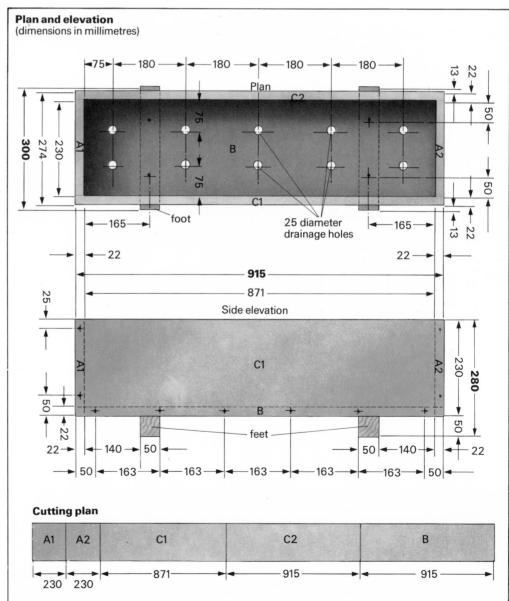

Plan and elevation
(dimensions in millimetres)

Plan

25 diameter drainage holes

foot

Side elevation

feet

Cutting plan

Techniques

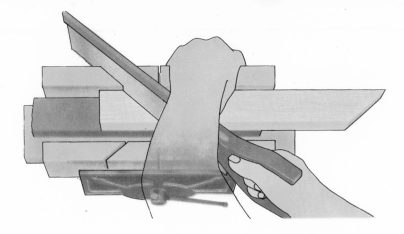

Dowel joints

A dowel is a circular-section pin used to hold two pieces of timber together. You can buy ready-made dowels but it is far cheaper to cut your own from lengths of hardwood dowelling rod, chamfering them at one end. A dowel should be about four times as long as its diameter, so an 18mm (¾in) diameter dowel would be about 75mm (3in) long.

You must check with a try square before starting work that the two pieces of timber you are joining are cut square and sit flush together.

To make a dowel joint, drill corresponding holes in the two pieces of wood being joined. Then glue the dowels in the holes and join the pieces of wood together over them. The job is straight-forward but it will only be successful if you take great care when marking and drilling the holes. Make sure you drill the holes square to the surface; a dowelling jig will help you to do this (see 2). The holes must be at exactly the right spot in each piece of wood and to the right depth. If they are not deep enough the wood will not join up over the dowels; if one hole is deeper than the other the joint will be weak. The diameter of the hole is critical, too, since the dowel must fit snugly into it.

Edge-to-edge

Make sure all surfaces are planed square. With hard pencil, mark guide-lines across both pieces of timber where dowels are to be sited. Intersect these with central line along each piece of wood to form crosses where holes to take dowels are to be drilled.

1 For drilling, mark centre of each cross with bradawl
2 Using correct size bit for dowelling, drill holes (with diameter about a third thickness of wood) to depth of not less than half dowel length (inset)
3 Cut dowels to length; with medium fine glasspaper slightly chamfer one end and saw shallow groove along each dowel to let excess adhesive escape (inset). Glue and insert dowels in one piece of wood, apply adhesive to protruding dowels and timber faces to be joined and fit other piece of timber over dowels. Finally clamp two together and remove excess adhesive while wet with clean dampened cloth

Edge-to-panel

4 When joining upright to panel or to bearer, mark dowel locations by clamping upright and bearer together at 90 degree angle or in 'L' shape, using scrap pieces of wood for protection. Check surfaces are flush with one another to ensure accurate marking. Make pencil crosses for drilling dowel holes as before
5 As pencil marks on upright are markers for inside of frame, turn upright round and continue guide-lines across top of faces to be joined
6 Mark each join A, B etc. to ensure right pieces stay together. Stagger holes if at right-angles to each other to allow sufficient clearance when making up frame
7 Drill holes to depth of not more than half thickness of upright (top hole) and with diameter about one third thickness of edge (lower hole). Glue and fit dowels as before

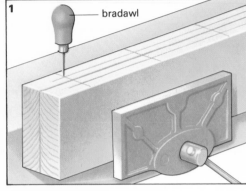

bradawl

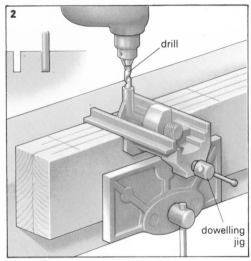

drill

dowelling jig

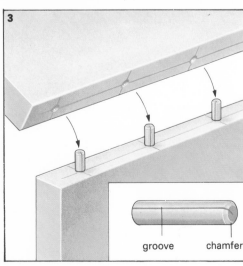

groove   chamfer

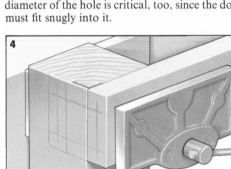

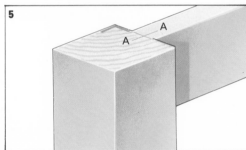

A   A

A

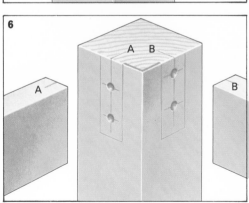

A   B

A

B

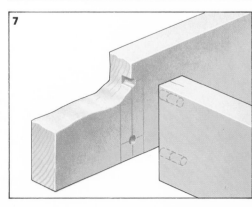

Rebate joints

One of the quickest and easiest ways of joining two pieces of timber to form a right-angle, rebate joints are often used when making drawers, boxes and other similar containers that will not be subjected to great stress.

This joint is made by cutting a rebate in one or both pieces of timber to be joined together so all surfaces are flush when the joint is complete. The joint is then secured with adhesive and often with nails or screws as well for additional strength. There are two basic principles to remember. First, never cut the rebate more than three-quarters, or less than half, the timber thickness. Secondly, always cut slightly to the waste side of the saw line to obtain a tight join, rubbing down with medium glasspaper afterwards to provide a suitable surface for the adhesive.

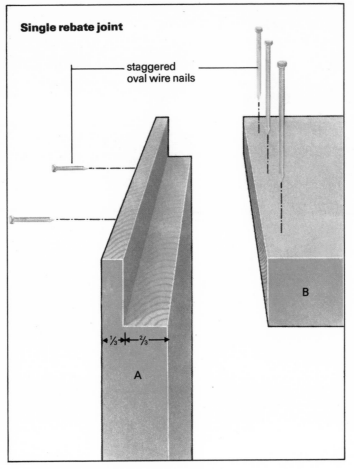

Single rebate joint

staggered oval wire nails

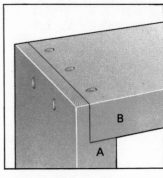

Single rebate

Using a measuring tape and try square, mark out the shape of the rebate in rail A. Cut the rebate squarely with a tenon saw to the same depth as the thickness of rail B. Smooth the saw cuts with medium glasspaper.

There is no cutting to be done on rail B so apply woodworking adhesive to the inside edges of the rebate in A. Place the end of B inside the rebate and glue and screw (or pin) through whatever will be the unexposed face when the work is complete. Wipe off excess adhesive with a clean dampened cloth.

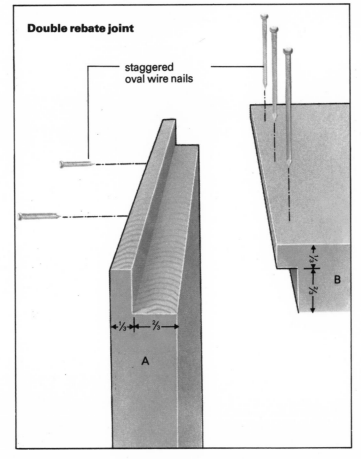

Double rebate joint

staggered oval wire nails

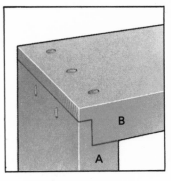

Double rebate

Mark out and cut the rebate squarely in rail A with a tenon saw to a depth of not more than three-quarters of the thickness of rail B. Trace the shape of this rebate onto rail B with a sharp pencil and then cut the rebate in B. Smooth all saw cuts with medium glasspaper, apply woodworking adhesive to one of the rebates and bring the two rails together screwing (or pinning) through the unexposed face. Wipe off excess adhesive.

Mitre joints

Mitring is a neat way of joining pieces of wood to form a rectangle and any right-angle framing. It is not difficult but, as with all woodwork, accuracy when cutting the wood is essential. Various jigs and guides are available to help you ensure precision cutting and we describe some of them here, with full details of how to use them to obtain perfect corner joints.

Mitre box

1 First secure the mitre box either by screwing it to your bench or by gripping the bottom 12mm ($\frac{1}{2}$in) in a vice. Mark the cut in pencil on the face of the wood to be mitred, allowing about 1mm ($\frac{1}{32}$in) for trimming

2 Place the wood in the box against the far side and on top of a piece of scrap wood to raise it above the bottom of the slots. The pencil mark should be just within the slot so you cut on the waste side of the mark (**inset**). Holding the wood firmly against the box, tenon saw carefully down the slot and through the wood, starting with the saw at a slight angle (tip downwards) and levelling it out as you near the bottom. Don't hurry the job as you may cut into the sides of the slot and make the wrong angle

3 To cut the opposite angle on the same piece of wood move the wood along the box and, with your left hand holding the wood firmly against the far side of the box, saw under your left arm, starting with the saw at an angle and levelling it out as before

4 For trimming, use your plane and a mitre shooting board to prevent splitting the wood

Mitre guide

5 A useful gadget for cutting mitres on wide planks of wood. It comprises an upright with a spring clip to hold a panel or backless tenon saw; the upright swivels

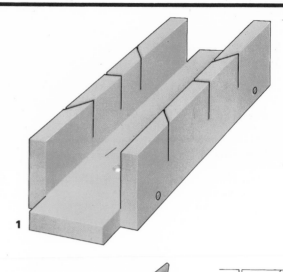

slot
pencil line —— saw cut
wastage

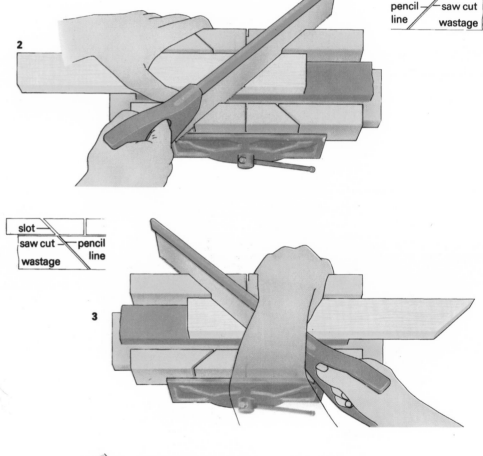

slot ——
saw cut —— pencil line
wastage

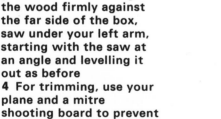

on a fixed base plate
which you screw to the
workpiece. You can set
the upright at any angle
for cutting mitres to fit
out-of-true corners.
First measure and mark in
pencil the wood to the
maximum length required,
allowing about 1mm
($\frac{1}{32}$ in) for trimming.
Select your angle, tighten
the swivel nut and screw
the base plate to the
wood. Position your saw
in the spring clip and

lower it onto the wood,
aligning with the pencil
mark
Draw the saw back to
make the initial cut at the
edge nearest you and saw
with the blade at a slight
angle, handle downwards,
levelling out as the base
of the cut is reached.
If mitring both ends of
the wood, make sure you
cut the angles in opposite
directions. Trim smooth
with a plane, using a
mitre shooting board

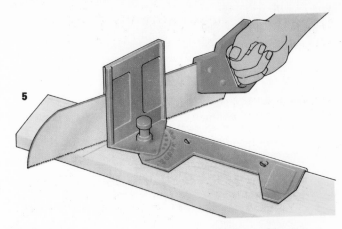

5

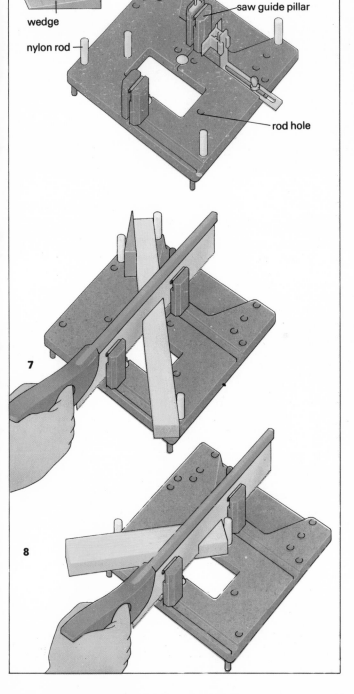

6

wedge

nylon rod

saw guide pillar

rod hole

7

8

Sawing jig
6 The jig shown here is a
Jointmaster. It comprises
a metal base with
strategically placed holes
on the surface to take
nylon rods which hold the
wood in position and
indicate angles of varying
degrees. On the base are
two slotted pillars to hold
the saw in place while
cutting. When using this
type of jig you alter the
position of the wood but
saw in the same direction
7 First insert a nylon rod
in the appropriate 45
degree hole and lay the
wood against the rod and
the far saw pillar. Ensure
precise positioning of the
cut by lining up the wood
under the saw, which is
held in position by the
nylon springs in the
pillars. You will find the
wedge (supplied with
this jig) useful for holding
the wood firmly in place.
Insert a rod in the nearest
convenient hole in the jig
so it presses the wedge
tightly against the wood.
Move the saw backwards
and forwards within the
guides, making light cuts
on only forward strokes
8 An alternative method
of cutting mitres with
this jig is to place a nylon
rod in each of the two
holes immediately in front
of the far saw pillar, with
another rod placed in the
appropriate near corner
hole. First cut one end of
the wood square and then
insert this end between
the two adjacent rods and
against the inside of the
near corner one. No
allowance need be made
for wastage with this
method of cutting the

mitre angle. If the wood
you are cutting is very
thin and liable to slip
between the two rods,
place another strip of
wood against the one to
be cut to make the whole
piece thicker

Joint fixing
9 There are several
methods of fixing, but the
simplest and most
common is gluing and
pinning. You will only be
able to join one corner at
a time so glue both
surfaces and clamp them,
between padding, in a
vice. This ensures that
when you pin through the
joint at right-angles to
each outer edge you do
not knock it out of
alignment. With your nail
punch, sink the pin heads
below the surface and fill
as required. If the wood
is too wide to take pins,
glue and dowel instead.

9

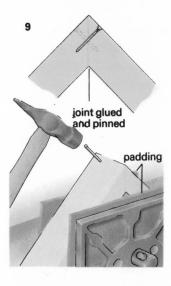

joint glued
and pinned

padding

Bridle joints

There are two main types of bridle joint—the mitred and the 'T'. One real advantage with these joints is they can withstand pressure from above and from the side. Mitred bridle joints are used to join pieces of timber of the same width and thickness—in making such things as mirror frames. 'T' bridle joints are used in general furniture making.

When making a bridle joint, the same basic principles apply as those for tenon joints; the thickness of the tenon should not be more than one third the thickness of the timber from which it is cut. If there are two tenons, the combined thickness should not be more than two thirds the thickness. If one tenon is more than a third the thickness, the other tenon should be correspondingly thinner. No tenon, however, should be less than a quarter the thickness of the timber from which it is cut.

You can further strengthen these joints once they are glued in place by pinning or screwing them together. Before marking and cutting out any joints, mark on both pieces of timber all face edges and face sides (see diagrams for symbols).

Mitred bridle joint

1 With a measuring tape, pencil and try square, measure and mark accurately on all four edges at one end of timber B the depth of the slot to be cut out, which will be the same measurement as the width of timber A from which the tenon will be cut. Also mark the depth of the tenon on A (the width of timber B). The depth of the slot in B will taper at an angle when the end has been mitred. Mark the mitre line across both sides from the top corner on the face edge to the depth line on the inside edge. Check the mitre angle is accurate with a

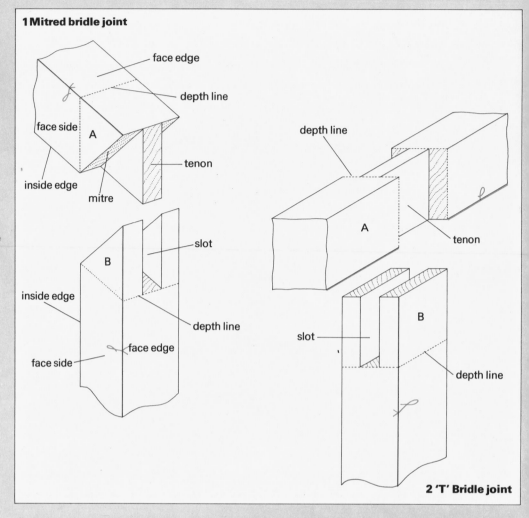

1 Mitred bridle joint

face edge
depth line
face side
A
inside edge
mitre
tenon

slot
B
inside edge
depth line
face edge
face side

depth line
A
tenon
slot
B
depth line

2 'T' Bridle joint

mitre square. Place timber B horizontally in a vice and saw through the mitre line.

With a mortise gauge set to the required width of the tenon, which in this case will be one third the thickness of timber A, mark out on the mitred face and the face edge of B the position of the slot down to the depth line. Remember to keep the stock of the gauge against the face side of the timber. Place the timber vertically in the vice and tenon saw down the slot lines to the required depth. Carefully remove the waste from the slot with a mortise chisel, working from both sides towards the centre. With the mortise gauge set as before, mark across the end and along the inside face edge of timber A the position of the tenon as far as the depth line. Mark out the mitre line to be cut as for timber B on both sides of A. Place the timber horizontally in the vice and cut down the the mitre line on each side of A as far as the lines marked

by the gauge. Place the timber upwards at an angle in the vice and saw down the lines marked by the gauge at the same angle as the mitre to remove the waste from either side of the tenon. Smooth all cut edges with medium fine glasspaper and fit the joint together, making sure it sits firmly. Glue the joint and secure it in a G-clamp until it has stuck. Alternatively glue and then pin or screw the joint.

'T' bridle joint

The 'T' joint can be used to join two pieces of timber that have at least one side the same measurement. One of the most common applications of this joint is where an upright timber joins a load-bearing horizontal timber.
2 To join two pieces of timber with dimensionally matching sides, face the larger sides of each piece (if they exist) to the front. Mark out accurately the position of the tenon on the horizontal timber A and the slot in the

vertical timber B in the same way as for the mitred joint. Remember the depth of the slot will be the same as the width of timber A and the width of the tenon must be about a third the thickness of A.

Place timber A horizontally in the vice with the face side upwards and cut down either end of the tenon as far as the line marked with the gauge. Turn the timber over and cut down from the other face in the same way. Remove the two waste pieces with a mortise chisel, working from both sides towards the centre. Place timber B vertically in the vice and cut down the lines marked by the gauge, which will correspond to the width of the tenon in A, to the depth line. Carefully chisel out the slot waste, working from both sides towards the centre.

Mortise and tenon joints

The strength of the mortise and tenon joint makes it ideal for use in heavy framing and general furniture work. To ensure a really strong T-joint the tenon must fit tightly into the mortise, so take great care when marking the timber and always cut on the waste side. The joint is made by shaping one end of a piece of timber into a tenon to fit into a slot (mortise) made in the other piece. The thickness of the tenon must never be more than one third the thickness of the timber in which it is cut.

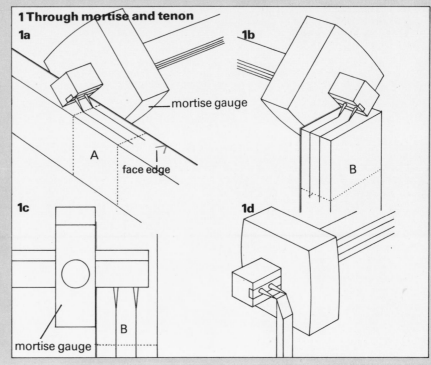

1 Through mortise and tenon

1a

1b

— mortise gauge

A

face edge

1c

B

mortise gauge

B

1d

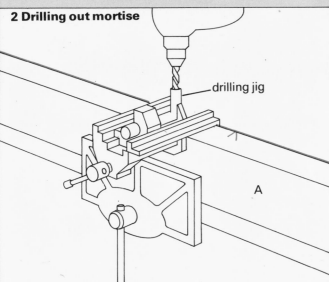

2 Drilling out mortise

drilling jig

A

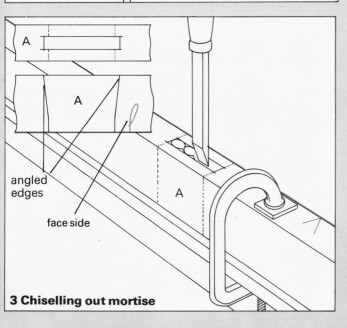

A

A

A

angled edges

face side

3 Chiselling out mortise

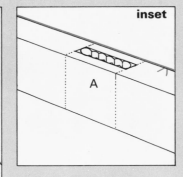

inset

A

There are several kinds of mortise and tenon joints. They all serve much the same purpose; some are stronger, while in others the joint construction is hidden.

Through mortise and tenon
Mark all face edges and face sides (**see diagrams for code**). On the face edge of timber A, mark the length of the mortise, which will be the same as the width of the piece of timber – B – from which the tenon is to be cut. With a pencil and try square mark lines where the joint is to be made, around all four edges of timber A (**see 1a**). The tenon for this joint must be of the same depth as the mortise. Mark this depth round the four edges of timber B (**see 1b**). Measure the thickness of tenon timber B, divide this by three and set your mortise gauge to that measurement (**see 1c**). Release the thumbscrews

holding the pointer and stock, adjusting these so the distances between each and the fixed pointer are one third the width of timber B. If using only a mortise chisel to cut out the mortise, check its blade is the same width as the distance between the pointers on the gauge (**see 1d**). This distance must be one third of the thickness of timber B.

Keeping the stock of the gauge up against the face side of the timber, mark out the mortise (**see 1a**) and the tenon (**see 1b**).

To drill out the mortise, clamp timber A in a vice and, with the aid of a jig, make a series of holes in the area marked (**see 2 and inset**). Use a drill bit slightly narrower than the final width of the mortise required and rest your work on a piece of scrap wood to prevent tearing the timber as you drill through. With a pair of G-clamps secure timber A to a workbench, making sure you put a piece of scrap wood underneath and padding between the clamps and the work (**see 3**). Chisel out the mortise with the correct width blade – if you have not already drilled holes. Angle it slightly to cut away from the mortise to allow space for wedges (to be inserted from opposite edge to face edge).

4 Cutting tenon
4a Sawing at an angle

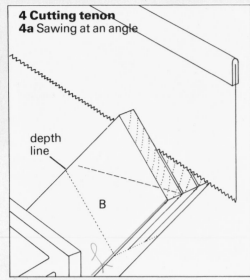

depth
line

B

4b Sawing parallel to depth line

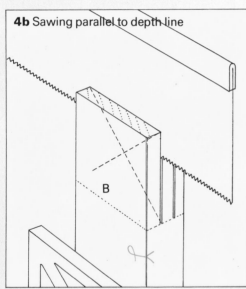

B

4c Removing waste

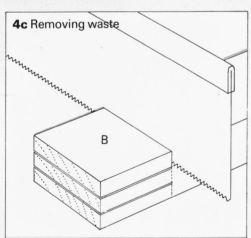

B

To cut out the tenon in timber B, place the timber at an angle in a vice and cut with a tenon saw at an angle down both sides of the tenon to the depth line already marked (**see 4a**). Turn the wood round and repeat the procedure. Secure timber B vertically in the vice and saw to the depth line on both sides (**see 4b**). Place timber B horizontally in the vice and remove the waste by cutting along the depth lines (**see 4c**).

5 Inserting wedges

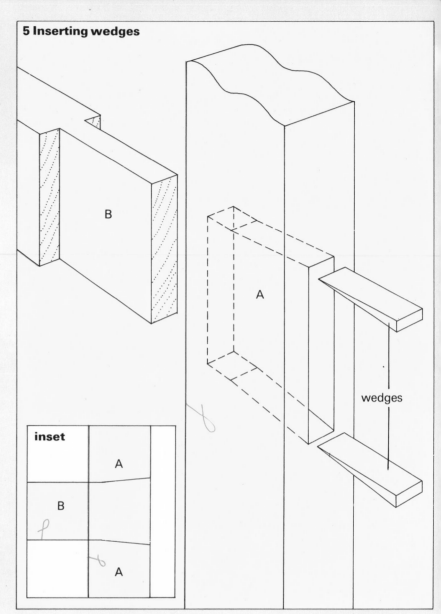

B

A

wedges

inset

A

B

A

6 Alternative wedging

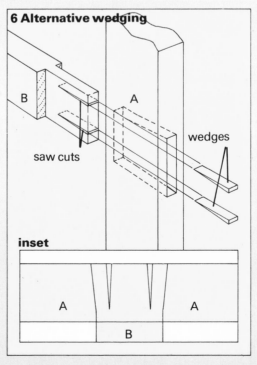

B

A

wedges

saw cuts

inset

A

A

B

Apply woodworking adhesive to the tenon and the inside of the mortise and fit them together. From matching wood cut two thin tapered wedges the same width as the mortise. Apply adhesive to the wedges and insert them in the gaps already cut, using a mallet or hammer and block of wood. Hammer the wedges alternately to keep the tenon straight in the mortise (**see 5**). Clamp the joint between padding until dry. Saw off the ends of the wedges and smooth the joint with fine glasspaper or a block plane (**see inset**). Another method of wedging (**see 6**) is to saw slots about two-thirds down depth of tenon, 4mm ($\frac{3}{16}$ in) in from edges. Tap wedges in slots to lock tenon in position (**see inset**).

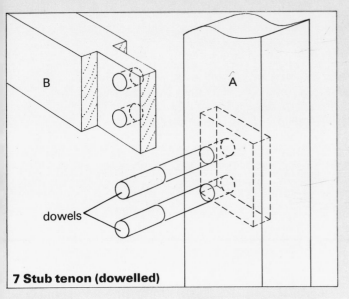

7 Stub tenon (dowelled)

dowels

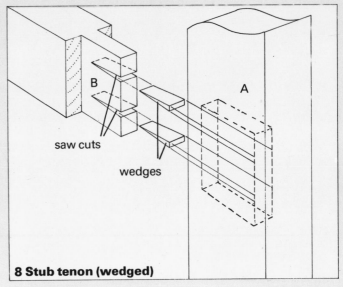

saw cuts

wedges

8 Stub tenon (wedged)

Stub tenon
A neater version of the mortise and tenon, since the tenon stops short and does not appear on the outside. The joint is strengthened by securing with dowels (**see 7**). Wedges can be used instead of dowels. Here you must partially insert the wedges first (**see 8**).

Haunched tenon
This is similar to the through tenon, but has a haunch (shoulder) on the top of the tenon – and a matching recess in the upper end of the mortise – for extra strength. The haunch piece protrudes no more than one quarter along the tenon and should be cut down the same

distance to form a square (**see 9**).

Double or multiple tenon
For use on really wide joints where a single tenon would give a weak joint. Any number of tenons may be cut as long as their widths and the gaps between are the same (**see 10**).

Twin tenon
Often used for the centre or lock rail of door frames. The tenons are linked by a haunch for greater strength and the mortise is 'stopped' to correspond (**see 11**).

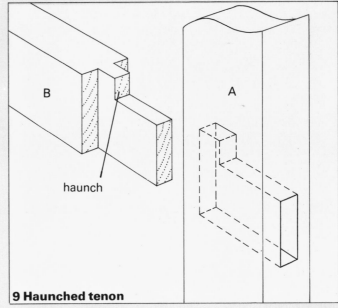

haunch

9 Haunched tenon

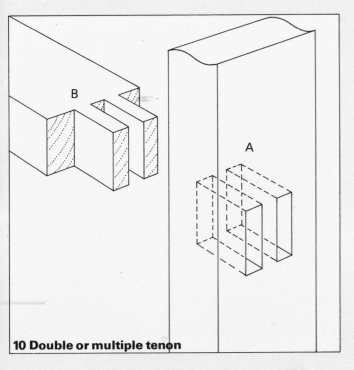

10 Double or multiple tenon

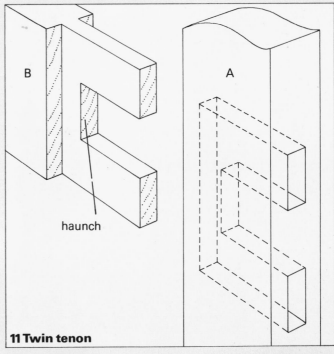

haunch

11 Twin tenon

Housing joints

The housing joint is used in cabinet work, furniture making and shelving systems, but should not be used when there is a risk of the timber bowing since this causes the joints to work loose. The uprights must be rigid and vertical (as in the confines of an alcove) and you may need to build in an extra upright or make the crosspieces shorter to avoid bowing. The joint is mostly used with timber of equal width and thickness, but the thickness and width of the upright should never be more than twice that of the crosspiece.

Simple housing

Using a try square, mark a line at the required height across the upright where the top edge of the crosspiece will enter the housing. Mark another line underneath this so the width of the housing is exactly the same as the thickness of the crosspiece to ensure a tight fit. Continue these lines onto both edges of the upright and mark on the depth line. If you are making a series of joints (such as for a shelving system), the depth lines must all be the same depth (about half the upright thickness); use a mortise gauge for accurate marking up.

Place the upright flat in a vice or clamp it to your work surface. Make two cuts with a tenon saw to the depth line, keeping the saw on the waste side (inside) of the line. Remove the waste from between the cut lines with a chisel; if the piece of timber is very wide, you will need to use a paring chisel.

Apply woodworking adhesive to the inside of the housing and insert the crosspiece, securing the joint by pinning, or screwing, through the upright into the end of the crosspiece. Wipe off excess adhesive with a clean dampened cloth.

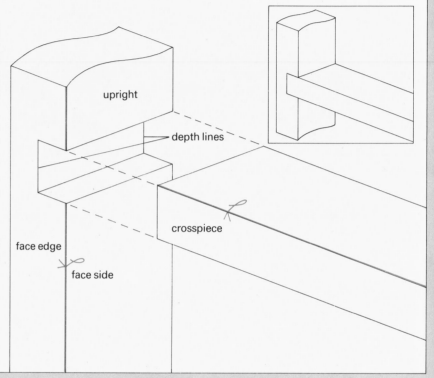

Stopped housing

Mark out the housing on the upright in the same way as for the simple housing joint but stop the lines the same distance short of the front edge as the length of the recess in the crosspiece.

Mark out the recess on the crosspiece, taking care to make it the correct size so the front edge of the two pieces of timber will be flush when joined. The width of the recess must never be more than one fifth of the total width of the timber in which it is cut and its depth must be equal to the depth of the housing. Cut out the recess with a tenon saw.

Place the upright flat in a vice or clamp it to your work surface and make two cuts with a tenon saw to the depth line, keeping the saw to the waste side (inside) of the line and at an angle to avoid removing the wood from the front edge where the housing stops. Remove the wood from this area by chopping down to the depth line with a chisel held vertically, bevel edge inwards. Apply adhesive to the inside of the housing and to the recess and bring the two pieces of timber together, securing the joint as before.

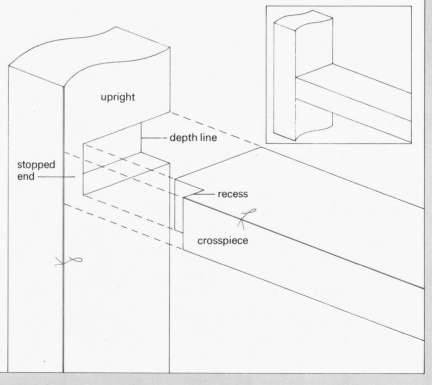

Box joints

Box joints are mostly used in the construction of furniture and cabinet work. Both pieces of wood being joined must be the same width and, ideally, the same thickness as well.

'L' joint

Using a measuring tape, pencil and try square, mark out an uneven number of tenons and recesses across the width of both pieces of timber. Make sure each tenon is at least 10mm wide; if less, the joint will be considerably weakened. In one rail there should be more tenons than recesses and less in the other rail, so when the rails are joined together the tenons in one fit neatly inside the recesses in the other rail. Place each rail vertically in a vice and cut down to the depth line with a tenon saw

where you have marked the tenons and recesses. Chop out the waste from between the cut lines with a chisel. Apply woodworking adhesive to the fixing edges of the tenons and recesses on both rails and join the two, clamping them (and pinning for extra strength if needed) until the adhesive has set. Wipe off excess adhesive with a clean dampened cloth.

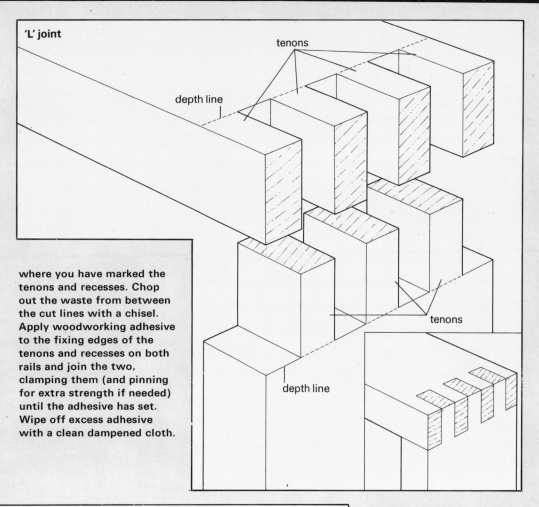

'L' joint

tenons

depth line

tenons

depth line

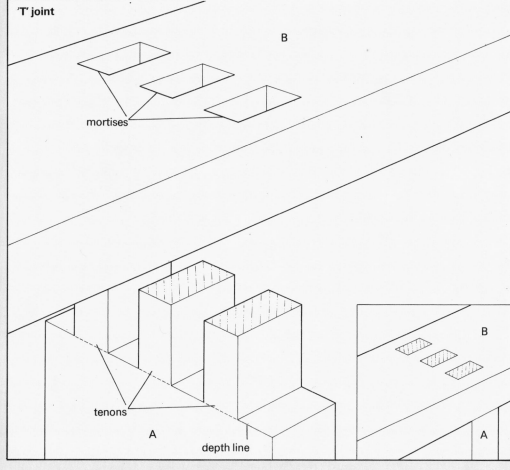

'T' joint

B

mortises

tenons

A

depth line

B

A

'T' joint

Mark and cut out the tenons and recesses in rail A in the same way as for the 'L' joint. Mark out the mortises in rail B to the same dimensions as the tenons in rail A; remove the waste from inside these lines by drilling a hole through the rail and chopping out the rest with a chisel. Apply woodworking adhesive to all the fixing edges on the tenons and recesses on rail A and to the inside surfaces of the mortises in rail B. Bring the two rails together, clamping them (and pinning for extra strength if necessary) until the adhesive has set. Wipe off excess adhesive with a clean dampened cloth.

For cabinet work where a hidden joint is required, a stopped 'T' joint is used. To make this, measure and cut the tenons and recesses in rail A half the thickness of rail B; the mortises in rail B must be the same depth as these.

Halving joints

One of the quickest and easiest ways to join two pieces of timber, halving joints are mainly used in constructing light frames where the joint will not be subjected to too much stress. The joint is made by cutting a recess in both pieces of timber so all surfaces are flush when the recesses are brought together and secured with woodworking adhesive. For extra strength the joint can be fixed with nails or screws as well.

'L' joint of timbers the same thickness

Top 'T' joint
Above Cross joint

'L' joint of timbers of different thicknesses

Mitred 'L' joint

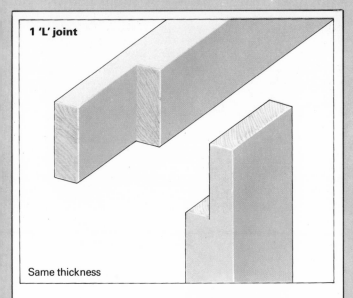

1 'L' joint

Same thickness

1 When both pieces of timber are the same thickness, cut each recess to half that thickness. Use your measuring tape, pencil and try square to mark out the dimensions accurately and cut out squarely with a tenon saw the recess in both rails.

Smooth all cuts with medium glasspaper. Apply woodworking adhesive to both recesses and secure the joint by screwing (or pinning) from the face that will be hidden when the structure is finished. Wipe off any excess adhesive.

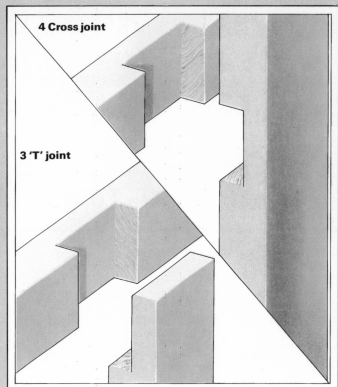

4 Cross joint

3 'T' joint

3 To make a 'T' joint, mark out the recess in one rail and cut squarely to the depth line with a tenon saw. Chisel out the wood from between the cut lines. Cut the same depth recess in the other rail. Smooth all cuts with

medium glasspaper, apply woodworking adhesive to both recesses and secure. **4** To make a cross joint, mark out, cut and chisel out recesses in both rails, apply woodworking adhesive to both recesses and secure the joint.

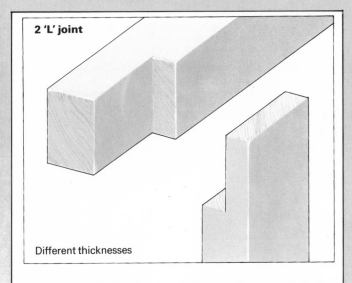

2 'L' joint

Different thicknesses

2 When the pieces of timber are not the same thickness, mark out and cut the recess in the

thinner rail to exactly half its thickness. Then mark and cut same depth recess in thicker rail.

Left The basic frame shown here is constructed entirely by using halving joints. A simple 'L' joint is used in each corner, but you could use a mitred 'L' joint for a neater finish. A cross joint is used in the middle of the frame and the remainder are all 'T' joints.

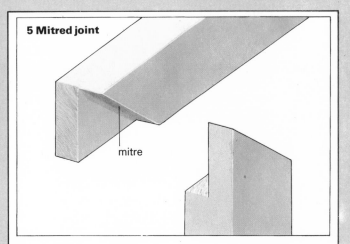

5 Mitred joint

mitre

5 To make a mitred 'L' joint, place one rail in a mitre box (or guide) and cut the mitre angle to half the rail thickness. Place the rail vertically in a vice and tenon saw the mitre angle to remove the waste. Place the other rail in the mitre box (or guide) and cut through the mitre angle. Mark the base

of the mitre squarely across the rail and cut along the base line to half the rail thickness. Place the rail vertically in a vice and remove the waste, keeping the saw parallel to the base line. Smooth all cuts with medium glasspaper, apply woodworking adhesive to edges and secure joint.

Joining wood end to end

These joints enable you to use up scrap wood and are therefore important for the economical use of timber. But they are never as strong as one complete length of timber and should not be used for load-bearing structures. The timbers should be of equal width and thickness; if the width of a piece of timber is more than twice its own thickness, these joints should not be used.

Lapped joint

Check the timber is square and mark the cutting lines on both rails, marking the depth of the recesses exactly half the thickness of the timber and the length of the recesses the same as their width. Use a marking gauge for accuracy. Place each rail in a vice and cut off the waste with a tenon saw, keeping slightly to the waste side of the line. Check the joint for fit (all edges should be flush) and, if necessary, remove more wood with a chisel or flat file. Apply woodworking adhesive to the fixing surfaces of both recesses and bring the two rails together, securing the joint with screws through one face. Wipe off excess adhesive with a clean dampened cloth.

Splayed joint

Check the timber is square and mark the cutting lines on both rails; make the length of the recesses the same as their width and their greatest depth exactly two-thirds the thickness of the timber, tapering to one-third the thickness at the end of both pieces.
Place each rail in a vice and cut off the waste with a tenon saw, keeping slightly to the waste side of the line. Check the joint for fit then glue and screw together, securing it with screws in the same way as for the lapped joint.

'V' joint

Check the timber is square and mark a line squarely across the width of each rail the same distance back from the square end as the width of the timber.
Draw a line centrally along the length of both rails and draw two more lines on each to mark the shape of the recess on one rail and the point on the other. Place each rail in a vice and remove the waste with a tenon saw, keeping slightly to the waste side of the line. Check the joint for fit then glue and screw together through each edge.

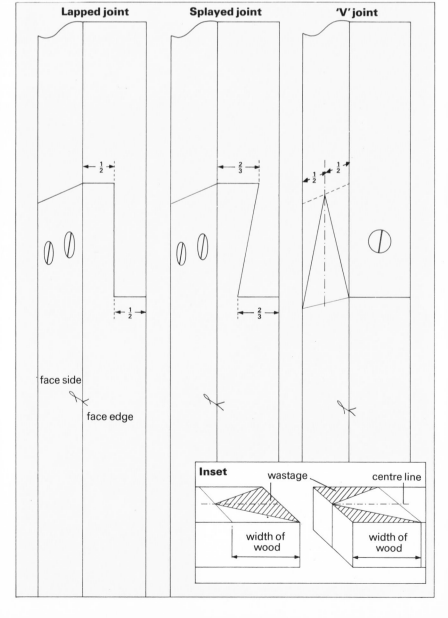

Fitting a recessed hinge

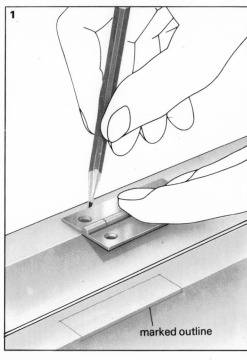

marked outline

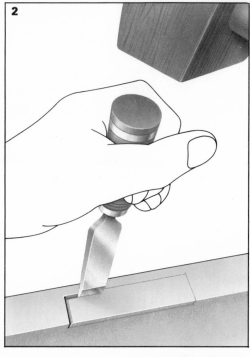

1 Using the hinge leaf as a guide trace the outline of the recess with a sharp pencil. The knuckle must lie just clear of the edge of the piece of wood. Mark the thickness of the hinge on the face of the wood down from the fixing edge

2 Score the outline of the hinge with a sharp knife. Hold the chisel vertically on the line with the bevel facing the waste side and tap the handle lightly with a mallet (or hammer if the chisel has a plastic handle) until the blade almost reaches the required depth

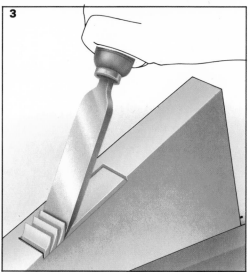

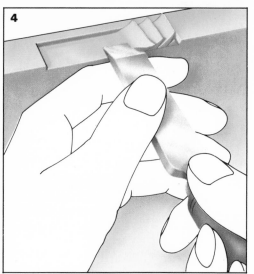

3 With the chisel bevel face downwards, clean out the recess making shallow-angled cuts to remove the waste wood to the required depth of the recess

4 Cut out any remaining slivers of wood from the recess by tapping lightly on the chisel (bevel face upwards) across the grain of the recess and along the base line

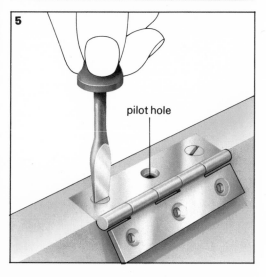

pilot hole

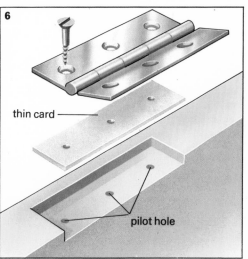

thin card

pilot hole

5 Place the hinge leaf in the recess to see if it has been cut to the right size and depth

6 If the recess is cut too deep, pack it with a small piece of card to bring the leaf flush with the wood surface. If it is not deep enough chisel out more wood

Making up Timesaver drawers

Front fixing detail
Four-sided construction

back profile

side profile

base

front profile

drawer front

front profile

drawer front

base

handle

fixing screws

front plates

drawer front

Four-sided construction

corner post

Three-sided construction

Front fixing detail
Three-sided construction

drawer front

front plate

handle

base

surface fillet

rebate and fillet

groove

This ingenious kit is both time and labour-saving — with it you can make up a drawer to any dimension, with a choice of depths: 100 or 120mm (4 or 4¾in). The 15mm (⅝in) PVC drawer profile is grooved on the inside to accommodate the runners. The choice includes a four-sided drawer using special corner posts and a handle to be glued and screwed into the drawer front profile groove, or a three-sided drawer to which you fit your own drawer front with special front plates (see assembly diagram).
You also have the choice of fixing your own decorative front directly to the drawer front profile on the four-sided type.
You fix the plastic or wood runner at the required depth to the panel ends (or dividers) of your drawer unit (see 1).

To estimate the total length of drawer profile required, measure your lengths and three (or four) sides, allowing for clearance and a drawer stop at the back. With the profile laid flat, cut it to size with a fine tooth veneer or tenon saw. Smooth the cut edges with fine or medium fine glasspaper. With the drawer groove facing you, insert the two

back corner posts in the hollow at each end of the back profile, pushing them in as far as you can before ramming home with the heel of your hand. Join the two sides to these corner posts in the same way, making sure the grooves for the base in each side meet the one in the back.
Cut base from 3mm (⅛in) lacquered or plain hardboard or birch plywood (12.5mm/½in larger than the internal dimensions of your drawer) and insert in the assembled

three sides. If the drawer is larger than 840sq mm (13sq in) or if two sides are longer than 840mm and likely to support a heavy load, glue the base into position with woodworking adhesive.
If using a decorative drawer front with a three-sided drawer you must cut a groove on the inside face (or make a rebate and fillet, or fix a fillet strip) to act as a base support. Screw through the front plates into the drawer front with No 6 round head screws of the required length. Now join front plates to sides.
If using a four-sided drawer, follow the same method but join front corner posts to front profile and then to the sides, and fix the special handle through the front profile. Alternatively fix your own decorative drawer front and handle directly onto the front profile.
You must never use the front as a drawer stop since this weakens the joint between front and sides every time you close the drawer. A piece of runner fixed vertically at the back makes an adequate drawer stop (see 2).

1 Drawer runner fixing
(dimensions in millimetres)

2 Drawer stop fixing

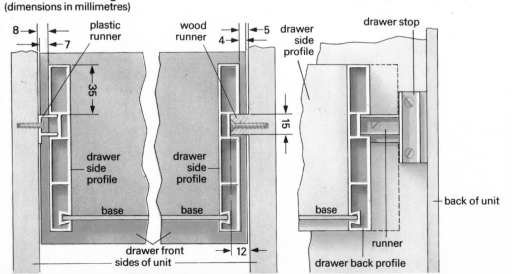

plastic runner

drawer side profile

base

wood runner

drawer side profile

base

drawer front
sides of unit

drawer side profile

drawer stop

base

runner

back of unit

drawer back profile

Appendix

Metric conversion charts

Metric prefixes and abbreviations

The metre is used as an example below. The same prefixes apply to litres (l or lit) and grams (g). The abbreviation lit is used for litre when unqualified to avoid confusion with the numeral 1.

millimetre (mm)	0.001	one thousandth metre
centimetre (cm)	0.01	one hundredth metre
decimetre (dm)	0.1	one tenth metre
metre (m)	1	one metre
decametre (dam)	10	ten metres
hectometre (hm)	100	one hundred metres
kilometre (km)	1000	one thousand metres

Length (linear measure)

Fractions of 1 inch in millimetres

Thirty-seconds, sixteenths, eighths, quarters and one half

in	mm
1/32	0.8
1/16	1.6
3/32	2.4
1/8	3.2
5/32	4.0
3/16	4.8
7/32	5.6
1/4	6.3
9/32	7.1
5/16	7.9
11/32	8.7
3/8	9.5
13/32	10.3
7/16	11.1
15/32	11.9
1/2	12.7
17/32	13.5
9/16	14.3
19/32	15.1
5/8	15.9
21/32	16.7
11/16	17.5
23/32	18.3
3/4	19.0
25/32	19.8
13/16	20.6
27/32	21.4
7/8	22.2
29/32	23.0
15/16	23.8
31/32	24.6
1 inch	25.4

Twelfths, sixths and thirds

in	mm
1/12	2.1
1/6	4.2
1/4	6.3
1/3	8.5
5/12	10.6
1/2	12.7
7/12	14.8
2/3	16.9
3/4	19.0
5/6	21.2
11/12	23.3
1 inch	25.4

Note

Find the Imperial figure you wish to convert in the **heavy** type central column and read off the metric equivalent in the right-hand column and vice versa.
For example:
10 inches = 254 millimetres and
10mm = 0.39in.

Conversion from inches is only taken up to 40 in the chart below, see next chart for continuation.

Inches/millimetres		
in		mm
0.04	**1**	25.4
0.08	**2**	50.8
0.12	**3**	76.2
0.16	**4**	101.6
0.20	**5**	127.0
0.24	**6**	152.4
0.28	**7**	177.8
0.31	**8**	203.2
0.35	**9**	228.6
0.39	**10**	254.0
0.43	**11**	279.4
0.47	**12**	304.8
0.51	**13**	330.2
0.55	**14**	355.6
0.59	**15**	381.0
0.63	**16**	406.4
0.67	**17**	431.8
0.71	**18**	457.2
0.75	**19**	482.6
0.79	**20**	508.0
0.83	**21**	533.4
0.87	**22**	558.8
0.91	**23**	584.2
0.94	**24**	609.6
0.98	**25**	635.0
1.02	**26**	660.4
1.06	**27**	685.8
1.10	**28**	711.2
1.14	**29**	736.6
1.18	**30**	762.0
1.22	**31**	787.4
1.26	**32**	812.8
1.30	**33**	838.2
1.34	**34**	863.6
1.38	**35**	889.0
1.42	**36**	914.4
1.46	**37**	939.8
1.50	**38**	965.2
1.54	**39**	990.6
1.57	**40**	1016.0
1.97	**50**	
2.36	**60**	
2.76	**70**	
3.15	**80**	
3.54	**90**	
3.94	**100**	
7.87	**200**	
11.81	**300**	
15.75	**400**	
19.68	**500**	
23.62	**600**	
27.56	**700**	
31.50	**800**	
35.43	**900**	
39.37	**1000**	

Imperial measurements are expressed below in yards, feet and inches rather than in decimals for convenience if converting with rulers or measuring tapes which do not include decimal readings.

Feet/metres				Yards/metres				
ft	in		m	yd	ft	in		m
3	3	**1**	0.30	1	0	3	**1**	0.9
6	7	**2**	0.61	2	0	7	**2**	1.8
9	10	**3**	0.91	3	0	10	**3**	2.7
13	1	**4**	1.22	4	1	1	**4**	3.7
16	5	**5**	1.52	5	1	5	**5**	4.6
19	8	**6**	1.83	6	1	8	**6**	5.5
23	0	**7**	2.13	7	2	0	**7**	6.4
26	3	**8**	2.44	8	2	3	**8**	7.3
29	6	**9**	2.74	9	2	6	**9**	8.2
32	10	**10**	3.05	10	2	10	**10**	9.1
65	7	**20**	6.10	21	2	7	**20**	18.3
98	5	**30**	9.14	32	2	5	**30**	27.4
131	3	**40**	12.19	43	2	3	**40**	36.6
164	0	**50**	15.24	54	2	0	**50**	45.7
196	10	**60**	18.29	65	1	10	**60**	54.9
229	8	**70**	21.34	76	1	8	**70**	64.0
262	6	**80**	24.38	87	1	6	**80**	73.2
295	3	**90**	27.43	98	1	3	**90**	82.3
328	1	**100**	30.48	109	1	1	**100**	91.4

Quick conversion factors – length

Terms are set out in full in the left-hand column except where clarification is necessary.

1 inch (in)	= 25.4mm/2.54cm
1 foot (ft)/12in	= 304.8mm/30.48cm/0.3048m
1 yard (yd)/3ft	= 914.4mm/91.44cm/0.9144m
1 mile (mi)/1760yd	= 1609.344m/1.609km
1 millimetre (mm)	= 0.0394in
1 centimetre (cm)/10mm	= 0.394in
1 metre (m)/100cm	= 39.37in/3.281ft/1.094yd
1 kilometre (km)/1000m	= 1093.6yd/0.6214mi

Quick conversion factors – area

1 square inch (sq in)	= 645.16sq mm/ 6.4516sq cm
1 square foot (sq ft)/144sq in	= 929.03sq cm
1 square yard (sq yd)/9sq ft	= 8361.3sq cm/ 0.8361sq m
1 acre (ac)/4840sq yd	= 4046.9sq m/0.4047ha
1 square mile (sq mi)640ac	= 259ha
1 square centimetre (sq cm)/ 100 square millimetre (sq mm)	= 0.155sq in
1 square metre (sq m)/ 10,000sq cm	= 10.764sq ft/1.196sq yd
1 are (a)/100sq m	= 119.60sq yd/0.0247ac
1 hectare (ha)/100a	= 2.471ac/0.00386sq mi

Quick conversion factors – volume

1 cubic inch (cu in)	= 16.3871cu cm
1 cubic foot (cu ft)/ 1728cu in	= 28.3168cu dm/0.0283cu m
1 cubic yard (cu yd)/ 27cu ft	= 0.7646cu m
1 cubic centimetre (cu cm)/ 1000 cubic millimetres (cu mm)	= 0.0610cu in
1 cubic decimetre (cu dm)/ 1000cu cm	= 61.024cu in/0.0353cu ft
1 cubic metre (cu m)/ 1000cu dm	= 35.3146cu ft/1.308cu yd
1cu cm	= 1 millilitre (ml)
1cu dm	= 1 litre (lit) See **Capacity**

Index